Gender, Science, and Authority in Women's Travel Writing

LATIN AMERICAN GENDER AND SEXUALITIES

Series Editor: Carolina Rocha,
Southern Illinois University, Edwardsville

The Latin American Gender and Sexualities series is a timely addition to current scholarship on gender and sexuality. In the last decade, a number of Latin American governments are showing openness to new kinds of sexualities through public policy. The study of gender and sexuality also developed during that time to examine questions of power, nationalism, and changing identities within the social fabric of Latin American countries. Because of its appeal ranging from gender and feminist studies to queer theory, this series is a vibrant component of Latin American studies looking at the intersection of gender and culture. Works include book-length studies and essay collections that combine the methodologies and insights of cultural studies and literature with those of history, anthropology, and other social sciences.

Recent Titles in This Series

Gender, Science, and Authority in Women's Travel Writing: Literary Perspectives on the Discourse of Natural History
By Michelle Medeiros

Writing Terror on the Bodies of Women: Media Coverage of Violence against Women in Guatemala
By Sarah England

White Middle Class Men in Rio de Janeiro: The Making of a Dominant Subject
By Valeria Ribeiro Corossacz

Resistant Bodies in the Cultural Productions of Transnational Hispanic Caribbean Women: Reimagining Queer Identity
By Irune del Rio Gabiola.

Unbecoming Female Monsters: Witches, Vampires, and Virgins
By Cristina Santos

Negotiating Gendered Discourses: Michelle Bachelet and Cristina Fernández de Kirchner
By Jane L. Christie

Gender, Science, and Authority in Women's Travel Writing

Literary Perspectives on the Discourse of Natural History

Michelle Medeiros

LEXINGTON BOOKS
Lanham • Boulder • New York • London

Published by Lexington Books
An imprint of The Rowman & Littlefield Publishing Group, Inc.
4501 Forbes Boulevard, Suite 200, Lanham, Maryland 20706
www.rowman.com

6 Tinworth Street, London SE11 5AL, United Kingdom

Copyright © 2019 by The Rowman & Littlefield Publishing Group, Inc.

All rights reserved. No part of this book may be reproduced in any form or by any electronic or mechanical means, including information storage and retrieval systems, without written permission from the publisher, except by a reviewer who may quote passages in a review.

British Library Cataloguing in Publication Information Available

Library of Congress Cataloging-in-Publication Data

Names: Medeiros, Michelle, author.
Title: Gender, science, and authority in women's travel writing : literary perspectives on the discourse of natural history / by Michelle Medeiros.
Description: Lanham : Lexington Books, [2019] | Series: Latin American gender and sexualities | Includes bibliographical references and index.
Identifiers: LCCN 2019001171 (print) | LCCN 2019012968 (ebook) | ISBN 9781498579766 (electronic) | ISBN 9781498579759 (cloth) | ISBN 978-1-4985-7977-3 (paper)
Subjects: LCSH: Women in science. | Women travelers—History. | Travel writing—History. | Travelers' writings—History and criticism. | Latin American literature. | Natural history.
Classification: LCC HQ1397 (ebook) | LCC HQ1397 .M44 2019 (print) | DDC 500.82—dc23
LC record available at https://lccn.loc.gov/2019001171

Contents

Acknowledgments	vii
Introduction	1
1 Shaping Scientific Knowledge: Maria Graham's Travels in Nineteenth-Century Brazil	21
2 Gertrudis Gómez de Avelleneda's Travel Writings: Beyond Optical Illusions of the Soul	53
3 Nísia Floresta Voyages through Europe: Transatlantic Perspectives on Nature, Progress, and Women's Education	93
4 Beyond the Laboratory Walls: Doris Cochran's Strategies to Build a Reputation as a Scientist in the Early Twentieth Century	139
Conclusion	181
Credits	187
Works Cited	189
Index	201
About the Author	213

Acknowledgments

My deepest gratitude goes to the staff of the many libraries and archives around the world who facilitated the access to the materials included in this book. My special thanks goes to the staff of the Smithsonian Institution Archives, especially Heidi Stover and Tad Bennicoff, who met my countless requests and demands and helped me to bring Doris Cochran to light. Special thanks are also due to the staff of the National Museum of Rio de Janeiro for bearing with my constant requests for endless documents and notes buried deep in their archives. Jorge Dias da Silva Júnior, who found and scanned more than 100 letters between Doris Cochran and Bertha Lutz and continued to support me even after the devastating fire that happened there. Thanks to him and to this research project, these letters were preserved. I also would like to thank Cochran's cousin, Sarah Schneider, for her willingness to help with the project. Stela Maris Scatena Franco also deserves my special acknowledgment for kindly providing invaluable material to support this project.

I would also like to acknowledge the staff and faculty at Marquette University for their encouragement and support, especially Anne Pasero and Eugenia Afinoguenova for advising and guiding me in the process of writing this book.

I am also in debt to my friends: Shannon Derby, for reading my chapters late at night and early in the morning, always providing new insights and provocative questions; Daniela Calvo, for reading my chapters and encouraging me to keep going; and Patricia Gevert, for reminding me that there is life out of academia. I deeply appreciate their friendship in so many ways. Thanks also to my dear friends Boubakary Diakite and Laura Oprescu for their help with the French translations. Marcia Stephenson, my friend and mentor, who believed in this project before anyone else did, also deserves my special acknowledgment.

I am also grateful for the support from my family: Henry, for putting up with me in the process of writing this book; and Bernardo and Gabriel, who constantly remind me, unknowingly, that despite its challenges, life is worth it. Lastly, I would like to thank my late grandmother, Iva Marquardt, the first woman traveler I met in my life, who inspired me to investigate other women like her.

Introduction

"If someone were to ask you this question offhand,—What is one of the most characteristic sounds of Brazil, one which would probably attract the notice of a foreigner visiting the tropics for the first time? . . . if you go away . . . into the country . . . you will hear the true voice of Brazil—the chorus of singing frogs" ("Frog Collecting"). The opening remarks of a talk the American scientist and explorer Doris Cochran gave to the members of the Women's Club in Washington, D.C., in 1936 evidences her attempt to bring her passion for herpetology to the attention of her public. As a woman scientist, she could not deliver her speeches to professional societies around the world. Her unique condition as a traveler allied with her expertise in natural history, however, allowed her to create a novel way to disseminate her knowledge among other women and with the general public without transgressing the boundaries of her gender.[1]

Gender, Science, and Authority in Women's Travel Writing: Literary Perspectives on the Discourse of Natural History aims to analyze the interrelations among authority, gender, and the scientific discipline of natural history in the works of transatlantic women travelers from the nineteenth and early twentieth centuries. The purpose of this book is to shed new light on our understanding of the literary perspectives of the discourse of natural history and how these viewpoints had a surprising impact in areas that went beyond scientific fields. It advances the study of travel writing and gender in new directions by bringing together Latin American, European, and American women travelers who actively engaged in natural history discussions in their writings. By demonstrating how these women were only able to participate in intellectual enterprises by embarking on transatlantic voyages, this book discloses how the work produced by these travelers challenged and reshaped dominant discourses, bringing a new point of view to nineteenth- and twentieth-century studies in Latin American history, literature, cultural studies, and history of science. Moreover, this book analyzes to what extent the approaches employed by female travel writers who wanted to engage in the production of knowledge has changed since the mid-nineteenth century, and to what degree such changes could be considered positive and more productive.

The emergent discipline of natural history in vogue during the early nineteenth century was an outgrowth of many factors, including, most particularly, the scientific expeditions to the Americas that were initiated toward the end of the eighteenth century. As Mary Louise Pratt explains, travelers provided material for the new scientific discoveries, which in turn stimulated new expeditions to exotic places. That is, the explosion of natural history and the scientific expeditions fomented the construction of knowledge on both sides of the Atlantic (*Imperial* 15). Natural history cannot be easily defined, however, and it has covered a range of different subjects (Secord 654). As Nicholas Jardine and Emma Spary observe, natural history as a field of inquiry has developed over the course of several centuries "as the product of conglomerates of people, natural objects, institutions, collections, finances, all linked by a range of practices of different kinds" (8). Natural history was not merely a discourse which represented nature because the "boundaries between the natural and the conventional, artificial and social have been continually contested and relocated" (Jardine and Spary 12). Rather, natural history was a mode of representing reality that implied a discourse which was informed by many different frameworks. What Nancy Leys Stepan calls a "passion for the tropics" came about mainly from the political opportunity of extending European domination, and the knowledge produced in the process was more a reflection of what the travelers wanted to see than of what they actually found (33–34). Sara Mills also notes that in the nineteenth century many European travelers were looking for objects and new species to further legitimate the scientific knowledge that was being produced ("Knowledge" 34). The new species of plants and animals found in America over this period were classified and named in honor of Europeans and extracted from their environments to be exhibited in museums and gardens in Europe: "Thus, those writers who produce scientific knowledge are fundamentally connected to European imperial expansion and the promotion of a view of the world that sees European activities as fundamentally civilizing" (Mills, "Knowledge" 35). Therefore, natural history became a tool to authorize the European reappropriation of the Americas that ultimately served as an endorsement to Eurocentrism.

Critical literature in the field has shown that whereas European scientific travelers used natural history discourses to validate imperialist expansion, Latin American writers used it to forge new national identities. Jorge Cañizares-Esguerra discusses how natural history expeditions played a key role in Latin America mainly because, in the late colonial period, travel narratives became a useful tool for political leaders to create an image of the nation as a productive, resource-rich, unique entity (*Nature* 46). Besides, the representations of American nature proposed by the Latin American political and intellectual elite from the end of the eighteenth century were elaborated from a Eurocentric vision. From this perspective, the jungle has been defined in these geographic and historical coordinates as a space available for expropriation and capitalist exploitation. The necessity of portraying nature as controlled was a way to insert it into the logics of capitalism (Martínez Pinzón 10–15). In that sense, dichotomies of civilization and barbarism were replicated for example by the widespread presence of Botanical Gardens throughout the continent in an attempt to demonstrate the idea that nature could be controlled, forging a civilized Latin American model. Pratt also notes that scientific travels were a turning point on both sides of the Atlantic and that the rhetoric of the reinvention of America offered an alternative to the Creole elite to shape their own national identities (*Imperial* 172). Ángela Pérez-Mejía, in her compelling study *A Geography of Hard Times* (2004), analyzed travel accounts about South America from 1780 and 1849 to demonstrate how these narratives contributed to create a map of the emerging Latin American nations to the rest of the world. Pérez-Mejía argues that in this precise historical period, 1780 marks the beginning of the end of the colonial era whereas in 1849 the first official maps of the new Latin American nations were commissioned. In the interval between these two symbolic dates, while the independence battles were taking place, several European travelers went to Latin America propelled by the curiosity about the new continent fueled by the scientific expeditions of the previous century (Pérez-Mejía 3). Ranging from scientific to sentimental travel narratives, travelers such as Louis Agassiz, Charles N. Bell, Theodore Roosevelt, among others have repeatedly emphasized the exoticness of Latin American nature in their writings. The capitalist vanguard, by its turn, also traveled to the continent seeking to access the economic opportunities that emerged from the independence of its nations (Pratt, *Imperial* 48). But the most important inspiration for the projects of nation of the new Latin American nations came from the travel accounts produced by Alexander von Humboldt (1769–1859). A German geographer, he traveled to South America in 1799 and remained there until 1804. In 1816, he began to publish his accounts, which would become the source of knowledge about Latin American geography and nature throughout the nineteenth century. Humboldt sought to measure and quantify the nature of the continent, using instruments such as barometers, compasses, and astrolabes (Pérez-Mejía 15).

Humboldt's writings had a clear pedagogical intent and became an authorized source of American "reality." The new America portrayed in his accounts "is the one that nascent capitalism needs: white, mistreated, and ready to accept European aid" (Pérez-Mejía 51). But his main interest rested on American nature, "which he represented in dimensions that the human eye can barely take in" (Pérez-Mejía 51). This monumental nature was more important than its inhabitants, and Humboldt was the mind who was able to understand, observe, and give meaning to it. Nature was a character created and forged by European knowledge based on prior scientific traditions, but corrected and augmented: "That is the America seen by Humboldt and painted within the liberal pro-independence parameters of the emergent governing class which would thank the traveler for his scientific work in a decidedly nationalistic tone" (Pérez-Mejía 55). This new proposal served well the emerging Creole elites of Latin America, in hopes to create their own projects of nation. Humboldt omitted valuable empirical and local scientific knowledge and his decision to ignore the legacy of the indigenous people gave space to the Creole elites to forge the main premises of the independence discourses: the barbarism versus white civilization (60). Moreover, Pérez-Mejía claims that the pictorial and narrative representation of the native as naked attributes to them a lack of civilization and knowledge, systematizing a geography in which knowledge no longer belonged to the locals (71). Finally, such projects did not involve women, relying solely in the alliances between white men and Europeans. Hence, Humboldt's narratives served as means to validate the independence projects in Latin America, endorsing and reinforcing a confrontation of civilization and barbarism, erasing the local knowledge, and eliminating women from the equation (Pérez-Mejía 68–71).

Thus, I employ the expression "natural history discourse" in this book to refer to the powerful and often competing rhetorical devices used to describe the world beyond Europe due to the fact that these narratives were necessarily based on the discourses circulating at the time they were produced. I draw this concept from the idea that discourse, in its Foucauldian sense, is a form of power that circulates in the social field and can attach to strategies of domination as well as to those of resistance (Sawicki 185). Foucault believed that no discourse was objective and each had an ideological purpose. Natural history, in particular, was the discourse that granted its user the power to organize and categorize nature (160). From this perspective then, the production of knowledge propelled by the natural history discourse was connected with power and specific agendas that regulated and determined truth (Acker 105). Moreover, natural history also furthered a complex patriarchal agenda (Mills, "Knowledge" 42).

The gendered character of scientific discourse, as historians of science such as Londa Schiebinger observe, has often portrayed women as incapable of intellectual production and as being naturally suitable only for reproduction and motherhood. Schiebinger demonstrates how several women had their scientific work neglected for many years just because of their gender. Many women scientists had to have their writings signed by their husbands or even adopt a male pen name in order to have their observations acknowledged in the field. She mentions the example of Marie Curie (1864–1934), the first person to win two Nobel prizes, who had her membership in the prestigious Académies des Sciences denied solely because she was a woman (*The Mind* 2). Schiebinger states that some women, however, managed to participate actively in fields that were almost exclusively male-dominated. She analyzes the rise of science in the seventeenth and eighteenth centuries to better understand how the exclusion of women took place: "The nature of science is no more fixed than the social relation between men or women. Science too is shaped by social forces" (*The Mind* 9). Therefore, Schiebinger blames the institutionalization of science and its promotion of biological determinist explanations to support the notion of women's inferiority in relation to men as the main reason women were gradually excluded from the scientific community (*The Mind* 3). Toward the end of the nineteenth century, many women were increasingly forbidden to join academic and scientific societies because of their gender and were prevented from participating in scientific practices and in the construction of knowledge at large. Scientific theories portrayed women as incapable of performing academic tasks, therefore being only allowed to perform their roles as wives and mothers. In other words, the scientific discourse largely supported the agenda of the patriarchal society (*Plants* 15). Lila Marz Harper discusses the professionalization of science and the strategies women had to employ as these changes took place. Harper emphasizes the importance of bringing travel narratives to light in order to uncover women's scientific discoveries: "travel narratives served as means by which women could gain a foothold in a traditionally masculine-dominated field, even as that field became increasingly more restrictive" (14). Although women were allowed to write, they could only do so about certain topics such as their domestic life and children. Women travelers, however, found themselves in an advantageous position that broadened their perspectives and allowed them to engage additional topics. They could discuss issues related to their observations in their travels, a logical outcome of which was to use the discourse of natural history to talk about them. Because it was considered inappropriate for women to write about scientific matters, they could not engage the discourse in the same ways that their male counterparts did.

As Pratt suggests, the heterogeneity of travel narratives as a genre facilitated "its interaction with other kinds of expressions" (*Imperial* 11).

Margaret Rossiter's comprehensive research on American women scientists demonstrates that the professionalization of science that took place at the end of the nineteenth century reasserted male domination over the feminine presence.[2] Although women began to seek employment in the scientific fields in significant numbers around the 1880s, their opportunities were very limited. As a result, despite the fact that they were slowly incorporated into the scientific world, they were still segregated within it. By 1910, the feminist and suffragist movements in Europe and the United States had gained significant proportion, and women scientists contributed to both movements by doing research to refute "scientific" opinions about women's abilities, protesting about their conditions in the scientific community, giving public support, or engaging in local politics to win the vote for women. In 1920, although women were finally allowed to vote, neither their research initiatives nor their protests against discrimination resulted in noticeable improvements in their ability to pursue scientific careers (Rossiter 100). Thus, in the beginning of the twentieth century, even though the situation of women who wanted to become professional scientists and participate in the construction of knowledge had greatly improved in comparison to the previous century, they still had to face strong resistance to engage in scientific careers. By the 1920s, women with higher education degrees pursuing scientific careers still had limited opportunities and became confined to entry-level positions: "Rather than broadening the subsequent opportunities open to these highly educated women, employers and advisers of various sorts, instead tried to dissuade them from aspiring to full equality or advancement through a pattern of 'restrictive logic'" (Rossiter xvii). This restrictive logic created barriers and inconsistencies that affected all women pursuing careers in any scientific field. To resist this exclusion, women scientists employed many strategies, which tended to be either idealistic and confrontational or "realistic" and conservative. The former consisted of "writing angry letters and otherwise documenting the 'unfairness' of the unequal opportunities open to men and women" (Rossiter xviii). The latter consisted of accepting the inequalities and sexual stereotypes, "but using them for short-term gains such as establishing areas of 'women's work' for women. Strategists for this approach emphasized that women had 'unique skills' and 'special talents' that justified reserving certain kinds of work for them" (Rossiter xviii). Rossiter points out that in the United States by the 1920s, although the idealists had failed to obtain equal rights, the realists had made some progress and secured a place for women in more specific feminine fields: "They advocated such virtues as patience, self-discipline, and stoicism, which, rather than the liberals' protest and confrontation, remained the women scientists' dominant values until fairly recent times" (xviii). Also, certain scientific fields, such as botany and anthropology, were considered "feminized" and therefore allowed women to participate (Rossiter 295–96). Thus, women's success in scientific careers was only possible if they operated within the patterns of segregation and exclusion imposed on them to carve their space as professional scientists. In that sense, the institutionalization of science that took place in the nineteenth century ultimately served to consolidate the exclusion of women, mainly because science became mostly restricted to spaces in which they were not allowed to participate.

In Latin America, the situation was even more complicated, considering that very few women were able to pursue education, let alone employment in scientific activities. Across the continent, they continued to be strongly associated with their roles as mothers and with the responsibility of upbringing their sons and daughters. Throughout the nineteenth century, as the Latin American countries became independent, the process of nation-building heavily relied on a patriarchal system that excluded women from the public sphere (Jacinto and Scarzanella 12). By the beginning of the twentieth century, lack of education continued to be a major problem, and the incorporation of women into the educational system only started to take place after 1920 in most Latin American countries. Even so, women's educational opportunities were still limited to fields traditionally considered more "feminine," such as nursing, teaching, and social work. The feminist and suffragist movements had some impact on the gradual inclusion of women in the educational system in Latin America, but ultimately failed to accomplish comprehensive changes regarding their engagement in scientific careers. In 1910, the first Argentinian feminist congress attracted much attention and was attended by fifty-one professional women, 20 percent of them practicing medicine in the country (Ramacciotti and Valobra 37–38). They continued to advocate for women's rights and, in 1936, created the Argentinian Federation for University Women. Likewise, in Uruguay, many activists organized themselves to protest against the inequalities they faced as women in their fields, but with the start of the dictatorship of Gabriel Terra in the country in 1933, much of the efforts of the feminists and suffragists were suppressed (Sapriza 74). Thus, although some women were able to establish a scientific career in Latin America in the beginning of the century, their vindications did not disrupt the prevailing dynamics that excluded them from scientific issues in the following years. Despite this context, a few women scientists were able to overcome these gender barriers to establish their authority and reputation in their fields. But how did they accomplish that and to what extent were their strategies similar to those used by their counterparts from the previous century? How did travel narratives assist women in their endeavors to engage in scientific debates from a more literary perspective, despite their exclusion from the mainstream scientific fields?

AUTHORITY, GENDER, AND NATURAL HISTORY IN TRAVEL NARRATIVES

In the early nineteenth century only the findings of those authorized to produce knowledge were recognized as valid. Many male travelers journeyed throughout the world with the purpose of bringing new knowledge back to Europe. Women travelers, on the other hand, were not permitted to contribute to the production of scientific knowledge. As Tim Fulford, Debbie Lee, and Peter J. Kitson contend, publishing scientific findings required a number of alliances and negotiations among patrons, press, and the public. These alliances were particularly restricted to women: "the few women who had the opportunity to practice science were mostly presented as assistants to their male relatives or explicators of the original research of men" (3).

Thanks to recent studies in gender history, however, the findings of women travelers are emerging from the archives and we are rediscovering the history of science from this new perspective. Schiebinger has demonstrated, for example, how natural history can be categorized as a gendered discourse by analyzing the history of science from a post-structuralist feminist approach ("Gender" 3). Taking recent scholarship on the ways gender has impacted the history of science as point of departure, this book examines the situation of women travelers who desired to participate in the established circuits of knowledge production since the beginning of the nineteenth century, but were largely prevented from doing so due to the exclusively male world that was constructed among scientists.

Travel narratives are unavoidably influenced by the changes in perspective and new experiences that take place as travelers cross national, political, and cultural boundaries. By analyzing the writings of the British botanist Maria Graham (1785–1842), the Cuban-Spanish author Gertrudis Gómez de Avellaneda (1814–1873), the Brazilian writer Nísia Floresta (1810–1885), and the American naturalist Doris Cochran (1898–1968), this book demonstrates how their unique condition as travelers offered them unparalleled opportunities to participate in debates on natural history carried out by prominent male authors of their time. As transatlantic travelers who visited the same places described by their male predecessors and counterparts, these women gained authority to challenge recognized ideas and viewpoints, and by doing so, they managed to establish their own female authority.[3] Mills observes how British women travelers from the nineteenth century used their identity as imperialist subjects to achieve a position of authority in the contact zones. Pratt suggests the term contact zone "to refer to the space of colonial encounters, the space in which people geographically and historically separated come into contact with each other and establish ongoing relations . . ." (*Imperial* 6). Pratt, hence, created the term, which is broadly used in this book, to explain the associations between the traveler and the local people who come into contact and establish relationships which are not always symmetric (*Imperial* 7). Mills argues that women travel writers engaged in specific discourses that complied with the imperialist agenda to align themselves with Imperialist forces (*Discourses* 71–72). She advocates that women's travel writing should be analyzed taking into account the discourses surrounding them since these texts are complex and reveal a sophisticated negotiation permeated by power relations related to gender. For Mills, the contact zone offered women travelers unprecedented opportunities to use their race in their favor. In other words, the contact zone seemed to be a perfect environment for women to surpass gender limitations. Therefore, overseas, European women seemed to have more chances to construct their authority as writers. Although neither Mills nor Pratt explicitly discuss how women travelers engaged with the natural history discourse in their narratives, they do offer valuable tools to start this discussion.

Several studies on women's travel writing have been published in the last few years. For example, the recent *Transatlantic Travels in Nineteenth-Century Latin America: European Women Pilgrims* (2015) by Adriana Méndez Rodenas offers a comprehensive study of how European women travelers challenged the standard paradigms of travel writing. In her study, she analyzes the writings of Frances Erskine Inglis, Maria Graham, Flora Tristán, Fredrika Bremer, and Adela Breton, emphasizing how the trope of pilgrimage shaped the female travel narratives she discusses. Most of the scholarship about Latin American women travel narratives have given more visibility to these travelers, although focusing almost exclusively on the nineteenth century and generally addressing the travelers' impressions about the societies they visited, and the implications of race and class in the colonial space. *Peregrinas de outrora: viajantes latino-americanas no século XIX* (2008) by Stela Maris Scatena Franco offers a historical account of three Latin American women travelers focusing mainly on the autobiographical aspects of their writings. A few works bring together European and Latin American women travelers. Among these studies is *Mujer y literatura de viajes en el siglo XIX: entre España y las Américas* (2011) by Beatriz Ferrús Antón, which analyzes travelers such as Helen Sanborn, Ella Hoffman, Laura de Montoya, Gertrudis Gómez de Avellaneda, Clorinda Matto de Turner, Eduarda Mansilla, and Concha Espina to highlight their role in the construction of the new Latin American independent nations. More recently, Nina Gerassi-Navarro published *Women, Travel, and Science in Nineteenth-Century Americas: The Politics of Observation* (2017), an insightful study bringing together travelers from the United States, Brazil, and Mexico. She analyzes the travel narratives of Frances Calderón de la Barca and Elizabeth Cary Agassiz and shows how their writings include a social dimension to their observations on nature, culture, race, and progress in Brazil and Mexico. An influential study about Latin American travel writing in the twentieth century by Claire Lindsay, *Contemporary Travel Writing of Latin America* (2010), explores the narratives of several male and female writers, including Silvia Molina and María Luisa Puga. The book discusses contemporary issues related to mobility, representation, and globalization. Scholarship specifically analyzing the use of natural history discourse in women's travel narratives in the nineteenth and twentieth centuries is still very limited and this book complements and dialogues with the current scholarship in an attempt to bring the importance of women's endeavors to contribute to knowledge to the forefront.

Thus, this book draws from these and many other studies to specifically address the discourse of natural history in European, American, and Latin American women travel writers with the purpose of uncovering the specific strategies they used to become part of intellectual currents. Moreover, it includes a substantial analysis of unpublished archival materials, such as letters, memoirs, and photographs that had not been considered before in the analysis of women's travels and the construction of knowledge. This book aims to advance these studies by showing that although imperialist identity may have played its role in the construction of the authority of European women travelers, this model alone is insufficient to explain how women who lacked this imperialist identity were still able to achieve authority in the contact zone.[4] Although Pratt generally uses the term "contact zone" to refer to places outside of Europe, this concept applies equally well when colonial subjects travel to that continent and establish relations there. Despite the fact that the women travelers analyzed in this book belonged to somewhat privileged social classes, the point of intersection among them was neither their imperialist identity nor the whiteness of their skin, but rather, I argue, their transatlantic subjectivity. Being a transatlantic subject, as opposed to being English, American, Brazilian, or Spanish/Cuban, is what put these women in a position of authority on both sides of the Atlantic. Analyzing these women travelers together is not an attempt to homogenize them; instead, it is an opportunity to examine each of them in her own particularities, considering the impact that their travels had on the establishment of their authority as writers. Méndez Rodenas defines "transatlantic perspective" as "the comfort (and dis-ease) of inhabiting two worlds at once" (43). She contends that European travelers, male or female, although from different angles, produced their gaze leveraging their singular positions as inhabitants of a transatlantic space, each one from his or her own unique perspective. For the author, "European women enacted a two-way transatlantic transit by their acknowledgment of the Other, sensitivity to local customs, and awareness of the historical present" (11). At the same time, Méndez Rodenas evokes the transformative power of the encounter to highlight the effects of travels on the travelers themselves and on the places they visited (11). My notion of transatlantic subjectivity, as it will be further clarified below, encompasses the idea of transatlantic perspective proposed by Méndez Rodenas as one of the many assets of the transatlantic subject. Vanesa Míseres in her *Mujeres en tránsito: Viaje, identidad y escritura en Sudamérica (1830–1910)*, contends that traveling allowed Latin American women the opportunity to establish simultaneous ties with different spaces and nations without strictly belonging to one or the other. The transnational imaginary proposed by these travelers worked, then, as a response to the ideas prevailing in the nineteenth century about the nation, understood under these systems of oppositions that sought to discriminate between what belongs and what remains outside each region. From this perspective, the transnational becomes a cultural phenomenon that spreads across several nations and the act of traveling becomes a tool to generate transnational links between subjects who cross political, geographical, and cultural borders. The idea conveyed by Míseres is related to the fact that the women she analyzed, who traveled while national identities were being conceived in their own nations, found in travel writing a space to offer a perspective of this process from the outside. She proposes that through a "transnational imaginary," these women challenged the notions of gender, class, modernity, and cultural homogeneity of their time. Whereas Míseres' concept is concerned with the specific context within which Latin American women traveled, I argue that simply traveling was not sufficient to overcome the literal and metaphorical confinement imposed on them because of their gender. My analysis thus encompasses specific rhetorical and discursive strategies women travelers, regardless of their nationality or place of origin, employed to overcome their gender limitations.

Therefore, the concept of transatlantic subjectivity proposed in this book is an endeavor to explain the complex negotiation that led women to acquire an unusual authority as a result of their travels. To become a transatlantic subject meant to successfully negotiate their gendered condition in order to gain a prominence which would eventually overcome their gender constrains. This is not to say that all women travelers, Europeans or otherwise, were able to become transatlantic subjects. This unique status was only possible to achieve if she could successfully fulfill at least two conditions in her travel narratives: mobility and presence. Such conditions, although apparently diametric opposites, were interconnected, and together they offered the traveler the opportunity to establish herself firmly on both sides of the Atlantic, while simultaneously accentuating her ability to overcome certain spatial and textual constrains. Finally, because this transatlantic subjectivity derived from the negotiation of the female traveler's exclusive gendered condition, it is not equally applicable to male travelers. Besides, both European and non-European women were able to become transatlantic subjects, provided that they were able to firmly ascertain their mobility, and within that, their own presence in their travel narratives.

Mobility seems to be a logical condition when one refers to traveling. As Charles Forsdick writes, "travel writing is the most physical of all literary genres primarily as a result of its very subject matter which involves the passage of the body through varying configurations of time and space" (68). However, to establish the ability or capacity to move in a travel narrative was not straightforward for women as space was defined and regulated differently for them, and even the act of leaving home required justification (Foster and Mills 178).[5] Doris Massey points out that women's gendered identity was linked with the immobility of the confinement to the domestic sphere: "The attempt to confine women to the domestic sphere was both a specifically spatial control and, through that, a social control on identity . . ." (11). If gender notions are spatially produced by the binary association between public and private defined as masculine and feminine, these conceptions of space are challenged by mobility. Simply put, the "disruption of the association of women with the spaces of home . . . proves to have a profound effect on both a woman's sense of self and the way in which she is regarded by others, both at home and away" (3).[6] Women travelers established their mobility by moving within the contact zones, occupying various spaces, from the private to the public spheres, from the city to the countryside, constantly engaging in physical mobility. To become a transatlantic subject meant to challenge the fixity of women's identity, but this mobility also needed to be negotiated due to gender constraints. As Massey puts, "the challenge is to achieve this whilst at the same time recognizing one's necessary locatedness and embeddedness/ embodiedness, and taking responsibility for it" (11). In other words, mobility also meant a constant negotiation of gender roles, many times looking for alternate ways to establish authority.

Analyzing the complex correlation between gender and mobility is a difficult undertaking, as both concepts are permeated by cultural, political, geographical, and power relations. Massey contends that the gendered characteristic of space is not stationary and therefore cannot be analyzed without taking into consideration its dependence upon the cultural context that surrounds it (186). The concept of mobility considered here goes beyond geographical movement and encompasses meaning, practice, and potential, all aspects related to gendered disparities, and each one of them contributing to the production, reproduction, and contestation of these constraints (Cresswell and Uteng 2). As Tim Cresswell and Tanu Priya Uteng put it, "understanding mobility thus means understanding observable physical movement, the meanings that such movements are encoded with, the experience of practicing these movements and the potential for undertaking movements" (2). More than simply moving across the Atlantic, the travelers analyzed in this book attributed meaning to their mobility by engaging in travel narratives to record their enterprises. Such narratives asserted their experience of practicing these movements and their potential to do that. As Massey explains, "the mobility of women does indeed seem to pose a threat to a settled patriarchal order . . . one gender-disturbing message might be—in terms of both identity and space—keep moving!" (Massey 11). If traveling meant to challenge this spatial control, the comprehensive and perpetual meaning of mobility encoded in their travel narratives seemed to be the best way to overcome their spatial limitations. Moreover, "at the core of individual social mobility lies the ability to encounter, connect, and engage in relationships with other agents, objects and places," resulting in social mobility and social interaction (Cresswell and Uteng 23).[7] Therein lies the importance of complying with the second condition to become a transatlantic subject: locate their presence within their narrative of mobility.

Then, to become a transatlantic subject, women travelers had to establish a strong presence on both sides of the Atlantic, a presence which, situated within a narrative of transatlantic mobility, needed to convey the idea of a subject inhabiting two worlds at once. As Edward Said puts, in these narratives, "both the old and the new environments are vivid, actual, occurring together contrapuntally" (186). Therefore, this presence encompassed not only the fact or condition of being physically present in both words, as the concept of transatlantic perspective proposed by Méndez Rodenas or the idea of the transnational imaginary posed by Míseres imply, but also a noteworthy quality of poise and effectiveness. The writings of the women travelers analyzed in this book reveal that they affirmed their presence in both senses, and therefore stated their authority as travelers by engaging in specific rhetorical strategies to occupy the gendered terrain of travel narratives.

Because women travelers had to constantly negotiate their own gendered condition, their approaches to establish their transatlantic presence also had to be constantly negotiated. As Mills observes, they either rejected or reinforced several textual mechanisms employed by their predecessors, therefore the heterogeneous nature of their writings (3). The discourse of natural history permeating the travel narratives of male travelers dictated the conventions of travel writing. To be able to build a reputation as a travel writer meant to successfully engage oneself with these conventions to minimize the risk of producing a non-reliable account. The women analyzed here engaged, challenged, and subverted many of the travel writing tropes employed by their male peers, seeking to create a space for themselves as narrators. They engaged with the male hegemonic rhetoric of racial superiority, since presenting themselves in terms of race rather than gender was an effective strategy to undermine the biased preconceptions that limited their authority as writers (Foster and Mills 94). Nevertheless, while some of the travelers analyzed in this book could take advantage of the intrinsic racial superiority perpetuated by the accounts of their male predecessors, as was the case of Graham and Cochran, Latin American women travelers, such as Gómez de Avellaneda and Floresta, equally forged this superiority leveraging their own differences. To assert the quality of their presence, these women employed the discourse of natural history, sometimes replicating and sometimes deconstructing hegemonic tropes of discovery and adventure, employing specific mechanisms to forge fantasies of mastery and possession, even if occasionally mocking them. More important, they employed the high-status discourse of natural history in their narratives to engage in intellectual dialogues with other travelers by discussing, refuting, confirming, or updating previous opinions, therefore circulating information from one place to the other. However, instead of adopting a competitive and threatening position, they created their own way to approach this subject without transgressing the limits of their own femininity. By using literary and non-literary genres considered more appropriated for women, such as biographies, poems, letters, and personal notes, they feminized the natural history tropes to create a space for themselves to participate and circulate knowledge. What is more, they used this space to challenge and refute scientific beliefs, demystifying more masculine forms of discourse. Finally, to establish their presence in both sides of the Atlantic, these women formed strategic networks both in their home countries and in the contact zone to endorse their enterprises, verbalize their projects, and engage in intellectual debates. Leveraging their condition as travelers, they forged an expertise and offered insights on matters not previously available to them. All these textual mechanisms and strategies, combined with each traveler's purpose and particularities, provided them the opportunity to achieve the status of transatlantic subjects, granting them a unique position of authority for a woman traveler. Moreover, this transatlantic subjectivity provided them with an unusual visibility at the public sphere. Considering that mobility meant to keep overcoming these gender constraints, all women analyzed in this book capitalized from their travel experiences, negotiating their prominence to create alternate forms of visibility to participate in the intellectual debates of their time.

Paola Bertucci argues that Mariangela Ardinghelli (1730–1825), an Italian translator and naturalist who facilitated the circulation of knowledge between Italy and France in the nineteenth century, "constructed layers of selective visibility that allowed her authorship to be identified by specific audiences, while protecting herself from social isolation or derision" (Bertucci 226). If "going public" was potentially dangerous for women authors at her time, Ardinghelli was able to develop original strategies to avoid retaliation while creating her own space of action and authority. As a skilled mathematician and translator of male scientific works, she published many of her works anonymously, choosing not to be fully visible in the public sphere to comply with contemporary rules of social behavior (228). Drawing from Bertucci's discussion, considering the risks that "going public" presented to women, the concept of alternate visibility proposed in this book consists of the mechanisms women, travelers or scientists, used to carve their images to the public opinion. Akin to Ardinghelli, who never traveled, these women used their authority as travelers to negotiate their visibility by carefully selecting the subjects they would discuss and the means to impose their authorities on their readership and male counterparts. Using their travel narratives and other alternative genres that were considered more acceptable for female writers, all the women analyzed here created an alternate visibility that ultimately allowed them to discuss their scientific findings, therefore crossing boundaries into genres that had strong gender restrictions, while still preserving their authorship. Working within the limitations imposed on them, instead of openly defying them, this alternate visibility provided these women travelers an opportunity to contribute to the construction of knowledge and advance in their careers.[8]

This book consists of four chapters discussing each of the aforementioned travelers, considering their idiosyncrasies, the context in which they produced their narratives, how they approached the natural history discourse, and the careful negotiation their writings reveal about the process of becoming transatlantic subjects. Chapter 1, "Shaping Scientific Knowledge: Maria Graham's Travels in Nineteenth-Century Brazil," discusses the travel narratives of Graham's voyages to Brazil between 1821 and 1823, as well as her correspondence and personal notes. Although she did benefit from of her imperialist identity to establish her superiority and create a social network in Brazil, she still had to use specific mechanisms to establish her authority as a traveler. Graham cleverly took advantage of her position as a social explorer, a common female role in travel narratives (Pratt, *Imperial* 157), and employed the discourse of natural history to create an opportunity to discuss more scientific subjects and refute the impressions of Latin America made by her male predecessors. Her narrative displays an example of how a woman traveler from the early nineteenth century took advantage of her opportunity to travel to contribute to science. Although she was never able to become a professional botanist, her feminized perspective of the natural history discourse allowed her to deliberately blur the line between gender and genre. She employed genres such as biographies and religious books to produce narratives that effectively disclosed her scientific interests and contributions. This strategy allowed her to explicitly, but also cautiously, engage in scientific debates in order to establish her own authority as a scientist and travel writer.

Chapter 2, "Gertrudis Gómez de Avellaneda's Travel Writing: Beyond Optical Illusions of the Soul," takes the discussion to the other side of the Atlantic to examine the work of the Cuban traveler Gertrudis Gómez de Avellaneda, with particular emphasis on her travel accounts and periodical contributions. The chapter demonstrates how Gómez de Avellaneda used travel narratives as a tool to assist her in the establishment of both her transatlantic subjectivity and literary authority. I compare and contrast two of her travel accounts: *Memorias* (1836–1838), which describes her first voyage to Europe, and *Mi última excursión por los Pirineos* (1860), which comprises her annotations about the voyage she made to the Spanish and French Pyrenees twenty-five years later. As these accounts represent two very distinct moments of her career, they enlighten the development of Avellaneda's transatlantic subjectivity and the formation of her literary authority. Analyzing these accounts makes it evident that over the time span separating the publication of both works, Gómez de Avellaneda was able to achieve a voice that allowed her to speak, although many times not explicitly, about subjects not necessarily considered appropriate for a woman. Therefore, Gómez de Avellaneda used travel narratives as a means to challenge the discursive conventions of natural history and participate in scientific debates while she was also establishing and reaffirming her own authority as a writer. The chapter, then, focuses on the analysis of her magazine "Álbum cubano de lo bueno y de lo bello (Cuban Album of the Good and the Beautiful)," published in 1860, to demonstrate that her periodical writings became a means for her to discuss scientific ideas and promote herself as a mediator of the transatlantic world between Europe and Latin America.

Chapter 3, "Nísia Floresta's Voyages through Europe: Transatlantic Perspectives on Nature, Progress, and Women's Education," focuses on the voyages of the Brazilian educator and writer Nísia Floresta to Europe between 1856 and 1865 to demonstrate how she used the discourse of natural history to depict her travels and to inscribe herself in this tradition, creating an authority that would give her literary visibility in Europe. In her travel narratives, she dialogued with her male counterparts, and displayed a distinctive way to depict European nature and civilization. Unable to continue her career as a writer and educator in Brazil, she used her narrative as a space to propose an educational model for girls, which would include the necessity of the empirical experience provided by travels. She created her own feminized version of the Grand Tour, the social ritual in which upper-class English men participated in during the 1800s, and subverted this tradition, creating a feminine perspective of this practice in which she integrated nature and culture to create a unique educational model for girls. Ultimately, she used the alternate visibility provided by her travels to engage in intellectual debates involving women's education both in Europe and Brazil. Although Floresta was not a professional scientist, she approached scientific subjects in her travel narratives, novels, and essays to offer her insights and challenge current beliefs on issues such as biological determinism.

Chapter 4, "Beyond the Laboratory Walls: Doris Cochran's Strategies to Build a Reputation as a Scientist in the Early Twentieth Century," returns to Latin America and focuses on the American herpetologist of the Smithsonian Institution, Doris Cochran, and her strategies to overcome the gender constraints that still prevailed in the American scientific community in the early twentieth century. Although she was a scientist with a respectable position as a naturalist at the Smithsonian, her ability to participate in and contribute to the field of science was still shaped by her gender. In the beginning of the century, although women were slowly incorporated into the scientific world in the United States and elsewhere, they were nevertheless segregated. Cochran's travel narrative demonstrates that her journey to Brazil in 1935 became a remarkable opportunity to transcend the limits of the laboratory walls, while at the same time allowing her to surpass the limits of her own gender constraints. Through a collaboration with the Brazilian scientist and feminist Bertha Lutz, Cochran took advantage of the strategic transcontinental and transatlantic networks both women created in order to have access to privileges that facilitated her scientific travels that later granted her a significant visibility at home. Moreover, upon her return, Cochran created a public image of herself, "the frog lady," demystifying the stereotype of the scientist as white and male. The chapter demonstrates that, not surprisingly, women scientists in the early twentieth century still had to employ similar approaches used by their counterparts in the previous century to create their authority as writers of travel narratives.

By analyzing the work of these women together, this book introduces a novel perspective of the female transatlantic subject. All four women analyzed here, despite originating from different nations, with diverse educational backgrounds and scientific interests, benefited from the social leverage offered by the transatlantic world between Europe, Latin America, and the United States and used travel narratives as means to establish themselves as transatlantic subjects, forging an authority which included aspects that would never have been possible had they stayed in their native countries. By doing that, they sought to achieve recognition, either as a botanist, in the case of Graham, a writer, in the case of Gómez de Avellaneda, an educator, in the case of Floresta, or as a scientist, in the case of Cochran. Unable to participate in scientific discussions with the same authority men were granted, their transatlantic subjectivity allowed them to achieve visibility in less professional and therefore less restrictive fields. Their alternate visibility was an attempt to obtain recognition back home, thereby continuing to challenge their gendered confinement and maintaining their mobility. By creating an image of themselves that allowed their participation in intellectual and scientific dialogues without necessarily assuming a formal authority that was only allowed to men, they managed to make their contributions to knowledge without fully transgressing their gender boundaries. These women left their homes so that they could find a space for themselves to have a voice and contribute to the construction and dissemination of knowledge on both sides of the Atlantic. Moreover, by encompassing women travelers from a time span of one hundred years, this book stresses the importance of transatlantic travels to the possibility of making intellectual contributions to the field of science well into the twentieth century. The women explored in the chapters that follow had to overcome certain social limitations to make their work seen. For these women then, their alternate visibility created a unique, yet gendered, space to make intellectual contributions.

NOTES

1. The watercolor painting displayed in the front cover of this book represents another example of Cochran's attempt to share her knowledge and passion for frogs employing alternate genres.

2. Rossiter's seminal study documents American women scientists' efforts to establish themselves in the scientific community and their struggles to be able to fully participate in the sciences in the early twentieth century. For more details, see Margaret W. Rossiter, *Women Scientists in America: Struggles and Strategies to 1940* Baltimore: Johns Hopkins University Press, 1984.

3. Although strictly speaking Cochran did not cross the Atlantic, the position of the United States in relation to Latin America replicated to a great extent the European imperialist model. For consistency, I will refer to her travels as transatlantic in this book.

4. Throughout the book, I also draw on the valuable contributions of several other scholars who analyzed the travel writing of the women chosen for my project, such as Jennifer Hayward, Stella Maris Scatena Franco, Constância Lima Duarte, Maria Soledad Caballero, Charlotte Hammond Matthews, Regina Akel, Monica Szurmuk, Vanesa Míseres, Beatriz Ferrús Antón, Angela Pérez Mejía, and Adriana Méndez Rodenas, among others.

5. Foster and Mills observe that different groups of women had different relations with space. They specifically discuss the differences between high- and middle-class British women, explaining that the latter had more access to public spaces if compared to the former in the nineteenth century (178). However, all travelers analyzed in this book faced similar restrictions in terms of space and gender.

6. For a detailed study about mobility and space in Francophone Literature, see *Exiles, Travellers and Vagabonds: Rethinking Mobility in Francophone Women's Writing,* edited by Kate Averis and Isabel Hollis-Touré.

7. For more details, see *Gendered Mobilities*, edited by Tanu Priya Uteng and Tim Cresswell.

8. This approach was well aligned with the realist approach suggested elsewhere by Rossiter, p. 177 (note 1 above).

Chapter One

Shaping Scientific Knowledge
Maria Graham's Travels in Nineteenth-Century Brazil

"We walked down to the foot of the hill, and . . . most of us carried home something. Fruit and flowers attracted some; Langford got a number of diamond beetles, and a magnificent butterfly, and I a most inadequate sketch of the scene . . ." (Graham, *Brazil* 166).[1] This passage transports the reader to the beginning of the nineteenth century and to the exciting world of scientific expeditions.[2] One might imagine that this account could be found in the diary of a celebrated traveler and naturalist such Humboldt, who spent several years in South America and whose writings became famous throughout the world.[3] The use of the word "inadequate" to describe the narrator's sketched rendition, however, would unlikely be seen in one of Humboldt's accounts. Instead, this quotation comes from the diary of Maria Graham (1785–1842), the daughter of a British naval officer who had the chance to travel abroad well before other better-known women voyagers, such as Mary Kingsley, were even born. Adjectives such as "inadequate" are very common in Graham's narratives whenever she referred to her own work. Graham's choice of words was not innocent but instead an ironic deployment of self-deprecating language; one of the many strategies she utilized to construct her authority as a writer and a traveler. Thus, this passage illustrates well the discourse Graham deliberately employed in her travel accounts. A woman traveler who explored the New World, she endeavored to bring home more than simple travel accounts; her ultimate goal was to share the knowledge she acquired with the rest of the world. Hampered in these scholarly efforts by her gender, Graham had to forge the means to be able to accomplish this goal.

By focusing on Maria Graham's travel diaries and some unpublished manuscripts, this chapter shows that one of her greatest goals was to cross the boundary of the masculine world of natural history. This analysis of Graham's writings offers a new perspective on her contributions to travel literature and science; in addition, by showing how she made use of her status as a British woman to produce an imperialist discourse, I demonstrate that she strategically exploited her imperialist identity with the intention of constructing her transatlantic subjectivity and producing a more literary and "feminine" form of scientific discourse. Ultimately, her reputation as a travel writer offered her the opportunity to take advantage of an alternate visibility: as a writer of travel narratives, Graham was allowed to publish her scientific findings avoiding the use of more masculine and restrictive forms of discourse. By discussing how she accomplished that it is possible to further unveil women's strategies to contribute to science during the early nineteenth century.

BOOKS, TRAVELS, AND SCIENCE: A SHORT SKETCH OF MARIA GRAHAM'S LIFE

Maria Graham was born Maria Dundas in the United Kingdom in 1785, and starting at a young age she accompanied her father on travels throughout the world. The daughter of Rear Admiral George Dundas, a British naval officer, Maria Dundas received an education similar to many middle-class girls from her time. She was sent to school in Richmond and used to spend the holidays with her uncle, Sir David Dundas. She recollected that these holidays were very agreeable and that his house was a center for scientists, literary men, and French émigrés. This environment actively inspired her to learn more about the world: "At Richmond too . . . I read many books of history, and now and then some portions of natural history, of which I was extremely fond, and books of travels into all parts of the world" (qtd. in Gotch 59). In 1808 she traveled to India accompanying her father: "On the thirtieth of December, 1808, I embarked with my father, my sister, and my youngest brother, on board His Majesty's ship Cornelia, rated two and thirty gun frigate, for Bombay, where my father was appointed Commissioner of the Navy . . ." (Gotch 93). Her voyage to India was recorded in a diary that she later published. While en route, she met British Lieutenant Thomas Graham whom she married in 1809. Years later, in 1821, Thomas Graham was assigned to travel to Brazil and Chile, and the couple embarked on an enterprise that changed Maria Graham's life forever.

In her travels, Graham wrote diaries that provided new perspectives on the society and politics of Latin America in the nineteenth century. She visited Brazil three times: the first time, between 1821 and 1822, accompanied by her husband; the second time, between 1822 and 1823, after her husband's death and a stay of seven months on her own in Chile; her third and final visit to Brazil took place in 1824 following a short stay in England. On the third trip Graham returned to Brazil specifically to tutor the daughter of the Brazilian Emperor Dom Pedro I, Princess Maria da Gloria, later crowned the queen of Portugal. She described the first two visits in her diary, published under the title *Journal of a Voyage to Brazil and Residence There, During Part of the Years 1821, 1822, 1823*. The third voyage was documented by Graham and titled "Life of D. Pedro." The manuscript was published in Portuguese under the name *Correspondência entre Maria Graham e a Imperatriz Dona Leopoldina e Cartas Anexas*.[4] The original manuscript was written in 1835 and now is part of the collections of the National Library of Rio de Janeiro.[5] In 1825 Graham sailed back to England and two years later she married the painter Sir Augustus Wall Callcott. Less than ten years later, in 1836, she fell ill and was unable to leave her house in Kensington during the last years of her life. She died as Lady Callcott in Kensington on November 21, 1842 surrounded by what she most loved in her life: her books, paintings, sculptures, and curiosities of natural history (Gotch 296).

A BRITISH LADY IN THE TROPICS: NETWORKS IN THE CONTACT ZONE

Drawing from Pratt's notion of the contact zone, it is possible to analyze how Maria Graham carefully constructed a social network of influential figures in the Brazilian society. The members of this network shared her interest in natural history and authorized her travels to the countryside, where she made most of her relevant scientific findings. Using her influence as a British woman, she was able to visit as many interesting and exotic places as her male counterparts.[6] The outcomes of these explorations were not only remarkable pages in her travel diaries; they also resulted in valuable ethnographical and geological observations and even the discovery of new specimens of plants. The strategies used by Graham to explore, publish, and therefore produce scientific knowledge inevitably intersected with the colonial context and the contact zone. Moreover, the contact zone seems to have made feasible the publication of her work, which gave her a remarkable visibility in the public sphere. Although women had more freedom before the Victorian era in many aspects of their lives, as critics such as Ann B. Shteir have observed, their role in society was still very limited to less professional activities. In the late Enlightenment period, although science was part of the education and recreation of young ladies, women's scientific work was largely shaped by the influences and protection they received, commonly, from their fathers or husbands. With rare exceptions, their work remained outside of the public records (Schiebinger, *Cultivating* 51).

Given the constraints Graham encountered as a woman of her time, the colonial environment provided an uncommon space for her to take advantage of her European status, as Mills writes: "women align themselves with colonial forces and thus potentially with a predominately male and masculine force" (*Discourses* 25).[7] By aligning themselves with male forces, British women travelers in colonial spaces were able to use imperialist power to their advantage and achieve more than they could in their own nations. From this perspective, given that the scientific space was not feminine and the practice of science was considered "an unwomanly act" (Watts 55), the contact zone provided a space in which it was easier for women to join the world of natural history in a smooth and natural way. However, although they were allowed to travel as long as they were accompanied by their male protectors, women were not supposed to explicitly attempt to make scientific contributions. Hence, simply aligning themselves with the masculine imperialist power was not sufficient for them to enter the world of science, and they had to find alternative ways to achieve this goal. In fact, the natural imperial superiority was just a way to define themselves as the other, an essential condition in the establishment of a transatlantic subjectivity. The contact zone was a place where women travelers such as Maria Graham could take advantage of their status as European citizens to achieve this superiority in relation to the other, albeit not without remaining within the boundaries of their gender. Indeed, Graham used her imperialist identity and employed an imperialist discourse to present herself as a prominent person, somehow above gender limitations.[8] Pérez-Mejía observes, in the case of Flora Tristán and Maria Graham, that "if these women suffered discrimination in their travels for the fact of being women, however, their European origins and their white skin allowed them to assume a position of superiority as narrators with respect toward any other race . . ." (78). Graham often made such superiority explicit in her narrative:[9]

> I have met with two or three well-informed men of the world, and some lively conversable women; but none of either sex that at all reminded me of the well-educated men and women of Europe. Here the state of general education is so low, that more than common talent and desire of knowledge is requisite to attain any; therefore the clever men are acute, and sometimes a little vain, feeling themselves so much above their fellow-citizens, and the portion of book-learning is small. (Graham, *Brazil* 147)

As this passage indicates, Graham defined the other in terms of race rather than gender. Even if her statement refers to the level of education of the Brazilians regardless of their gender, by emphasizing that "well-educated men and women of Europe" were superior, her statement was racial. By using this rhetoric, women travelers undermined their own gendered condition to grant themselves an intrinsic superiority (Mills 94). Therefore, in their voyages to America, travelers (especially women) could construct a new identity, which was subject to social structures and relations that differed to some extent from those of Europe (Pratt, *Imperial* 169).

By establishing the other as inferior and reaffirming her own superiority, Graham could transcend her role as woman. This superiority allowed her to create a complex social and intellectual network that, among other things, enabled and legitimated her explorations. When she first went to Brazil in 1821, to the city of Recife, Graham began to establish the contacts that would eventually enable her to enter the royal residence in Rio de Janeiro three years later. Arriving in the middle of a revolution, since the country was at the peak of the conflicts that would culminate in its independence in 1822, Graham witnessed and narrated important historic events of these pre- and post-independence years. In this unstable environment, she became friends with Madame do Rego, wife of Luís do Rego, a Portuguese general who was the governor of Pernambuco, a Brazilian province in the northeastern part of the country. His objective, although ultimately unsuccessful, was to avoid the revolution. Madame do Rego was the daughter of the Viscountess of Rio Seco, an Irish woman with important connections in Rio de Janeiro. As a result, when Graham arrived in Rio de Janeiro on December 15, 1821, she began to make use of the network of acquaintances and friends she had formed in Pernambuco. Due to these connections, she soon became friends with the Viscountess of Rio Seco, wife of the Viscount of Rio Seco, who was responsible for the Royal Treasury. Intimate friends with the Royal Family, the couple would be the perfect bridge between Graham and the Princess Maria Leopoldina a few months later. The turbulent environment of the revolution prevented Graham from getting closer to the Royal Family at that moment. However, her friendship with the Viscountess introduced her to the upper classes in Brazilian society: "I went ashore last night to the opera, as it was again a gala night, and hoped to have witnessed the reception of the Prince and Princess. The Viscondessa do Rio Seco kindly invited me to her box, which was close to theirs; but, after waiting some time, notice arrived that the Prince was so busy writing to Lisbon, that he could not come" (*Brazil* 189).[10]

Indeed, the revolutionary environment offered Graham the perfect opportunity to strengthen her ties with the Rio Seco family. As noted, the Viscount was an important man to the Portuguese Court. Because of the instability provoked by the movements for independence, people with connections with the Portuguese Crown naturally felt threatened. Graham took advantage of the situation and offered protection to her influential friends: "I went ashore with an officer as early as I could . . . determined to call on the Viscountess of Rio Seco in my way, to offer her refuge in the frigate. We found her in a Brazilian dishabille and looking harassed and anxious . . . we promised her, that on her making a signal from her house, or sending a message, she should have protection" (*Brazil* 184). As Graham indicated here, the unstable environment in the colony allowed her to offer help to influential people in Brazil. Graham used the imperial forces, represented here by the frigate, to present herself as someone in a position of superiority, who had the power to grant protection. The use of the pronoun "we" served to align herself with the British forces because ultimately it was their protection that was being promised. The portrayal of the Viscountess as fragile and harassed endorsed her necessity of protection. Graham noticeably used her influence and imperial power to get close to the Viscountess and to win her trust and friendship. In fact, this event marked a turning point for Graham. From then on, she attended balls, receptions, and meetings of the high society in Rio de Janeiro, and consequently, further expanded her network of friends and contacts.[11]

When Graham returned to Brazil after spending almost a year alone in Chile, she reconnected with the friends she had made during her first visit. Now a widow, since her husband had died on their way to Chile, she was well aware of the importance of having protection in order to be able to move freely throughout the country and conduct her scientific explorations. Given the calmer post-independence atmosphere of this second voyage to Brazil, Graham finally was able to meet and become close to the now Empress Maria Leopoldina. This valuable contact came about thanks to her relationship with the Viscountess of Rio Seco, to whom Graham had earlier offered protection. The Viscountess was a good friend of José Bonifácio, a minister and adviser of D. Pedro I, and a scientist himself: "Soon after I arrived here, in March . . . I felt that, as a stranger here, and situated as I am, I was peculiarly unprotected, and therefore I spoke to the minister Jose Bonifacio, telling him my feelings; and saying, that from the amiable character of the Empress, I should wish to be allowed to wait on her, and to consider her as protecting me while I remain in the empire" (Graham, *Brazil* 248). To establish her need for protection, she relocated Brazil to an imperial position, strategically emphasizing her gendered condition as a woman to justify her need to meet the Empress Leopoldina. After consulting José Bonifácio in person, on May 19, 1823, Graham was in fact introduced to the Empress, whose friendship would last until the latter's death in 1826, only a year after Graham took leave of Brazil for the last time. Importantly, however, the friendship with the Empress turned out to be not just for protection. Maria Leopoldina shared a great interest in science and Graham knew she could count on the Empress' help to achieve her objective of becoming a scientific explorer in Brazil.[12]

The Empress Leopoldina became the greatest friend Graham made in Brazil, and the interest of both women in natural history sealed their camaraderie. They exchanged several letters that clearly document their many common interests: "The catalogue of shells which I sent you will enable you when in London to procure me the kinds and species which are wanting in my collection. I shall be glad to send you in return whatever may be curious or precious to illustrate the natural history of Brazil" (Graham, *Life* 111). Graham and Leopoldina, therefore, not only exchanged letters, but they also conspired in the task of attempting to acquire objects and books in a field that was not willing to allow for women's participation. Despite this wider context of the male-dominated field of inquiry, it is still surprising to note that the Empress of Brazil, unquestionably the most powerful woman in the country, had to depend on Graham to be able to obtain such objects. Her willingness to send, in exchange, any object to illustrate the Brazilian natural history shows that she would use all her influence to satisfy the scientific interests of her friend.

It is worthwhile to analyze Graham's network of local connections because it illustrates her exposure to many different contact zones in Brazil. Furthermore, it suggests that she had to use different social strategies to take full advantage of the opportunities that each friendship provided, leveraging her imperial identity while negotiating her gender constrains. Evidently, her British superiority allowed her to be treated with privilege within the country, along with the men on her ship: "This day several of the officers and midshipmen of the Doris accompanied us to dine at the governor's, at half-past four o'clock. Our welcome was most cordial I was seated . . . between M. and Madame do Rego. He seemed happy to talk of his old English friends . . . and she had a thousand enquiries to make about England, whither she is very anxious to go" (*Brazil* 112–13). As mentioned above, whereas Graham used her British superiority to become acquainted to the Rio Seco family, she was aware that it would be presumptuous to make a similar offer to the Empress. Thus, she wisely changed her strategy and presented herself as a vulnerable and defenseless woman who herself now needed to be protected, but without undermining her imperial superiority: "She [the Empress] spoke to me most kindly; and said, in a very flattering way, that she had long known me by name, and several other things that persons in her rank can make so agreeable by voice and manner; and I left her with the most agreeable impressions" (249). Graham's reputation had preceded her and, despite the Empress' rank, she treated her in equal terms. It is apparent that Graham's goal was to become close to the Empress not only because she could protect Graham as a lonely, vulnerable widow but also because she could offer her protection as a woman with an interest in carrying out intellectual pursuits, which notably was also a quality of the Empress:[13] After a conversation with Leopoldina, she commented: "Her Imperial Majesty conversed easily with every body, only telling us all to speak Portuguese, which of course we did. She talked a good deal to me about English authors, and especially of the Scotch novels, and very kindly helped me in my Portuguese; which, though I now understand, I have few opportunities of speaking to cultivated persons. If I have been pleased with her before, I was charmed with her now" (319). The passage indicates that Graham considered the Empress a knowledgeable woman, with whom she could have a high-level intellectual conversation. Her remark indicates an air of superiority, suggesting that only the Empress was able to fulfil the standards of what she considered a "cultivated person." The common knowledge and interests they shared sealed their bond of friendship and, as a result, Graham ultimately was offered an opportunity of employment to become the tutor of the daughter of the Empress.[14] Her extensive network of friends, aligned with her nationality and level of education, along with her friendship with the Empress, allowed Graham to make strong connections within many contact zones in the Brazilian society, firmly, but carefully, establishing her presence as a transatlantic subject.

Considering Graham's wide-ranging social circle, it is evident that she also aspired to be what Pratt calls a "social explorer," a woman traveler interested primarily in the social and political aspects of the places she visited (Pratt, *Imperial* 160).[15] However, Graham took advantage of her position as a social explorer to extrapolate this role. For Pratt, the social explorers were the female versions of the capitalist vanguard, the European travelers who massively went to Latin America in the beginning of the nineteenth century, mainly after the independence movements within the continent. Propelled by the economic opportunities provided by the newly independent nations, these travel writers legitimized this neocolonial territory of European expansionism (Pratt, *Imperial* 148). Pratt adds that, in contrast with the explorers and naturalists who employed a rhetoric of discovery on their travel accounts, "their writings were a goal-oriented rhetoric of conquest and achievement" (*Imperial* 148). However, the enterprise of the capitalist vanguards was highly gendered, a male and heroic world not available for the women who traveled along them or alone in the same period. Within this context, the female travelers defined by Pratt as social explorers created their own rhetorical possibilities, considering the goal-oriented nature of the narrative of conquest proposed by the capitalist vanguard (Pratt, *Imperial* 157). Their narratives, instead, were urban-based accounts focusing on their social and political lives, displaying a strong ethnographical interest, and their identity and authority were established through their independence and social interactions (Pratt, *Imperial* 159). Graham indeed took advantage of her independence, privileges, and social interactions to establish her identity in the contact zone. However, as opposed the social explorers, she did not necessarily reject adventure and scientific erudition in her travel account. On the opposite, she offered many comments which underscore her scientific interest and expertise, evidencing that social explorer was not the only role she performed in her travel account. The documentary evidence available indicates that she benefited from her position as a social explorer to pursue her scientific and intellectual endeavors.[16]

On her second stay in Brazil, she undertook an expedition to Santa Cruz, on the surroundings of Rio de Janeiro, which was only possible because of her network: "The Visconde do Rio Seco had kindly furnished us with a letter, and mentioned that the object of the journey was mere curiosity, so that the Capitão told us that he would next day do all he could to satisfy us" (Graham, *Brazil* 283). During this trip, Graham used her status, either as a socialite or as a British citizen, to have doors opened to her, sometimes literally: "A mulatto serving-man came round cautiously to *reconnoitre* from the back of the house, when having ascertained that we really were English travelers benighted and wet, the front door was opened" (276). Her visit to the sugar cane plantation, *Engenho dos Affonsos,* also was only possible because of her network:[17] Her social network and imperial superiority ultimately facilitated her explorations as a professional traveler, and Graham made it very clear that this adventure was only possible because of her situation as a British traveler with important connections in Rio de Janeiro. In the manuscript "Life of D. Pedro" she also described in much detail her expedition to the Macacu farm where she made several botanical observations and collected many specimens, which she later sent to London. The expedition was, once again, facilitated by her role as a social explorer since the farm belonged to the prominent Lisboa family, which had strong connections with the imperial court and to which Graham became acquainted through her relationship with the Empress Maria Leopoldina. This same family offered her a cottage where she lived after leaving the Royal Palace in 1825. While in this cottage she collected many plants and seeds, built an herbarium, and sent many specimens to England. This is very well documented in her unpublished correspondence with Sir William Hooker, a celebrated botanist who became the director of the Kew Garden years later.[18] As these and other instances indicate, Graham used her social relations and powerful friends to authorize her scientific explorations.

A SOCIAL EXPLORER WITH SCIENTIFIC ASPIRATIONS: NEGOTIATING AUTHORITY AND TRANSATLANTIC SUBJECTIVITY

Although to a great extent Graham's narrative fit the model of the social explorers described above, she also leveraged her position as a British socialite to engage in many scientific expeditions during her stay in Brazil. Unlike the role of social explorer, scientific expeditions required a taste of adventure, however, the role of the adventure hero was not easily available to women travelers simply due to its strong association with a British masculine subjectivity (Foster and Mills 255). Mills and Foster contend that within the role of adventure hero there are a few narrative possibilities for women travelers if they resorted to the specific position of explorers. However, they needed to adopt certain strategies to guarantee that their femininity would somehow be preserved within the narrative (259). To be able to engage in such scientific enterprises, Graham had to negotiate her gendered position within the narrative possibilities available to her as a woman traveler.

On August 20, 1823, she departed on the aforementioned expedition to Santa Cruz, in the countryside of Rio de Janeiro, and although her position as a socialite facilitated her enterprise, she was aware that her curiosity and desire for adventure could interfere with her identity as a social explorer: "I had long wished to see a little more of the neighborhood of Rio than I have hitherto done; and had resolved on riding at least to Santa Cruz, about fourteen leagues from hence, and as the road is too well travelled to fear extraordinary accidents, and I am not timid as to common inconveniences, I had determined to hire a black attendant and go alone" (274). Graham's willingness to visit the countryside indicates her need of mobility within the contact zone. However, this mobility needed to be negotiated to avoid undermining the "need for protection" which granted her the endorsement of the Empress. Whereas Graham's remark could represent a shift in her narrative, which could expose a subversion of her role as a social explorer, she balanced her discourse and avoided the risk of damaging her own femininity. Even though she declared her willingness to travel alone, and her lack of fear in undertaking such a trip, she also asserted that the road she chose was relatively safe, and that she would hire a companion to travel alongside her. Besides, Graham later added that although preferring to go on the trip alone, she eventually accepted the company of the brother of an English friend, and admitted that she was very pleased to have a "fellow traveler," especially when traveling on horseback (*Brazil* 274): "I confess I was very glad to be relieved of the absolute charge of myself, and not a little pleased to have the society of a well-breed, intelligent young man, whose taste for the picturesque beauties of nature agrees with my own" (274). By placing herself under British male protection, she stressed her femininity and complied with gender constrains. Interestingly, Graham presented her companion as a fellow traveler, who shared a similar level of intellectual capacity as hers to undertake the trip. However, over the course of the expedition her compatriot companion became almost invisible and she only referred to him when using the pronoun "we." This evidences the fact that although she did accept the male protection of her compatriot, she claimed her own agency in the expedition. Moreover, his presence turned out to be a mere narrative device to negotiate her transgression and remain within the limits of her role as woman and social explorer.

Graham's social explorations often took her readers to the center of Rio de Janeiro's urban life, visiting palaces, museums, attending fancy dinner and operas, as well as to visits to prisons, markets, and religious retreats for girls (Pratt, *Imperial* 157). To comply with her femininity, even though she adopted the role of the male explorer in her expedition, Graham leveraged her position as a social explorer interested in the politics and societies she visited, giving a certain ethnographical character to these narratives. In her expedition, although she was visiting a more rural and exotic environment, she engaged in social interactions to have conversations with the locals, eat their food, and observe their behaviors and habits. Still in Santa Cruz, when visiting an Indian settlement, she commented:

> I enquired one of the women, in whose hut I sat down, if she knew whence her tribe came: she said no; she had been brought, when a mere child, from a great distance to Taguahy, by the fathers of the [Jesuit] company; that her husband had died when she was young; that she and her daughters had always lived there; but her sons and grandsons, after the fathers of the company went, had returned to their fathers, by which she meant that they had resumed their savage life. This is not surprising. . . . Many of the Indian women have married the creole Portuguese; intermarriages between creole women and Indian men are rare. . . . The Indian huts at Taguahy are very poor; barely sufficient in walls and roof to keep out the weather, and furnished with little besides hammocks and cooking utensils; yet we were everywhere asked to go in and sit down: all the floors were cleanly swept, and a log of wood or a rude stool was generally to be found for a seat for the stranger, the people themselves squatting on the ground. (285)

If the narratives of the male explorers tended to reinforce rigid racial stereotypes that further validated their imperial agenda, Graham challenged assumptions of savagery, instead justifying the natives' primitive state by exposing their poverty and exploitation. Her ethnographic interest is also related to scientific inquiry, as she was very systematic and methodological when collecting information about the living conditions of the natives. Still, the native Indians behaved as colonized in relation to her, willing to respond to all her questions and offering the best seats (Pratt, *Imperial* 163). Moreover, the movement across the space in the contact zone, ranging from the urban to the rural environments, further emphasized her freedom within the contact zone.

However, at times, her role as a female social explorer was deliberately suppressed in the narrative. Instead of social interactions and political opinions, a narrative of exploration, curiosity, and adventure emerged from the pages of her diary. Her excitement with the exploration of the unknown was evident from her descriptions, as she contemplated nature. She even admitted that the excursion offered her an entire new perspective of Brazil, one that she had not seen before (257). However, this so-called "entire new perspective" was not completely new to her audience:

> And above all these the mountains rose in the distance, and lower hills more near, between which, long valleys stretched themselves till the eye could follow them no farther; and the foregrounds were filled up with gigantic aloes, streams, and pools, and groups of passing cattle and their picturesquely clad conductors. Near Campo Grande, the scenery is diversified by several little green plains, with only an insulated tree here and there, decorated with air plants in bloom, and scarlet creepers. Beyond this lies one of the most beautiful spots I ever saw, namely, Viaga; where the rocks, trees, plains, and buildings, seem all placed on purpose to be admired. (281)

Graham's mapping gaze of the scene reproduced the point of view of the Eurocentric nineteenth-century colonial exploration accounts, which granted significance to what otherwise would be in fact a non-event on her narrative (Anderson 104). As Pratt puts, the gaze of the colonial explorer aestheticized the landscape and represented the sight as a painting, a symmetric and ordered rendition. At the same time, it conferred to this landscape a "density of meaning," which revealed its material and symbolic richness. This gaze reproduced the fantasy of mastery over what was being observed (Pratt, *Imperial* 204). The scene was subordinated to her gaze, like a painting or a diorama in a museum, intended to be possessed and admired. By resorting to this rhetoric, Graham legitimized herself as a colonial observer, a necessary maneuver to establish her presence as an European and a traveler, and by extent, her transatlantic subjectivity.

As a matter of fact, an even more masculine form of discourse emerged in the narrative when she exposed her intellectual capacity and desire to engage in more scholarly and scientific subjects. Over the course of the expedition, she made several botanical observations, mentioning the particularities of the plants she described. However, Graham highlighted her awareness of gender constraints through her negotiation of this scientific authority:

> Every time I pass through a grove in Brazil, I see new flowers and plants, and a richness of vegetation that seems inexhaustible. To-day I saw passion-flowers of colours I never observed before; green, pink, scarlet, and blue: wild pine apples, of beautiful crimson and purple: wild tea, even more beautiful than the elegant Chinese shrub: marsh-palms, and innumerable aquatic plants, new to me: and in every little pool, wild-ducks, water-hens, and varieties of storks, were wading about in graceful pride. (286)

Although she employed a non-technical language to refer to her botanic observations, she was still exposing her interest in more scientific subjects and expanding her gaze beyond political and social matters. Her scientific comments about the Brazilian landscape were not only related to her botanical interests. For example, in the passage below, she made some geological observations, further exposing the negotiation needed when adopting more scientific forms of discourses in her narrative: "I observed on the beach to-day a line of red sandy-looking matter, extending all along the shore, and tinging the sea for several feet from the edge. At night this red edge became luminous.
. . . It is the first time I have seen it here, and I cannot find that anybody has paid any attention to it. Perhaps it is not worth noticing . . ." (298). Graham's interest in making such a scientific statement, once again, reveals her taste for erudition and science, even if she rejected her own expertise by claiming that perhaps her observation was not worth mentioning. Although she avoided the use of more technical language and the mention of scientific names, at times, an unusual authority surfaces in her narrative. When visiting the Botanical Garden of Rio a few days after returning from Santa Cruz, she declared: ". . . the head gardener . . . showed us the cinnamon they have barked here, and the other specimens of spice: the cloves are very fine, and the cinnamon might be so; but the wood they have barked is generally too old, and they have not yet the method of stripping the twigs: this I endeavored to explain, as I had seen it practised in Ceylon" (297). Her remark reveals that her botanic expertise was more extensive and broader than she made it sound in her narrative, and that she had valuable knowledge to share even with professional male botanists. Her comment also implicitly grounded her expertise and knowledge with her imperial identity, since she mentioned Ceylon, granting a natural superiority to her remark. Even though she was referring to her own expertise more assertively, she was not necessarily claiming a more professional status to her observations, preferring to emphasize her empirical knowledge instead.[19] Regardless of the negotiations she had to make when adopting a more scientific voice, her narrative confirmed her capacity to observe, analyze, report, therefore reaffirming her intellectual curiosity and daring enterprise (Smith 19–20). In other words, her expedition provided her an opportunity to position herself as a capable observer and a credible narrator engaged in the geological and botanical debates of her time. As will be discussed below, taking part in this kind of debate using a more professional approach most certainly would cause great controversy among male scientists, especially when Graham tried to report her non-professional observations to them.

Determined to establish her presence as a transatlantic subject as well as her credibility as a travel writer while trying not to transgress her status as a social explorer, Graham's narration of her scientific expeditions served the purpose of further establishing her presence as in both sides of the Atlantic, which granted her the authority to engage in the construction of knowledge. Moreover, these expeditions confer to her subjectivity a certain mobility within the contact zone, which was an essential requirement on the establishment of her authority as a travel writer. By extending her gaze beyond political and social affairs, she challenged the immobility of her own status as a woman in society.

CROSSING THE BOUNDARIES INTO THE MASCULINE WORLD OF SCIENCES

Schiebinger has discussed the many ways in which science can be seen as gendered: "Feminists have enjoyed great success in revealing gender inequalities in the humanities, social sciences, and life sciences, where subject matters are sexed or easily imagined to have sex and gender" ("Creating" 468). The gendered character of the scientific discourse has often portrayed women as incapable of intellectual production and as naturally suitable only for reproduction and motherhood. Women travelers, however, found themselves in an advantageous position to engage on topics beyond their domestic life and children. They could discuss issues related to their travels, a logical outcome of which was to use the discourse of natural history to frame their observations. However, because it was considered inappropriate for women to write about scientific matters, they could not engage the discourse in the same ways as their male counterparts. Through the use of travel narratives, women could describe the world beyond Europe and, by emphasizing their ability to observe, place themselves in a position of authority almost impossible to achieve for a woman who remained at home at that time (Harper 160). Men, on the other hand, were fully engaged in travel and science in the eighteenth and nineteenth centuries.[20] For example, Humboldt, as discussed in the introduction of this book, was the most important name in the field of scientific travel writing in the eighteenth century, achieving the status of a hero after his expeditions through America (Dettelbach 288). His narrative style and his sketches were imitated over and over again following the publication of his *Personal Narrative* (Méndez Rodenas 176). Peter Hulme and Tim Youngs also recognize that Humboldt's travels "marked a turning point in travel writing," serving as a model followed by many after him (5). In fact, Humboldt's authority was never contested either in America or in Europe. Pratt observes that, besides landscape sketching, he used many other visual innovations in his travel accounts, reinventing the use of charts, graphs, and tables (*Imperial* 119). Humboldt, then, was a reference in travel writing whose authority was unquestioned.

Graham's work was closely related to those of her male counterparts who were traveling and producing knowledge in the specific areas of science which also interested her and to which she desired to contribute. In her writings, she explicitly mentioned, and sometimes even criticized, the findings of prominent male scientific explorers of her time such as Humboldt, Jean Baptiste Aublet, and Aubert du Petit-Thouars. Although scientific works almost always presented references to the works of other scientists, Graham, as a woman, was not considered a scientist, and therefore her intellectual conversations with her male predecessors offered peculiar characteristics, revealing her necessity to negotiate her authority to discuss topics considered unappropriated for her sex (Foster and Mills 89). Simply taking advantage of her imperial identity would not be sufficient to grant her authority to establish these conversations. Instead, she leveraged her transatlantic presence, reiterating her unique condition as eyewitness and observer of the same places visited by them. At the same time these dialogues located her in Latin America, they also placed her on the other side of the Atlantic, as a reader of the accounts she was dialoguing with, asserting her presence as a transatlantic subject. By engaging in an explicit dialogue with the accounts of contemporary male scientists, then, she conferred herself an authority as a writer-scientist, subverting the gender paradigms she would otherwise have had to face if she had remained home.

In Graham's diaries there are many sketches of the landscapes of Brazil which are in a clear dialogue with the Humboldtian scientific discourse. In that sense, these drawings manifest an intertextuality with travel accounts written by men in the nineteenth century, particularly Humboldt, who popularized the use of sketches in travel narratives. While in Tenerife, she followed his itinerary and visited the same sites he had visited just two decades before her. While contemplating the famous dragon tree of Humboldt's account, she observed:

> "After a pleasant but hot ride, we arrived at the villa about noon . . . to see one of the wonders of the island, the famous dragon tree. Humboldt has celebrated this tree in its vigour, it is now a noble ruin. In July, 1819, one half of its enormous crown fell: the wound is plaistered up, the date of the misfortune marked on it, and as much care is taken of the venerable vegetable as will ensure it for at least another century . . ." (Graham, *Brazil* 84).

Graham narrated her perspective of the dragon tree, located in a private garden which belonged to the Marquis Franchi, referencing the name of Humboldt. In his account about the tree, Humboldt noticed both the growth rate and age of the same tree: "As this plant . . . grows extremely slow, it is probable, that the dragon-tree of Orotava is older than the greater part of the monuments of which we have given a description in this work" (Humboldt,

Researches 209). Humboldt's conclusion was based mainly on the fact that the tree had attained its current state in the fifteenth century, when the Spaniards arrived there. Graham, on the other hand, mentioned the exact date its decay began, 1819, only a few years after Humboldt's visit, and estimated that the tree would last another 100 years with proper care. She added: "The dragon tree is the slowest of growth among vegetables; it seems also to be slowest in decay. In the fifteenth century, that of Oratava had attained the height and size which it boasted till 1819. It may have been in its prime for centuries before; and scarcely less than a thousand years must have elapsed, before it attained its full size" (Graham, *Brazil* 84). Many women travelers chose to visit sites previously mentioned by Humboldt, and to dialogue with his own observations: "This tacit acknowledgement of Humboldt as reliable source often filters the author' private encounter with Nature almost as if it was necessary to tread his vision's footsteps in order to authenticate their own literary wanderings" (Méndez Rodenas 37). Méndez Rodenas adds that these women often offered their unique emotional or aesthetic response to the site being observed (37). When Graham mentioned Humboldt in her description of the dragon tree, she not only attempted to prove she was a knowledgeable woman who had read his accounts, but she also emphasized the fact that she could offer a more accurate account of the tree. Her detailed estimate of the age of the dragon tree dismissed Humboldt's conjectures about its age as well as his comparison to the other monuments he saw. In that sense, Graham's response to Humboldt's account could be considered ironic, because whereas he celebrated its vigor, emphasizing its slow growth, Graham highlighted its slow decay. This oppositional irony can be further analyzed by comparing the way Graham and Humboldt sketched the dragon tree, as illustrated in figure 1.1.

Figure 1.1. Dragon tree by Humboldt (left) and by Maria Graham (right).
Atlas pittoresque du voyage: vues des Cordillières. Amsterdam: Theatrum Orbis Terrarum, 1910, plate 69. *Journal of a Voyage to Brazil and Residence There, During Part of the Years 1821, 1822, 1823,* 135.

Méndez Rodenas considers Graham's rendition of the dragon tree a reflection of a "Byronic sensibility and an obsession with ruins as a sign of the ravages of time . . ." (37). In fact, Graham's sketch does not even resemble Humboldt's representation. Whereas Graham's tree was depicted as part of a dense, disorganized, and chaotic backdrop, downplaying its grandiosity and emphasizing its decay, Humboldt's rendition focused on its monumental and sublime aspect. The presence of the men, diminished in relation to the tree, served only to further highlight its grandiosity. The tree was isolated, almost removed from its environment, as if it existed on its own. Instead of simply adding her own aesthetic response to the tree, she challenged Humboldt's authority by creating a response in almost diametric opposition to his rendition. Furthermore, Graham's apparent Byronic response, when considering her remarks quoted above, seems more like a response to Humboldt's exaggerated and romantic mode of representation of American nature. Whereas it is true that Graham's focus on the decay of the tree could be echoing the Byronic feelings suggested by Méndez Rodenas, her insistence in rationalizing its decay with numbers and dates can undermine this interpretation. Instead, her rendition can be also considered an ironic and updated response to Humboldt's account of the tree. Further, it could represent her attempt to deconstruct more romantic and subjective responses to the landscape. She added: "I sat down to make a sketch of it; and while I was drawing, learned from Mr. Galway the following history of the family of its owner, which a little skill in language and a little adorning with sentiment might convert into a modern novel" (*Brazil* 85). Graham proceeded to summarize the story of the now abandoned private garden in which the tree was located, due to an inheritance dispute between the daughter of the owner and his brother. Her mentioning that the story could become a novel was another layer of her ironic remarks about the tree. From this perspective, she was in fact denying sentiment, and simply trying to offer a more scientific and accurate portrayal of the tree, including the reasons why the garden was abandoned. By resorting to her capacity to update Humboldt's account, she created a unique possibility of scientific authority for herself. This was only possible because she was able to use the transatlantic subjectivity which provided her the means to engage in scientific debates.[21] The passage below further illustrates Graham's open criticism of Humboldt's imagination.

In her analysis of the writings of Maria Graham, Pratt argued that the traveler constructed herself as an "interactive seeker of knowledge" who used non-technical language and adopted an "infantile rather than patriarchal position" (*Imperial* 63). For Pratt, the scientific discourse was replaced in Graham's writing by an explanatory language. Although this is often true, it is also possible to find in Graham's work many passages in which she adopted a very authoritative tone. For example, again during her visit to Tenerife, she once more mentioned Humboldt, but this time to openly criticize his conclusions about the sepulchers of the Guanches, the aboriginal inhabitants of the Canary Islands. After examining some of the beads found in the sepulchers of the Guanches, and concluding that they were made of hard baked clay, she noted:

> Mr. Humboldt, whose imagination was naturally full of South America, has conjectured that they [the beads] might have been used for the same purpose as the Peruvian *quipos*, but they are inconveniently large for that use. They are not unlike the beads Belzoni found in the mummy pits in Egypt, and they closely resemble some of the many kinds of beads with which the Bramins have counted their muntras time immemorial. The Oriental custom of dropping a bead for every prayer having been adopted by the Christians of the west . . . appears, on that account, too common to deserve the notice of a philosophical traveller; and therefore the Guanche shepherds, or goatherd kings, are rather supposed, like the polished Peruvians, to have recorded the annals of their reigns with clay beads, than allowed to tell them with their orisons, like the Bramins of the Ganges, the shepherds of Mesopotamia, or the anchorets of Palestine and Egypt, because the modern monk does the same. (Graham, *Brazil* 88–89)

In his *Personal Narrative of Travels to the Equinoctial Regions of America*, to which Graham refers in this passage, Humboldt explicitly compared the Guanches with the tombs he saw in Ataruipe: "The Atures have almost entirely disappeared; they are no longer known, except by the tombs in the cavern of Ataruipe, which recall to mind the sepulchers of the Guanches at Tenerife" (Humboldt and Bonpland 240). Graham provided a correction to his "conjectures" and offered him a lesson about the differences between them. By labeling him a philosophical traveler, she dismissed his scientific objectivity, subtly criticizing his Romantic empiricism (Smethurst 232). Once more, she not only referred to, but also dismissed famous remarks by male travelers to claim authority for her own observations. Regarding this very same passage, Regina Akel similarly observed that Graham dismissed Humboldt's expertise. Akel argued that "by setting aside Humboldt's authority . . . she opened a space for her own narrative persona" (98). The passage indeed shows that Graham gave a very accurate account about the tombs and contextualized her description, offering a more complete explanation than the Prussian naturalist. From this perspective, her language, rather than "infantile," could be seen as authoritative and even "patriarchal," to use Pratt's words. In the field of botany, Graham also challenged some of her male counterparts, especially in the case of what she considered to be inaccurate or incomplete descriptions of plants or seeds. For example, in her "Life of D. Pedro" she commented that she found three species of trees mentioning their scientific names (of the genus *Lecythis*) and some nuts they produce that she had never seen before. She referenced Aubert du Petit-Thouars,[22] noting that in his *Mélanges de botanique et de voyage* he described some species of the same family, but according to her, "he was unfortunate in not visiting South America in a time of year or under circumstances permitting him to ascribe to each the proper fruit, flower or leaf" (Graham, *Life* 186–87). She not-so-subtly demonstrated with this commentary that she had visited the place in the right season and, for this reason, was able to provide a more comprehensive account than Petit-Thouars, a celebrated French botanist.

Jennifer Hayward has also observed that Graham frequently criticized her male counterparts in order to create her own authority, noting that she had to use "strategies to defuse the threat of a female writer" (Hayward 301). One of the strategies Graham utilized was to deftly and strategically maneuver a double image of herself that allowed her to keep a low profile when challenging her male counterparts. If, on the one hand, she criticized and updated the work of her male predecessors, on the other hand, she constantly used expressions to diminish her own work. However, almost immediately afterward, she presented indications that she in fact knew well what she was doing. Referring back to the passage which opened this chapter, for example, her use of the adjective "inadequate" to describe the sketch she made is in clear contrast with the quality and accuracy of the sketches she presented throughout her work.[23] Therefore, Graham's writings similarly illustrate strategies common to those found by Sandra Gilbert and Susan Gubar in the work of nineteenth-century women writers: "these authors managed the difficult task of achieving true female authority by simultaneously conforming to and subverting patriarchal literary standards" (73). By the same token, as Mills had observed, women travelers produced their writings aware of the discursive constrains surrounding them (72). Graham's narrative maneuvers went beyond operating within these gender constrains; unable to achieve prominence as a scientist, she used her authority as a traveler to create an alternate visibility and published her findings using less prestigious and authoritative literary genres, which allowed her to smoothly cross gender boundaries.

REVISITING GRAHAM'S WORK

Many works have shown the numerous strategies women used to try to compete in scientific fields. For example, Mary Orr has analyzed the work of the nineteenth-century scientist Sarah Bowdich (1791–1866). According to Orr, "Bowdich employed the vehicle of biography to overcome the obstacles that discouraged women from entering scientific disciplines.... Through these publications, Bowdich succeeded in disseminating her own scientific contributions in field-based research" (Orr 277). Similar to Bowdich, other women were able to contribute to the fields of science, but they were aware that they had to be cautious in order to avoid retaliation from the scientific community. In the case of Bowdich, she had a husband who helped her, and lent her his name to publish her work. Women who lacked male protection, on the other hand, were seen as transgressing their limits, mental as well as physical, being therefore classified as non-women (Benjamin 43). Maria Graham, unlike Bowdich, did not have a male protector who could endorse her work, not only because her husband died while they were traveling, but also because he had not been a man of science and, therefore, was not able to help Graham accomplish her goals. Her strategies to achieve recognition without being considered unfeminine consequently had to be more sophisticated.

As explained previously, Maria Graham explicitly dialogued with her male counterparts and indirectly became part of what one might call a scientific discussion. As Fulford, Lee, and Kitson observe, before the professionalization of science, which occurred only in the later nineteenth century, establishing a "scientific" dialogue required both rhetorical and political abilities because "the definition of the properly scientific was, in part, a political and social construct" (2). They add that gender was also an important obstacle, since women were simply not allowed to take part in such discussions, unless they were just participants in the discoveries of their male protectors (2). Hence, as the example presented below will clarify, taking part in such scientific discussions was something that could not be done by a woman using what were considered to be the standard approaches. Therefore, she had to negotiate her participation at the risk of having her observations considered mere "traveler tales" (Fulford, Lee, and Kitson 2). In 1822, while Graham was in Chile, there was a large earthquake that destroyed the coast of Valparaiso. She took careful notes on the event including the time and frequency of the tremors in her *Journal of a Residence in Chile during the Year 1822, and a Voyage from Chile to Brazil in 1823*: "Friday, November 22nd.—Three severe shocks at a quarter past four, at half past seven, and at nine o'clock. After that there were three loud explosions, with slight trembling between; then a severe shock at eleven; two or three very slight before one o'clock; and then we had a respite until seven p.m., when there was a slight shock" (Graham, *Chile* 153). After the incident, Graham wrote a short report entitled "An Account of Some Effects of the Late Earthquakes in Chili [sic]" solicited by Henry Warburton of the London Geological Society. Her report was published in the 1824 volume of the *Transactions of the Geological Society* becoming the first female-authored piece to be published in that journal.[24] Among the details of the event, Graham's report also described an apparent elevation in the continent: "It appeared on the morning of the 20th that the whole line of coast from north to south, to the distance of above 100 miles, had been raised above its former level. I perceived from a small hill near Quintero, that an old wreck of a ship which before could not be approached, was now accessible from the land, although its place on the shore had not been shifted" (Graham, "Earthquake" 153). Carl Thompson notes that in 1830 Charles Lyell cited Graham's report in his influential *Principles of Geology*, using it to support his theory that earthquakes could cause the elevation of landmasses.[25] This theory was, however, opposed by George Greenough, then president of the Geological Society, and it gave rise to a great controversy ("Earthquakes" 335). As Martina Kölbl-Ebert observes, "George B. Greenough . . . publicly accused Mrs. Graham . . . of willful falsehood, thus starting a dispute which, among male opponents, might easily have ended with a choice of pistols on the field of honour" (Kölbl-Ebert 36). Kölbl-Ebert adds that Graham's theory of the elevation of the land was very reasonable even at that time and concludes that she was criticized solely because of her gender. This helps to explain why Graham's efforts to contribute to science through the geological field were eminently condemned and never accepted as valid during her time.[26] In other words, Graham's only attempt to directly address scientific subjects more professionally was frustrated. Thus, her approach of resorting to more refined means in order to achieve her goals and participate in scientific debates was significantly more effective.

Dea Birkett observes that women were only allowed to participate in nonscientific and amateur pursuits and adds that if an area of study became established as a science, women's participation would automatically be restricted (82). Despite such a hostile context, women travelers sought to have their work accepted: "They were faced with the dilemma of how to give authority to their work when they lacked the broad academic background of male contributors" (Birkett 82). For these very reasons, therefore, in her attempts to enter the world of natural history, Graham had to produce a complex narrative that essentially consisted in a feminization of the discourse of natural history. In other words, she used the alternative visibility provided by her travel writing as well as her transatlantic subjectivity to create a more feminized way to report her scientific findings. Similar to Sarah Bowdich, Graham also used biography as one venue to disseminate her discoveries. In her manuscript, "Life of D. Pedro," she subverted the biographical genre to create a space for her own scientific voice. Accordingly, Graham dedicated several pages of the document to the description of plants and vegetation, geography, zoology, and to provide ethnographic observations. In one instance, she mentioned her visit to a sugar cane plantation, describing in detail not only the several plants she saw (including their scientific names) but also the usage of the land and the habits of its residents. As a result, she managed to have her work published under her own name, and although it was not formally recognized as valid by the scientific community, she contributed to the construction of knowledge in several areas, especially botany, and the circulation of knowledge on both sides of the ocean. Since botany was one of the few fields in which, to some extent, women were able to participate, it functioned as a bridge for them into the masculine world of science (Shteir, "Botany" 31–43). In fact, this was the field to which Maria Graham made her main contributions; she collected and sketched several plants and seeds and took advantage of her travels to extend her knowledge on the subject.

Later, in 1835, she published *Scripture Herbal*, a book in which she highly feminized botany through the use of the religious discourse, another acceptable form of writing for women. In the preface, she defined her book as a description of the "natural history of the bible" or "the unwritten book of God" (Graham, *Scripture* v). Bringing together science and religion seems to have been the only way she could find to have her botanical findings and expertise finally published under her name. Reading the work closely, it is possible to see how her sophisticated explanations and professional sketches communicate an extensive knowledge in the botanical sciences, converting the work in an effective alternative way to participate in the construction of knowledge. In the introduction, she made it obvious that her work, rather than an amateur job, was the result of years of research and travels. She also demonstrated her expertise by commenting on many of the works she had read. Again she challenged her male counterparts, and as a consequence, claimed authority to herself: "Dr. Harris's *Dictionary of the Natural History of the Bible* is most carefully and conscientiously compiled, and it is an admirable book for the table of every reader though it is not, as the ingenious writer imagines, so perfect as to supersede the necessity of any other" (Graham, *Scripture* ix). She also made it clear that she was able to make good use of both her knowledge on botany and of her network of social contacts and friends in the preparation of the book: "But were I to name every friend to whom I owe plants or prints to copy, and every book I have consulted, this notice would become unreasonably long" (Graham, *Scripture* v). Her remark also suggests that she was involved in botanical conversations and exchange of specimens with other professionals, conferring further authority to her own work.

The feminization of botany becomes even more apparent if we consider not only the concept of the book itself, but also how her narrative aligned science and love: "The collecting the figures and drawing them on the wood-blocks, as it was a work of labor, so it was a labor of love" (Graham, *Scripture* ix). The expression "labor of love" sounds very domestic and inoffensive, appropriate for the introduction of a cookbook, indicating her attempt to reaffirm her femininity. The intentional use of this kind of language guaranteed that her work would not offer any threat to her male counterparts or indicate an attempt to compete with their more professional writings. However, the contents of the book show more scientific organization and methodology than she apparently implied in her introduction. The book, similar to many of the botanical handbooks published by her male contemporaries, was organized in alphabetical order, and offered a detailed description of each plant, its origins, scientific names, location, etc. It also included the Bible chapters where they were specifically mentioned. Graham made sure to refer to the authors and botanical books which mentioned a particular plant, reinforcing her extensive knowledge of the field and a meticulous research method, both narrative devices typically present in scientific publications. Nevertheless, instead of merely replicating the information she found in other books, she inserted her own comments, demonstrating her expertise, proposing a dialogue, many times shedding new light on previous knowledge about the plants she was discussing: "Dr. Clarke, the accomplished traveler, finding the Cactus Ficus Indicus common in Syria and Palestine, imagined that it was indigenous there. . . . But the truth is that the cactus never was known until after the discovery of America, when the Spanish, Portuguese, and Dutch traders . . . introduced the thorny Cactus Ficus Indicus . . . the cactus soon took possession of the soil, and now passes for indigenous" (Graham, *Scripture* 484). In various entries of the book Graham referred to her own travels, leveraging her transatlantic subjectivity to emphasize the fact that she was able to see the plant she described. She used her own experience to support many of her claims, hence constructing her authority as a botanist demonstrating her empirical experience as a traveler.

For example, in the chapter about the Bramble (figure 1.2), a kind of blackberry, she mentioned how the plant was found frequently wild in most countries of the world. As evidence of her claim, she cited the Swedish traveler and naturalist Fredric Hasselquist and followed the reference with a note about her own observations: "Hasselquist found the Bramble among the ruins of Scanderette . . . and I have met with it wild on the top of a high mountain in Brazil" (Graham, *Scripture* 64). By exploiting her transatlantic subjectivity and mentioning her experiences as a traveler who had crossed the ocean and established her presence there, Graham put herself at the same level of her male counterparts to discuss scientific subjects. Moreover, when she stated that she found the plant "on the top of a high mountain," she implied that she too was capable of exploring a very high (and by extension, dangerous) mountain, which granted even more credibility to her discoveries. This self-claimed authority was not common or even necessary for a woman who was writing an innocent book about the Bible. These comments involving her expertise and travels came embedded in a text that was supposed to be merely a "labor of love." Graham's effort to compare herself with Hasselquist, who

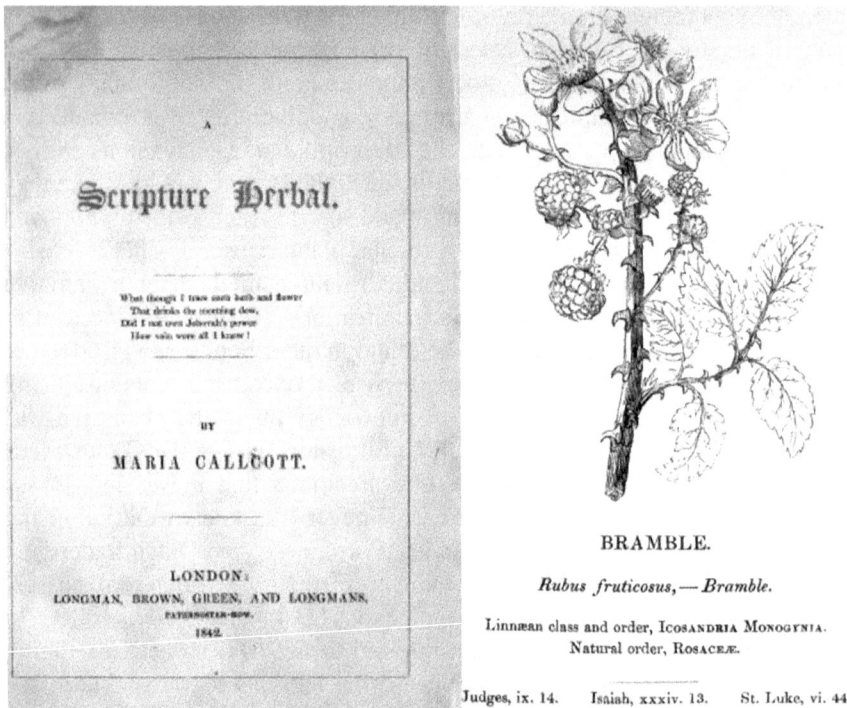

Figure 1.2. Graham's *Scripture Herbal* front page and her illustration of the Bramble.
Scripture Herbal, London, 1842, 44.

studied with Linnaeus himself, was not merely meant to establish her expertise. She described him as a young man devoted to travels in Palestine who "did much for Scripture botany," noting that he overcame difficulties to be able to reach Syria and Egypt and died as "a martyr to science" (Graham, *Scripture* vii). Nevertheless, she made the pointed observation that he was never able to recover from the heat and fatigue of his journeys to Palestine. Thus, while she evidently recognized the achievements of Hasselquist, she nevertheless presented him as a fragile man. This subtle association inevitably brings to mind a comparison with Graham herself, someone who was not frightened and was capable of climbing high mountains. What is implicit in her discourse is that, unlike Hasselquist, she was able to withstand the hardship of her travels and return home safely. By implying Hasselquist's fragility against her own resilience, she was also subtly contesting the patriarchal and scientific discourses about women's natural inferiority.

In a sense, Graham's journeys and explorations were not unique. Instead, they were part of a larger, but not necessarily manifest, project which took advantage of the interest many women who traveled as companions to their husbands had in botany to assign them the task of collecting new specimens of plants to send home. In fact, in 1790, botany was one of the subjects middle-class girls learned and practiced. Shteir contends that many aristocratic women and military wives traveling to accompany their husbands benefited from their journeying around the world and sent home botanical reports, created herbariums, and so on: "Colonial wives were enlisted in projects for imperial botany. William Hooker honored his correspondents by his attentions, gave them status, and validated their interests in supplying specimens for world floras" (Shteir, *Cultivating* 192). Shteir recognizes that although these women botanized "within the gender economies they brought with them from home," colonial encounters allowed them "to step outside conventional gender boundaries" (Shteir, *Cultivating* 193). Therefore, although botany was considered appropriate for women, their participation was restricted, and in the nineteenth century, botanists who described and named new specimens were almost exclusively male. Although upper-class women could work as botanists, they were only allowed to collect plants but never to catalogue them because that was an exclusively male activity (Schiebinger, "Gender" 170). Moreover, the Royal and Linnaean Societies never admitted women as its members at that time. The few women who studied plants were hardly recognized by the botanic associations in Europe: "Women were encouraged to dabble in botany, certainly, but not to excel in it" (Bennett 113).

Notwithstanding this context, at least two plants and one entire genus catalogued in renowned botanical works were named after Maria Graham (Hagglund 51). As previously mentioned, Graham corresponded with William Hooker, and frequently sent him reports about her botanical investigations and findings. Birkett observes that her correspondence with Hooker further motivated Graham to draw the plants she found in Brazil. However, as her diaries indicate, Graham's interest in observing, drawing, and collecting plants preceded her correspondence with Hooker: "In case of the fading of the colours of the specimens might it not be advisable for me to add rough sketches—say just an outline with the real colour of a petal and a leaf? I do not habitually draw flowers but I could do that and also any peculiar form of seed. Only let me know how I can be useful and I will try to be so" ("Letters to Hooker" 1824). As a transatlantic subject, she was occupying a privileged position that conferred her an authority on both sides of the Atlantic: while her presence in Latin America granted her the eyewitness position to collect and observe botanical specimens, she was also able to report her observations and send the specimens back to Europe. This unique position offered her the opportunity to establish an active collaboration with a renowned male scientist. Although reaffirming her lack of expertise in the letter, she was certainly aware of the difficulties involving the preservation and transportation of botanical specimens and offered to sketch them in their current state (Bravo 343).[27] She also mentioned that she was not used to drawing flowers, when it is clear that she already was an amateur botanist when she wrote the letter. Her rhetoric of modesty, self-deprecation, and lack of expertise, along with her transatlantic subjectivity, were therefore part of a careful attempt to collaborate with Hooker, while remaining within the limits of her own gender. As a result of her extensive collection activities, she produced a detailed *Book of Botanical Illustrations*, which was never published and can be found at the archives of the Kew Gardens, demonstrating that her ability to produce botanical sketches and scientific descriptions were very sophisticated (Birkett 81). Unable to publish her own botanical findings professionally, her collaboration with Hooker seemed to be the best way for Graham to make some valuable contributions to the field of botany.

In fact, in 1841 Hooker published *Botanical Miscellany*, in which he included the plants collected by Graham. He mentioned her name on a footnote as one of the sources who sent him material for the chapter "Contributions Towards a Flora of South America and the Islands of the Pacific" (Hooker 129). The chapter includes a plant named *Escallonia Callcottiae*, derived from Callcott, Graham's surname following her second marriage (figure 1.3), named by Hooker in recognition of Graham's botanical work (Birkett 80). However, his acknowledgment is almost insignificant, considering the multitude of specimens and information she sent him as well as her dedication to finding new materials to send home: "I am . . . supposing that you will not dislike to correspond with me occasionally in Brazil and that from time to time you will let me know how the Botanical world goes on and what is most wanted at home" ("Letter to Hooker" 1824). In exchange for the several plants she was willing to send, she only asked for an opportunity to participate in scientific dialogues, indicating her willingness to contribute to the construction of knowledge. Recently, in 1996, Thomas G. Lammers, a botanist at the Field Museum of Natural History in Chicago, published a detailed study of the flora of the Juan Fernandez Islands, belonging to Chile. According to his findings, Maria Graham was the first naturalist, man or woman, to collect specimens in the archipelago in 1823. He indicates the high quality of the collection she prepared and sent to Hooker in 1824 and the difficulty to collect these specimens, which are extremely rare, growing on steep to vertical rock exposures at 550–610 meters above the sea level. Among her collection, a few plants belonging to the family Campanulaceae indicated the discovery of a new specimens of the *Wahlenbergia* genus. Seven years elapsed and, in 1830, Candolle finally described a new species of *Wahlenbergia*, which he named *W. fernandeziana*. Despite the fact that several collectors traveled to the area searching for more materials, Graham's original specimen served as the lectotype for his description.[28] Much later, in 1884, in his account of the cruise of H.M.S. *Challenger*, Hemsley (1884) added another species, the *W. grahamiae Hemsl* (figure 1.3), which he named after her, also using Graham's sample she had collected in 1823 as the lectotype (Lammers 397–99).[29] Therefore, her work pointed the way to new botanical discoveries, and her original findings were the ones used to describe the new species, reiterating the high quality of her collection. Besides, Graham was also one of the collectors of Martius's *Flora Brasiliensis*,[30] which includes a list of botanical works and the itinerary of the herborizations she made in Brazil: in 1821 to Pernambuco, Bahia and Rio de Janeiro, and in 1823 to Rio de Janeiro, and Santa Cruz (Garcia 21). As a matter of fact, she was one of the two women, among the 65 authors and 135 collectors, who contributed to the project *Flora Brasiliensis* (Luna Peixoto and Filgueiras 992–98). These achievements, of course, provide ample proof that Graham's work was worthy of recognition in the field of botany during her time and that she deserves to be remembered as someone who helped to shape scientific knowledge about the New World in the nineteenth century, although she never received proper credit for her findings.

Maria Graham carefully developed a network in the contact zone that greatly facilitated her participation in the production of scientific knowledge. Perhaps Graham did use her imperialist identity to write a scientific discourse. Perhaps, as others indicated, science in the nineteenth century was already an imperialist endeavor, and so Graham also participated in imperialism to engage in science. As Youngs observes, "the question of whether women travelled as subjects or agents of imperial power, or as both, is one that involves an often difficult dialogue between feminist and postcolonial

Figure 1.3. *Escallonia Callcottiae* **(left) and** *Wahlenbergia Grahamae* **(right).**
The Board of Trustees of the Royal Botanic Gardens, Kew. Reproduced with the consent of the Royal Botanic Gardens, Kew.

theories" (Youngs 10). However, simply using her imperialist identity would not be sufficient to explain the authority Graham achieved in the contact zones and the visibility she eventually obtained back home. As I have demonstrated, analyzing the narratives of women traveling as subjects of imperial power naturally evokes a dialogue among feminism, post-colonialism, and science. Like her, many other British women engaged in travel, but few were able to achieve the prominence she attained as a travel writer. The process of acquiring this unique position of authority, instead, derived from her transatlantic subjectivity, a unique status only possible to achieve after a careful negotiation of her condition as a traveler within her gender constrains. To accomplish this objective, by traveling in South America, she avoided the trap of immobility imposed on women and found a space to renegotiate her gender role. She subverted her role as a social explorer and firmly established her presence as a transatlantic subject by building an influential network that would enable her explorations and botanical collections, and send them back home. Unable to take part in more formal scientific discussions, her remarkable reputation as a travel writer provided an opportunity to use this alternate visibility to engage in the construction of knowledge. Making use of literary genres considered appropriate for women, such as letters, diaries, travel narratives, and biographies, she feminized the so-called masculine discourse of science to create a space that allowed her to contribute to natural history, challenge male expertise, and create her own way take part in scientific discussions.[31] Moreover, Graham's feminine perspective of the natural history discourse was an effective way for her to blur the line between gender and genre. In other words, by using genres that were considered acceptable for female writers, such as biographies and letters, she produced narratives that effectively disclosed her scientific interests and contributions, thus crossing boundaries into genres that had strong gender restrictions. Even though it may be difficult to measure precisely to what extent Graham effectively contributed to science, it is safe to affirm, based on the legacy left by her, that the recognition she received is frequently insufficient. She is often presented as a traveler, a writer, an illustrator, but she is almost never acknowledged for her contributions to science. Most importantly, the analysis of Graham's writings and scientific contributions further clarify the reasons behind the fact that female travelers could engage in scientific enterprises and how they made that possible.

NOTES

1. This passage describes Maria Graham's visit to the Brazilian Botanical Garden. On this occasion, she was accompanied by Colonel Cunningham, acting British

consul-general, and his wife; Mr. Hayne, one of the commissioners of the slave trade commission, and his sister Miss Hayne; and by her midshipman, John Langford, who accompanied her on several of her journeys and expeditions.

2. This chapter is based on the article "Crossing Boundaries into a World of Scientific Discoveries: Maria Graham in Nineteenth-Century Brazil," 2012.

3. For more on Alexander von Humboldt, see the special issue on Alexander von Humboldt and America of *Studies in Travel Writing* 15.1 (2011).

4. In fact, the material was never published by Graham. However, part of her writings and letters was acquired by the National Library of Rio de Janeiro in 1938. The material was compiled and translated by Américo Jacobina and published in 1940. The volume is entitled *Correspondência entre Maria Graham e a Imperatriz Dona Leopoldina e Cartas Anexas* and presents the correspondence between Graham and the Brazilian Empress Maria Leopoldina, some additional letters, and also a short biography of Dom Pedro written by Graham.

5. In 2011 Jennifer Hayward and Maria Soledad Caballero published a new edition of Maria Graham's journal where they included the entire manuscript "Life of D. Pedro" among other archival findings. See Jennifer Hayward and Maria Soledad Caballero, *Maria Graham's Journal of a Voyage to Brazil*, 2011.

6. Humboldt himself never made an expedition to Brazil.

7. Although Mills writes about women travelers at the end of the century, in a more general sense, her model is useful, when used with caution, to discuss Graham's strategies in elaborating her own "discourse of difference" (Mills, *Discourses* 44).

8. Although Graham's nationality was her main tool to overcome her gender limitations, Jennifer Hayward observes that she essentially tried to portray herself as a person who was beyond gender using many techniques. In addition to her nationality, Graham also used her class or age for that purpose, although she never explicitly spoke of herself as masculine, as Mary Kingsley did (300).

9. Flora Tristán (1803–1844) was a French-Peruvian travel writer.

10. Prince and Princess refer to D. Pedro I and D. Maria Leopoldina before the independence of Brazil.

11. Evidently, Graham established a very strong network in Brazil. This network that she carefully built and maintained in the contact zone was fundamental for her to achieve the status of a professional traveler. Waldemar Valente observes that the social networks established by Graham in the Portuguese court in Rio de Janeiro were made up of important people. Among others, he lists: the Empress Maria Leopoldina, the Andrada brothers (José Bonifácio, Martin Francisco, and Antônio Carlos). Among the distinguished families cited by Valente are: the family of Viscount of Rio Seco, the family of Madam Lisboa, wife of the counsellor José Antônio Lisboa, and the family of the Viscount of Cachoeira. Among the English families is the family of the British consul Henry Chamberlain. Additionally, Graham maintained a strong friendship with the Baron of Mareschal, Rear Admiral Grivel (chief of the French station in Brazil), and with the consul of the United States (103).

12. Indeed, the creation of the Imperial Museum is attributed to her influence upon King D. João VI: ". . . one of the reasons often indicated for the creation of the Imperial Museum of Rio de Janeiro in 1818 was the interest in the natural sciences by the

future empress—D. Leopoldina—especially regarding her support for the naturalists that arrived here [in Brazil] in 1817, with the [then] archduchess" (Lopes 41). Leopoldina, then archduchess of Austria, sister of the second wife of Napoleon, arrived in Brazil in 1817 accompanied by the first naturalist mission officially authorized to enter Brazilian lands. The expedition was formed by scientists from different parts of Europe and was influenced by Humboldt's travels. Among the naturalists were the prominent Johann Baptist von Spix and Karl Friedrich Philipp von Martius, both from Bavaria. Six months after the arrival of Leopoldina in Brazil the first Brazilian Natural History Museum was officially founded (Lopes 41).

13. Although Leopoldina's interest in natural history was amateur, her personal correspondence reveals that she collected plants, animals, and objects. In several of her letters, she mentioned the Brazilian fauna and flora, and sent specimens to her family members and the Austrian Natural History Cabinet. She also mentioned the fact that she had killed and mounted the animals herself. Graham's friendship with Leopoldina facilitated her expeditions around the country and was instrumental for Graham to remain in Brazil alone after she left the Royal Palace. At that time, she collected many botanical specimens for Sir William Hooker. In a letter written on March 1, 1825, for example, the Empress mentioned that she sent Graham money from her own assets when she learned Graham was in need (Leopoldina, *Cartas* 320–436).

14. In the Archives of the Imperial Museum in Petropolis, Brazil, an unpublished letter (7 October 1824) from Graham addressed to the Brazilian Emperor D. Pedro I exposed her intentions about the education of the Princess.

15. Pratt uses the term "social exploratresses" (*exploratrices sociales*), coined by Hoock-Demarle, to refer to women travelers who were interested mostly in the social and political aspects of the places they visited (Pratt, *Imperial* 160).

16. For another approach which also challenges Pratt's perspective of Graham as a social explorer, see Adriana Méndez Rodenas, "Mapping the Unknown: European Women Travelers in Humboldt's New World," 2004. Méndez Rodenas agrees that Graham does not entirely fit the "social explorer" model, due to a more "reciprocal gaze" toward the other (43). However, she relied on her intrinsic superiority as an imperial subject, despite the heterogeneities on her discourse.

17. An *engenho* was a sugar cane plantation common especially in the northeast of Brazil until the nineteenth century. The mills where slave labor was used to transform sugar cane into sugar were deemed *engenhos*.

18. Sir William Jackson Hooker (1785–1865) was an English systematic botanist, who was a professor of botany at Glasgow University, and later was appointed as the Director of the Royal Botanic Gardens, Kew.

19. For a discussion of how the Botanical Gardens in Latin America in the nineteenth century represented and attempt to represent the American nature as controlled, forging a model of civilization closely related to Europe, see Felipe Martínez Pinzón's *Una cultura de invernadero: trópico y civilización en Colombia (1808–1928)* (Madrid; Frankfurt am Main: Iberoamericana/Vervuert, 2016).

20. Indeed, Fulford, Lee, and Kitson contend that between 1768 and 1833, although science was largely an amateur practice, due to social restrictions, it was performed only by "men (and not women) of science" (5).

21. This is not to say that Graham's criticism to Humboldt's observations were gendered, but instead it emphasizes the fact that she was attempting to engage in a scientific debate, even if it was not using the standard venues for that purpose.

22. Aubert du Petit-Thouars (1758–1831) was a prominent French botanist of the nineteenth century. See Aubert du Petit-Thouars, *Mélanges De Botanique et De Voyage* (Paris: A. Bertrand, 1811).

23. According to the classical formula of formal rhetoric, this strategy is called "affected modesty" and was frequently used by Sor Juana Inés de la Cruz. For more details see Stephanie Merrim's *Feminist Perspectives on Sor Juana Ines de la Cruz*, 1999.

24. As Carl Thompson, Betty Hagglund, and Esme Coulbert also observe in the Maria Graham project at Nottingham Trent University

25. See Charles Lyell, *Principles of Geology: Being an Enquiry How Far the Former Changes of the Earth Surface are Referable to Causes Now in Operation* (London: John Murray, 1835), 178.

26. The discussion continued for several years and it was only when later papers noted that Graham's reports had been confirmed by male witnesses of the earthquake that her work was accepted as accurate. See Kölbl-Ebert for further details.

27. Michael T. Bravo, *Culturals of Natural History*, observes that many collections were destroyed when transported to Europe due to climate, spray of sea water, and the crushing of the ship's timbers during a full gale (343).

28. Augustin Pyramus de Candolle (1778–1841) was a Swiss botanist who documented discovered, and named several new specimens of plants throughout his career.

29. A lectotype is a biological specimen or illustration later selected to serve as definitive type example of a species or subspecies when the original author of the name did not designate a holotype. For more details see Thomas G. Lammers, "Phylogeny, Biogeography, and Systematics of the Wahlenbergia fernandeziana Complex," 1996. It is important to observe that Graham's specimen was recognized as the lectotype only in 1996 thanks to Lammer's research.

30. *Flora brasiliensis* was produced between 1840 and 1906 by the editors Riedrich Philipp von Martius, August Wilhelm Eichler, and Ignatz Urban with the help of 65 experts from several countries. It contains taxonomic descriptions of 22,767 species, mostly Brazilian angiosperms, totaling 15 volumes, divided into 40 parts, in a total of 10,367 pages.

31. As Betty Hagglund observes, in the beginning of the nineteenth century, letters and diaries were not considered "low-status" or "private" genres and were widely used not only by women but also by men (5–6).

Chapter Two

Gertrudis Gómez de Avelleneda's Travel Writings

Beyond Optical Illusions of the Soul

In April 1836, at the age of twenty-two, Gertrudis Gómez de Avellaneda (1814–1873) embarked on the French frigate *Le Bellochan* to travel from Cuba to Bordeaux, France, in the first and possibly most remarkable voyage of her life.[1] She conveyed her feelings about this adventure in her well-known poem "Al Partir" (1836) and in her travel account *Memorias inéditas de La Avellaneda* (1914). The most extraordinary incident that occurred during her voyage was the hurricane that struck the frigate off the coast of Bermuda (Harter 23). As she recollected the episode in *Memorias*, she referred to the Cuban poet José Maria Heredia (1803–1839) and his "Oda al Niagara" (1824).[2] By employing an explicit intertextual reference to Heredia through the use of a similar trope of the hurricane and metaphors of the sublime, Gómez de Avellaneda expressed her understanding of the challenges she was about to encounter by crossing the ocean. As a woman who wanted to engage in intellectual enterprises, she knew at that very moment that it would not be easy to overcome the many obstacles she would face in her life. The hurricane foreshadowed her fate in the sense that it symbolized the resistance and the challenges she would find on her path to becoming a writer. Nonetheless, she used Heredia's words to make it clear that she was not afraid of danger; on the contrary, the threat excited her (*Memorias* 4).[3] By taking possession of the images and metaphors used by a well-known poet, she empowered herself and legitimated the process of creating her literary authority and presence. This voyage was only the first by a woman who would find in traveling the means she needed to forge the authority required to succeed as a writer. Fleshing out Gómez de Avellaneda's travel accounts, memoirs, and periodical writings sheds new light on our understanding of how this process took place.

As an affluent woman who received an outstanding education, Gómez de Avellaneda was aware of contemporary intellectual trends, and her writings were permeated with the subjects most in vogue at the time, such as science and natural history. In her poem "El viajero americano" (1846), for example, she dialogued with prominent scientists and travelers such as Humboldt, demystifying his visions of America and with writers such as the aforementioned José Maria Heredia, a well-known admirer of Humboldt's work (Pratt, "Las Mujeres" 58–59).[4] By dialoguing with Humboldt and Heredia, among others, she challenged their narratives and presented a feminine perspective on the discourse of natural history. As Marina Benjamin argues, women writers on science engaged in public forms of discourse and, therefore, cultural activities, by addressing female morals and manners (28). Although Gómez de Avellaneda was not explicitly committed to scientific endeavors, she participated actively in generating and circulating knowledge in the nineteenth century on both sides of the Atlantic. Hence, she constructed her authority as a transatlantic subject who worked as a conduit that transported information from one side to another and was eventually claimed by both Spain and Cuba as one of their greatest writers of all time.

GERTRUDIS GÓMEZ DE AVELLANEDA'S PATH TO BECOMING A WRITER

Gertrudis Gómez de Avellaneda was born in Puerto Príncipe, Cuba, on March 23, 1814.[5] The daughter of a distinguished Spanish family, she was educated by tutors and demonstrated her passion for reading novels, poetry, and drama. At twelve years old, she began writing odes and plays despite her mother's attempts to dissuade her from becoming a writer. At thirteen, she wrote her first novel, but she burned the manuscript herself. She was fluent in French, and one of her most prominent tutors was the poet José Maria Heredia himself, whose influence on her future poetic creations would be significant (Harter 21). In her youth, Gómez de Avellaneda was promised in marriage to a relative, but she refused to take part in the arrangement. This decision caused her family much trouble and culminated with her mother losing her inheritance. Soon after, Gómez de Avellaneda became ill and depressed, so much so that the family finally decided to leave for Europe in 1836. There, Avellaneda began attending balls, operas, and theaters; she also became an active writer. In Seville, Spain, her talents were soon recognized and her house became a place for intellectual meetings and poetry recitals. It was also in Seville that she met Ignacio de Cepeda, the great love of her life and her most bitter disappointment. Despite the strong attraction between the two, the relationship never became serious. Her letters to him, which were published years later, show how deeply in love she was, although they also reveal how she deployed romantic models of subjectivity to seduce her reader (Kirkpatrick 136). In the letters, she challenged some of the traditional representations found in Spanish Romanticism and gave "a new dimension—gender specificity—to the existing Spanish paradigms of the Romantic subject" (Kirkpatrick 134–35).

In 1840, Gómez de Avellaneda moved to Madrid, bringing with her several letters of recommendation. It was not long before the intellectual circles of Madrid became enchanted by her. In 1841, after publishing her first novel, *Sab*, she finally consolidated her name as a writer. By 1845, she was a well-known writer in Madrid and, a year later, she married the writer Pedro Sabater. The couple left for Paris, but only four months later Sabater died of cancer. After many other love affairs, another approximation with Cepeda, and a second marriage with Colonel Domingo Verdugo in 1855, she finally decided to return to Cuba (figure 2.1).⁶ In 1859, she sailed back to Spain accompanied by her husband, who died there in 1863. After falling once again

Figure 2.1. Portrait of Gómez de Avellaneda by Fernando de la Costa (1859–1864).
Archives of the Museo Nacional del Romanticismo, Spain. Reproduced with permission.

into deep depression, she convinced her brother to accompany her on a voyage to the United States. Following Heredia's steps, she visited the Niagara Falls and wrote a poem about the famous natural wonder. After two months traveling in the United States, she left for Europe, stopping first in London and then Paris, and finally settling in Seville, where she lived for another four years. Following the death of her brother in 1872, she returned to Madrid, where she died in 1873. In her will, written in 1872, she stated that she had forgiven the *Real Academia Española de la Lengua* for having denied her acceptance years earlier.[7]

GÓMEZ DE AVELLANEDA'S TRAVEL MEMOIRS: LEVERAGING THE TRANSATLANTIC SUBJECTIVITY

I will start my analysis by considering two travel accounts by Gómez de Avellaneda. The first is *Memorias* (Memories, 1836–1838),[8] the account of her first voyage to Europe, which she wrote in Seville in 1838. *Memorias* is especially significant because it precedes any of her publications as a professional writer and the recognition she would later achieve in Europe and Latin America. The second is "Mi última excursión por los Pirineos" (1860) (My Last Excursion to the Pyrenees), which consists of her annotations from a voyage she made to the Spanish and French Pyrenees.[9] In each case, travel narrative and natural history discourse appear camouflaged in genres that were not considered official venues for discussing such subjects. Instead, the former consisted of letters to a female cousin and the latter was a type of travel guide published in a Cuban newspaper. More than twenty years separate the two accounts. This makes them emblematic because they represent two distinct moments of her career: the first emphasized the need for establishing her literary authority and the second displayed an authority that had become internationally recognized, although she still had to overcome gender constraints. In addition, from the first to the second narrative, there was a noticeable difference: the letters consisted of a more private genre not intended for publication, whereas the periodical articles targeted a considerably wider audience.[10] This marked difference is a strong indicator that, during the twenty years that separated the production of both works, Gómez de Avellaneda achieved a voice that allowed her to speak, although many times not explicitly, about subjects not necessarily considered appropriate for a woman. She used travel narratives as a means of challenging the discursive conventions of natural history and participating in scientific debates while also establishing and reaffirming her own narrative presence and authority as a writer.

MEMORIAS: TRANSATLANTIC TRAVELS AND THE CONSTRUCTION OF LITERARY AUTHORITY

Gómez de Avellaneda depicted her first travelogue, *Memorias,* as notes wherein she offered descriptions, impressions, and opinions of the many places she visited, including Bordeaux, France, and Seville, Spain. In *Memorias'* opening pages, she clarified her itinerary, as well as her audience: "Since my departure from Cuba to my arrival in Seville, some notes on my travels. Dedicated to my friend and cousin Miss Heloysa de Artega y Loinaz" (*Memorias* 2).[11] Most striking about this passage is that she dedicated her travel notes to her cousin Heloysa. Travel accounts, especially the ones from the seventeenth and eighteenth centuries, were usually addressed to the authority who commissioned the traveler, usually a king or a royal society. This practice granted authority to the writer while endorsing the work (Beer 324). Gómez de Avellaneda's dedication of her travel notes to her female cousin can, therefore, be read as a parody of this practice and as an ironic way of presenting herself as a non-professional narrator. In this account, she observed Europe and described it to an explicitly Cuban and female audience instead of the traditional European male audience to whom such accounts were usually addressed.

In this epistolary travel account, she often used Cuba as a reference point point, and constantly compared the island to Europe. When she arrived in France, she started a series of comparisons with her homeland that continued consistently throughout the work. Gómez de Avellaneda attempted to deconstruct the dichotomies periphery/center and civilization/barbarism, since Cuba and by extension Latin America, usually the exotic object in many travelers' accounts, now occupied the opposite position (Albin 49). By using this approach when describing European landscapes and cities, she contributed to the debate regarding the knowledge about America circulating in Europe based mainly on European male travel narratives and established a strong presence on both sides of the Atlantic within her narrative. The unexpected word choice she employed to describe her first impressions about France supports this claim: "It was six in the afternoon when we arrived at the dock of Pauillac, and a crowd of people had gathered there to wait for the travelers. Each hotel owner made us aware of the advantages of their facilities, *eager* to be chosen; others *begged* us to allow them to carry our luggage, and the fruit sellers *surrounded* us with their baskets. This *craving* for money hit me unpleasantly, because this is still not common in our rich Cuba" (5).[12] This passage illustrates Gómez de Avellaneda's first arrival in Europe. Her choice of vocabulary was not innocent when she utilized words such as begged, surrounded, and eager, evoking an undomesticated side of Europe in contrast to a rich and civilized Cuba. She made it clear that she was completely shocked by the fact that she was surrounded by all these people begging for their money, as if they were uncivilized barbarians. In her opinion, the reception she received on her arrival was anything but refined, something she had never seen before in her "rica Cuba." The irony then becomes very clear, and her commentary about Europe turned into a deconstruction of the myth of barbarism attributed to Latin America. In other words, she directly challenged the "civilizing mission" forged by what Mary Louise Pratt calls the capitalist vanguard and its effort to reinvent America as "backward and neglected" (Pratt, *Imperial* 152).

Soon after this episode, Gómez de Avellaneda left for Bordeaux in a riverboat that sailed down the Garonne River. On the boat, she adopted the vantage point of the observer, something unusual for a woman, as women were not supposed to see but rather be seen (Pratt, *Imperial* 104). She subverted the politics of travel writing of the moment: whereas European scientists were traveling to America to rediscover and classify its resources, Gómez de Avellaneda took possession of the most prominent discourse of the time, that of natural history, and changed its perspective. In fact, it is not only the observer who changed but also what was being observed—a woman observing, comparing, and classifying Europe (as opposed to the stereotype of the male traveler and scientist of the time). In other words, the traditional subject became the object of observation (Albin 49):

> Nothing is as romantic and charming as the views and perspectives offered to the eyes of the traveler who journeys on the steam from Pauillac to Bordeaux in the summer months. I had seen Cuba's magnificent mountains and its virgin fields crowned with palms and mahoganies; I had looked out over its immense savannahs and contemplated its rich plantations. . . . However, I was enchanted by the delightful meadows adorning the superb banks of the Garonne [river]. (5)[13]

When describing the French landscape, Gómez de Avellaneda assumed the position of a female explorer who stood on the boat and returned the gaze that Cuba, and by extension Latin America, received from European travelers. She enumerated the many things she had seen in Cuba but emphasized that, despite the marvelous things she saw in America, her "traveler gaze" was still impressed by the European landscape. Her amusement was exactly what created distance between herself and the object-subject of her observation, that is, the other (Albin 49). Moreover, writing about the other in this case implied an act of resistance because the other was now Europe and colonial subjects lacked the authority to represent that continent (Pratt, *Imperial* 190).[14] For this reason, she had to negotiate this authority using the strategies that will be analyzed next.

In *Memorias*, as previously mentioned, Gómez de Avellaneda wrote an epistolary travel account addressed to her female cousin. In the letters, she constantly tried to diminish her own importance, stating that her intent was not to produce a professional account.[15] She clarified to her cousin Heloysa that she was writing solely from her memory and asked to be forgiven for her mistakes: "I see myself frequently confused when I describe an object merely relying on the memory that I have of it, there will be a thousand inaccuracies and mistakes for which I claim your indulgence" (2).[16] She also referred to her travel memoirs as "cuadernillos," another strategy to grant less professionalism to her writing. If the word "cuaderno" (notebook) in Spanish already implies an informal way of taking notes, using the diminutive exposes a certain sentimental and almost infantile tone. As Gilbert and Gubar observe, female writers had to be apologetic at the risk of being otherwise ignored: "If [the woman writer] refused to be modest, self-deprecating, subservient, refused to present her artistic production as mere trifles designed to divert and distract readers in moments of idleness, she could expect to be ignored or (sometimes scurrilously) attacked" (61–62). However, although Gómez de Avellaneda attempted to call the attention of her reader to the fact that she was not trying to write as a professional author, her narrative subtly revealed the opposite. In her first *cuadernillo,* she stated:[17] "Heloysa: I have thought of writing you curious outlines of my travels, consulting other travelers, taking notes about the history, traditions and local peculiarities of the places of which I speak; in short, beautifying these memoirs I have offered you, making them instructive and interesting, but I could not" (8).[18] A more attentive reader will notice she was, in fact, hinting at her intention of being a respected writer. The strategy of self-depreciation is evident in the passage; whereas the author explicitly diminished the quality of her work by stating she could not make it instructive and interesting, she implicitly did exactly the opposite by including not only comments about other travelers but also references to her extensive research about history, tradition, and other particularities of the places she described. In fact, only a few paragraphs later, she apologized for not being able to offer a more precise account of Cadiz and tried to compensate her reader for her flaw by offering a detailed description of Sevilla instead (*Memorias* 22). She added that she would be able to describe Sevilla accurately because she had informed herself and obtained books about the city's monuments (22). The variety of details she provided along with descriptions of the methods and sources she used to make her writings accurate and comprehensive prove she indeed attempted to produce a reliable account. This account eventually would be a source of knowledge to her compatriots.

According to Schiebinger, the production of knowledge that derived from the encounter between Europeans and Americans necessarily involved movement, mixing, triumph, and sometimes even extinction (*Plants* 12). Maria Soledad Caballero, in her article about Maria Graham, contends that the British traveler helped shape the knowledge about Latin America being disseminated in Britain. Moreover, Caballero recognizes that "women's travel narratives helped create public knowledge about foreign spaces" (115–16). At the time Gómez de Avellaneda reached Europe, her Cuban/American audience had limited access to information regarding that continent. Further, the knowledge they had about Europe was almost entirely produced by European auto-ethnographic accounts. In that sense, Gómez de Avellaneda returned the gaze and produced an authentic travel account about her encounter with the other in the Old World. Hence, she created a space to discuss topics that required using the authoritative discourse of natural history. When Humboldt traveled to America in 1799, Gómez de Avellaneda had not even been born. As mentioned elsewhere in this book, his travel writings consisted of a turning point for science, as they established new ways of observing the world. Gómez de Avellaneda, a well-educated woman, was familiar with his work and dialogued with him in several of her own texts. For Albin, the *cuadernillos* paradoxically imitated and deviated from the "conventional" travel writings of the period, such as the Humboldtian narratives. She contends that whereas Humboldt classified and described nature and used the aesthetic of the sublime in his descriptions, Gómez de Avellaneda tried to replace the scientific and historical discourses with an artistic/aesthetic language as a tool for acquiring the truth (53). Thus, Gómez de Avellaneda revised the rhetoric of the scientific discourse of Humboldt and created her own feminized way of depicting her travel observations.

When Gómez de Avellaneda arrived in Bordeaux, France, she admitted that seeing the city was a turning point in her life: "The days in Bordeaux are the line that divides my two existences: a divisor between the happy dreams of my first age and the agitating realities of these latest days of my life" (8).[19] As Humboldt praised the American landscape and reduced South America to pure nature (Pratt, *Imperial* 126), what most impressed Gómez de Avellaneda when she arrived in France was the modernity of the cities. In her visit to Bordeaux, she admired the progress represented by the bridge over the Garonne River, which she considered to be a great and daring work like the genius of the man who conceived it (*Memorias* 7). She listed many monuments, museums, objects of art, etc. with great excitement, and revealed an enthusiasm comparable to the Humboldtian narratives praising American nature: "When I arrived in Bordeaux, I experienced new kinds of emotions in my heart . . . I felt that kind of respect that is inspired by a commercial city in all its opulence" (5).[20] Gómez de Avellaneda employed Humboldtian tropes in her narrative to describe the city using a vocabulary similar to the one Humboldt employed to describe America's magnificence. However, she used this rhetoric to refer to the city, which was a novel way of using Humboldtian tropes and metaphors. In his personal narrative, for example, Humboldt stated:[21] "When a traveler newly arrived from Europe penetrates for the first time into the forests of South America, nature presents herself to him under an unexpected aspect. . . . He feels at every step that he is . . . on a vast continent, where everything is gigantic, the mountains, the rivers, and the mass of vegetation" (*Personal Narrative* 36). The paradoxical similarities between both excerpts are undeniable. The feelings both travelers experienced when they arrived at a new place are comparable. The idea of the sublime was implied in both statements, as both travelers felt diminished facing the opulence of what they were admiring. For Gómez de Avellaneda, the city's sumptuousness was comparable to the majesty of nature described by Humboldt and the grandiosity of nature was aligned with the genius of the man who projected the monuments she was admiring. The appropriation of the Humboldtian trope became even more evident in her second account, which focused more on European nature rather than its cities.

By returning the European gaze and deconstructing the binomial periphery/center, Gómez de Avellaneda established her narrative presence on both sides of the Atlantic and began the process of creating her transatlantic subjectivity. Her mobility as a traveler who was coming from across the ocean served as a tool that allowed her to invert the "colonizer/colonized" dichotomy. As previously discussed, imperial authority served as an apparatus women used to overcome gender limitations (Mills, Caballero, etc.). In the same vein, Melanie Hunter writes: "That authority, imperial in nature, whether as disseminating subject or dominating object, is negotiated, repositioned, manipulated, and reconfigured to serve the various projects of the writer traveling" (30). Mills also observed how British women travelers from the nineteenth century used their identity as imperialist subjects to achieve a position of authority in the contact zones (*Discourse* 44). However, Gómez de Avellaneda lacked this imperial identity and, for that reason, had to take advantage of her status as an "outsider" to align herself with imperial forces and grant herself authority as a writer. In other words, although she lacked the imperial identity that commonly granted authority to the subject, she took advantage of her status as a traveler-outsider to forge a similar authority. Albín observes that Gómez de Avellaneda tried to transcend her Creole condition by inscribing her voyage into a more cosmopolitan context, which included French, Spaniards, and English as her travel companions (53). Moreover, she explicitly aligned herself with British forces to incorporate some of the authority given to them because of their imperial power. An interesting and rather explicit example of this alignment can be found in her travel memoirs. Gómez de Avellaneda habitually visited cemeteries in the cities where her stay was extended. When she was in Corunna in Spain, she decided to visit the grave of a famous English general at the local cemetery. She mentioned that all English travelers passing by Corunna would generally stop by his tomb and she felt compelled to do the same:

> In the so-called Baluarte de S. Carlos, I saw the tomb of the famous General Moore, simple and elegant, which pleased me a lot. All the Englishmen who come to Corunna visit with great respect the grave of their ill-fated compatriot. I did the same without being English and I did not leave that place without saying with emotion this verse of a modern poem:
> Grateful and soft be this land to you;
> Even if it cannot be ever again
> Foreign land. . . . (15)[22]

By evoking the feeling of one contemplating the possibility of death far from home, she aligned herself with England and, by extension, its imperial forces. This rhetorical strategy allowed her to eliminate the differences between the English and other foreigners and subtly state her narrative presence. Her status as a foreign traveler placed her in a position of equality that enabled her to visit the English tomb, even though she was not from England. With the poem she quoted, she emphasized that the foreign status they shared put them in a condition of equality because Spain was a foreign land to both herself and the English general. This alignment cleverly granted her authority to displace Europe to a position of object, so she could take advantage of her status as a foreigner to describe in detail something that was completely new to her eyes. Moreover, this status would transcend gender, class, and race. However, this was only one of the strategies she used to forge her authority. She also had to craft ways to write without creating animosity among her male counterparts.

To justify her literary vocation and create her authority as a writer, Gómez de Avellaneda had to find a space within which she could participate in the intellectual debates of her time. Although she might not have anticipated that her memories would become public, they were, nevertheless, a powerful vehicle for disseminating knowledge and circulating information in the nineteenth century. The fact that she used an epistolary account as the means of delivering her travel narrative provided her more freedom to speak without being rejected or even attacked by her audience. In this process, her condition as a traveler in Europe assisted her in this endeavor. In the passage below in which she compared Cuban and Galician women, she established the distance between herself and her European counterparts: ". . . we, Latin-American women, in Galicia, are perceived as lazy and unfit for the domestic world; and I think it is undeniable that either because of the weather, or because of the education we receive, we are, in reality—Cuban women at least—more indolent than Galician women, and very few women in our country would happily submit to cooking in the kitchen in the morning . . ." (15).[23] This passage illustrates the expectations society had toward women in Spain and Latin America in the nineteenth century. In Spain, gender limitations clearly placed women inside the house, exclusively taking care of their husbands and children (Kirkpatrick 7). Gómez de Avellaneda justified her literary vocation in the sense that she demonstrated how the colonial environment privileged women, given that they did not "need" to complete household chores. She presented this fact in a natural way and attributed the personality of Cuban women to the weather or to the education they received. It also revealed class/race privileges as no middle/upper-class woman would have to work in the kitchen in her country. This more "civilized" practice would, once again, link the island, and by extension Gómez de Avellaneda, with countries such as England, where middle/upper-class women would not be responsible for these chores either, as servants were fundamental in Victorian England. By comparing Cuban and Galician women, Gómez de Avellaneda subtly stated she was unable to impersonate the Spanish patriarchal model for a woman. One could even imagine that she was indeed paving her way to justify her literary vocation. Gilbert and Gubar observe that the few women who managed to carve their literary authority in the nineteenth century share some characteristics. First, they created ways to write subtly, without alienating patriarchal society: "In effect, such women have created submerged meanings, meanings hidden within or behind the more accessible, 'public' content of their works, so that their literature could be read and appreciated even when its vital concern with female dispossession and disease was ignored" (72). Second, their works often seemed odd and did not fit literary standards: "Indeed, to many critics and scholars, some of these literary women look like isolated eccentrics" (72). Because Gómez de Avellaneda was Cuban, she could not impersonate models of women represented by the Galician ladies and, therefore, the only possibility for her was to become something else or, in her particular case, an artist. Women, either as writers or travelers, produced their narratives in the patriarchal context and, for that reason, they used numerous rhetorical strategies to create a literary persona who appeared to fit those patriarchal standards while they were, in fact, transgressing them (Gilbert and Gubar 73). Indeed, this strategy placed Gómez de Avellaneda somewhat above gender limitations. She proposed an alternative model of femininity that was not necessarily immoral, although she admitted it might be slightly odd. In *Memorias*, then, she used her condition as an "outsider" to justify her oddness and subtly state her authority as a writer.

"MÍ ÚLTIMA EXCURSIÓN A LOS PIRINEOS": AN UNUSUAL TRAVEL NARRATIVE

Almost twenty years later, Gómez de Avellaneda wrote a second travel account—this time, as a well-known writer in Cuba and in Spain. "Mí última excursión a los Pirineos" was composed of a series of articles published in the Cuban newspaper *Diario de la Marina*.[24] Establishing herself as a writer and using her social network allowed her to publish her articles in this important Cuban periodical.[25] The articles circulated between June 19 and July 28 of 1860 and addressed a wide audience. In the articles, Gómez de Avellaneda offered many details about the voyage she made to France accompanied by her husband, passing through many cities in the Pyrenees region before returning to Spain in the summer of 1859 (Ezama Gil 329). Besides giving information about the cities she visited, details of transportation, monuments, and their history, she provided particulars about lodging, amenities, and even the price range of such places. She also demonstrated a familiarity with tourist jargon: *tourist*, *cicerone*, *comfort*, etc. (Ianes 212). In fact, Gómez de Avellaneda mentioned many times in her narrative that she was a mere tourist that did not have a plan or an itinerary in mind when visiting the Pyrenees. She emphasized the fact that she was with a group, and that everyone would decide on the destination at the very last moment.[26] This uncertainty added a taste of adventure that enticed her reader to follow her next journey.

In the nineteenth century, there was a marked dichotomy between the authentic traveler and the vulgar tourist. The "beaten track" was the place where tourists were supposed to be found: "a region in which all experiences were predictable and repetitive, all culture and objects merely 'touristy' self-parodies" (Buzard 4). However, as James Buzard argues, the tourist experience could also be an authentic one if the more sensitive traveler could find the secrets hidden within the "beaten track" (6). In her narrative, Gómez de Avellaneda revealed her intention to have a valid experience in the Pyrenees that went beyond hotels, thermal baths, planned routes, and the preferred tourist attractions, despite her insistence to label herself as a tourist. For example, she showed great excitement when their group decided to make a "dangerous excursion" to Gavarnie (24). Although she presented herself as a tourist and did not deny the presence of a guide, she emphasized the need for courage to complete such an adventure, evoking Madam Roland's words when referring to her visit to Switzerland:[27] ". . . everyone who has a chance, but does not visit that place is unworthy to be called a man" (24).[28] Hence, her experience as a tourist was also an authentic one, as it required the courage to wander "off the beaten track." Nonetheless, Gómez de Avellaneda's choice of mixing her experience as a traveler with touristic observations was a rhetorical strategy that granted, at least on a superficial reading, less professionalism to her observations and, consequently, more freedom to use the rhetoric and tropes commonly employed in the discourse of natural history.

In several of her articles, then, Gómez de Avellaneda turned to the natural history discourse to represent European nature and the feelings it raised in the observer (Scatena Franco 222). However, there are several instances in which she refused the task of describing such feelings, which she claimed to be an impossible undertaking. Her breathtaking experience at Gavarnie could not be described with words:

> Do not expect my friends, however, that I attempt to describe the spectacle nature presented to my eyes, no; go and contemplate it if you have a heart, if you feel vibrant in your soul the harmonious cord that responds to everything beautiful, to the sublime. You will have to face difficulties and the fatigue, it is true; you will have to follow narrow gorges, paths that meander along the flanks of the mountain range suspended over abysses . . . ; you will be scared sometimes, even if you are brave, when you see yourself buried under immense vaults of colossal crags that threaten to collapse on your heads. . . . But in spite of these dangers—which do not harass the adventurous spirits, the impressions these places guard for you are such that no brush, no pen will ever be able to describe! (24–25)[29]

On her rendition of the French Pyrenees, although she emphasized the difficulties that the traveler faced in order to experience the sublime, neither she nor anybody else would be able to describe it precisely. As Daniela Bleichmar observes, natural history relied heavily on the necessity of visual representation of every place, plant, animal, or experience, for the natural historians believed this was the best way of spreading and disseminating knowledge (305): "Educated as observers and representers, naturalists and artists constructed a visual culture of natural history based on standardized ways of viewing nature and on pictorial conventions guiding its depiction" (Bleichman 308). Gómez de Avellaneda was evidently questioning homogeneous natural history discourses produced by European travelers, and suggesting that every explorer would have a unique experience. She summoned her readers to the adventure and, by doing so, she also invited them to formulate their opinions and impressions about the place being contemplated. Hence, she not only questioned the supposed objectivity of the hegemonic rhetoric of science and travel writing but also tried to demystify it, presenting her own experiences as a traveler/tourist. Moreover, the experience of climbing a European mountain was yet another attempt at returning the gaze of male European travelers and naturalists who climbed several mountains in Latin America and constantly resorted to comparisons to the Pyrenees when describing their own feelings and impressions.

In fact, it is possible to identify a subtle critique of Humboldtian tropes in Gómez de Avellaneda´s narrative. In his *Views of Nature*, Humboldt stated: ". . . let me hope that these 'Views' may afford the reader, at least some portion of that enjoyment which a sensitive mind receives from the immediate contemplation of nature. As this enjoyment is heightened by an insight into the connection of the occult forces, I have rejoined to each treatise scientific illustrations and additions" (*Aspects* x). For Humboldt, it was necessary to balance the aesthetic of the sublime with scientific illustrations, tables, and measurements with the purpose of explaining nature. At the same time, he believed the aesthetics of the sublime was necessary to complement science and to attempt to understand the "occult forces" that made nature work (Pratt, *Imperial* 121). Gómez de Avellaneda, on the other hand, believed the sublime was an individual experience for each observer, which implied that some of the "occult forces" simply could not be explained: ". . . there, where the ruins of the centuries are agglomerated without altering the primitive wilderness that is still displayed as on the first day of creation; there, in the presence of those peaks, of the ice as old as the world, and in the bosom of the august loneliness of which they are guardians, we all observed an involuntary respectful silence . . ." ("Mi última" 26).[30] For Gómez de Avellaneda, the real adventure was in the eyes of the explorer, who had no words to express his/her feelings. Thus, the paradoxical feelings the contact with nature caused in the observer made silence the only possible solution for her. In other words, she stated that neither art nor science was capable of describing that landscape. Only those who overcame all the difficulties of a journey would be able to experience the distinctive feeling the landscape raised on each observer. Moreover, the fact that she was rendering the European scenery indescribable indicates yet again the subversion of the dichotomy subject/other. In other words, the sublime was now emerging from the European landscape, reinforcing the argument that it was related to the unfamiliar and, for that reason, was also subjective, relying entirely on the eyes of the observer. Regarding Humboldt's methodology, he "urged to the traveler to cultivate a (masculine) discipline of both the senses and the intellect" as opposed to "the eighteenth century fascination with the (feminine-gendered) sentiments aroused by the American landscape" (Poole 72). In Humboldt's words: "When addressing the feelings and imagination, a firm hand is needed to guard the style from degenerating into an undesirable species of poetic prose" (Humboldt qtd. in Poole 72).[31] In other words, everything related to sentiment and emotion was considered feminine whereas reason was related to the masculine, and the strong hand of reason was needed to control these emotions. Gómez de Avellaneda, then, in contrast to Humboldt's method, proposed a feminized way of representing landscape that rejected the "firm hand" Humboldt urged to avoid: exactly what he considered "undesirable poetic prose."

Comparing these articles with her earlier *Memorias*, there is a marked difference in the way Gómez de Avellaneda shaped her literary persona and employed the discourse of natural history. In "Mi última excursión," Gómez de Avellaneda forged a European identity that authorized her narrative. In contrast with her situation when she wrote *Memorias*, she no longer needed to align herself with British forces because she could now use her well-established Spanish/European authority instead. In fact, she went so far as to dismiss the British alignment she employed before, even as mere travel companions. She mentioned that the group traveling to the French Pyrenees was composed of people from many nationalities, including Spanish and French, whom she praised as ". . . enthusiastic, penetrating, intelligent, cosmopolitan by instinct and by education, and possessors of that exquisite touch that appreciates and understands all the whims of feeling and imagination . . ." (25).[32] The English companions, on the other hand, were colder and had their own group, constantly avoiding interactions with everyone else. They alienated themselves and had a different perspective in terms of their impressions and emotions (26). Gómez de Avellaneda, then, made a strong separation between her group, the one composed of Spanish and French, and the other, composed of English travelers.[33] After twenty years in Spain, she aligned herself with the Spanish, automatically including herself in their group:

> It had been only three days we were together with the twelve or fifteen people on the excursion to Gavarnie and, in such a short time, we felt among all of us, not the affectionate intimacy *to which we Spaniards are prone*, but the harmony of taste, the similarity of impressions, the reciprocal need to please each other, which helped us to overpass the setbacks and contributed powerfully to foster a pleasant expedition, and to make us feel sad to see its end near. (26)[34]

The fact that Gómez de Avellaneda not only aligned but included herself in the Spanish group marked a sharp contrast with her memoirs where she affirmed her Cuban nationality at every opportunity (Scatena Franco 326). In fact, Scatena Franco contends that Gómez de Avellaneda displayed a Cuban identity in *Memorias* whereas, in these articles, she revealed a Spanish identity. She believes this is evidence of "ambivalence" in Gómez de Avellaneda's identity ("ambivalência identitária") because the author tried to be part of both Cuban and Spanish literary canons (327). However, her attitude toward her identity in both travel accounts was calculated, intentional, and, hence, cannot be called ambivalent. In that sense, Doris Sommer's solution seems more adequate regarding Gómez de Avellaneda's identity. Sommer observed that in her novel *Sab*, the protagonist is something singular, described as neither white, nor black, and concludes: "Sab, and by association, Avellaneda, is somehow foreign to established categories of representation"

(117). Thus, Gómez de Avellaneda, as a transatlantic subject who belonged to both sides of the Atlantic, was even more powerful than the imperial forces represented by England. If, in *Memorias,* she aligned herself with British forces to grant authority to her narrative and to establish a foreign status that would surpass gender, class, or race, here it is evident that her authority as a transatlantic subject was established as she dismissed such alignment.[35] Thus, Gómez de Avellaneda, at that point, had firmly established her literary authority through her transatlantic subjectivity. Furthermore, she transcended this authority to claim her identity as Spanish and Cuban at her own convenience on both sides of the Atlantic.

Hence, when Gómez de Avellaneda wrote these articles, she was already recognized as a writer in both Europe and America, and the necessity of self-affirmation was no longer urgent. However, she was still a woman and, for that reason, she had to negotiate her gender constraints when addressing some subjects. In this case, the writer protected herself using the shield she created when she disguised her articles as mere travel guides to tourists. In a letter to the editor of the *Diario de La Marina*, she wrote:

> As if I had a feeling that I should soon leave the soil of Europe, I wanted, on my last year's summer, to visit the most remarkable sites of the Spanish and French Pyrenees, taking notes of the traditions that inspired the poetic nature of those places. . . . Scrambled among other manuscripts, these *quick notes* I took in the excursion came with me, *so blurred*, by the way, and *so little intelligible*, that even myself needed memory efforts to decipher them, when it crossed my mind the idea that perhaps it would not be a bad idea for you to publish them. . . . But in the absence of beautiful descriptions . . . as *incomplete* and *disheveled* they might be, they are full of the *simplicity* and *truth* that characterizes everything that I write for myself, without pretensions *to embellish* and *polish* things with *fantasy* . . . (*Obras* 47)[36]

As she did in *Memorias*, Gómez de Avellaneda labeled her account with expressions such as "quick notes," "little intelligible," and "imcomplete," diminishing the merit of her travel notes. However, she displayed increased confidence in her own literary authority when she showed that her notes were also full of "simplicity and truth." Most remarkably, she subtly criticized the conventional rhetoric of travel writing, creating an opposition between "simplicity and truth" with an attempt to "fantasize" the truth. In other words, she challenged the established narrative conventions of travel writing. Even if she implied that she never intended to publish these articles, disguising any possible pretension to compete with more experienced male travelers, she addressed a larger audience, making several recommendations and suggesting itineraries to future travelers. Further, as the letter suggests, she created a space for herself to engage in the intellectual debates of her time without threatening her male counterparts. The publication of her travel account in Cuba also served to give her a considerable visibility in the island, to which she returned shortly after she wrote the aforementioned letter.

CIRCULATING KNOWLEDGE AMONG WOMEN: THE PERIODICAL WRITINGS OF GÓMEZ DE AVELLANEDA IN NINETEENTH-CENTURY CUBA

In 1859, Gómez de Avellaneda returned to Cuba after spending twenty-one years in Europe. Only a few months after arriving, in 1860, she became the first female on the island to edit a periodical publication, the "Álbum cubano de lo bueno y de lo bello" (Cuban Album of the Good and the Beautiful), a bimonthly magazine especially addressed to the women.[37] In the initial paragraphs of the magazine's first issue, Gómez de Avellaneda stated its purpose: to discuss many subjects that could interest a lady from the nineteenth century (3). By examining the magazine closely, it becomes evident that she also used the space to address some other aspects not necessarily considered appropriate for a woman at that time. By the 1860s, Gómez de Avellaneda had established her literary authority firmly on both sides of the Atlantic, and had created strategic social networks which gave her access to intellectual circles based on this privileged status.[38] She invited several important individuals from Spain and Latin America to contribute to "Álbum," including well-known male and female writers, scientists, and journalists. In fact, Gómez de Avellaneda used "Álbum" as a space to participate in debates on scientific topics, especially those that directly addressed and affected women. To discuss such subjects, both her contributors and herself employed a carefully calculated discourse that only apparently conformed to the patriarchal agenda. Thus, her magazine became a "counterpublic space" in the sense that it gave women access to alternative publishing as well as an opportunity to take part in transatlantic intellectual debates (Fraser 61).[39] In a sense, these female contributors took advantage of the alternate visibility provided by the magazine to discuss subjects not previously available to them. Above all, "Álbum" served as a space of interaction, a go-between of European/non-European networks of knowledge circulation.[40]

The word "scientist" was coined in the 1830s to identify the group of people who were studying the natural world, as science was becoming increasingly more professionalized (Cantor and Shuttleworth 2). The specialized scientific press was scattered and not accessible to the wider audience and, for that reason, it is fundamental to investigate venues in which science was not the main subject: "... by concentrating on specialized publications, which were mainly written both by and for members of the scientific elite, we ignore the main routes by which science was disseminated to the wider public" (Cantor and Shuttleworth 2). The periodical press was the most popular means of communication at that time and many of the articles published in it, although not directly addressing science, concerned topics informed by science (Cantor and Shuttleworth 2). Therefore, scientific knowledge circulated mainly through venues that did not necessarily have science as its main subject. Bernard Lightman investigates what he calls the "Victorian popularizers of science" who were not practitioners of science, but rather writers and journalists who wrote about the subject and interpreted it for their audience. Lightman adds that female popularizers of science used diverse genres to disseminate their message.[41] These writers frequently adapted scientific discourse to their audience while considering their readers' necessities and sensibility. The use of visual images provoked what Lightman calls a "sense of wonder" (135): "From the microscopic world to the awesome heavens, nature was depicted by these women as a spectacle and a feast for the senses" (Lightman 135). They also introduced poetry and literature as a means to discuss and represent nature, usually quoting well-known poets such as Byron and Coleridge (135). Their ultimate goal was to make their audience realize nature's beauty. In "Álbum," Gómez de Avellaneda applied, to a certain extent, some of the techniques Lightman identified in his analysis of the Victorian popularizers of science.[42] It is not surprising that she used literature and poetry to depict nature in her magazine. What is striking is that Gómez de Avellaneda often addressed science in her publication and seemed to impersonate a Spanish-Cuban version of the Victorian popularizers of science, offering a unique literary perspective of the natural history discourse.

The periodical press in Spain flourished in the nineteenth century and became more specialized toward the middle of the century. It "played a key role in developing a female readership," and many political papers started including sections dedicated to women, such as poetry, serialized novels, fashion, etc. (Kirkpatrick 72). Iñigo Sánchez Llama analyzes the printing press in Spain between 1833 and 1895, observing how the gradual appearance of more articles written by women revealed that these writers had more privileges during the time Isabel was the queen of Spain, a period he refers to as the "canon isabelino."[43] However, these writers had to adhere to the queen's agenda to acquire such privileges. Sánchez Llama contends that they would have prestige and a notable recognition as long as they displayed didactic and virtuous aesthetics, Christian idealism, or a neo-Catholicism of French origin on their writings. He adds that the fact they endorsed the nationalist and conservative foundations of the "canon isabelino" was paradoxically what gave them the prestige and, therefore, freedom to write (14).[44] As Cuba still belonged to Spain at the time Gómez de Avellaneda edited her "Álbum," the same rules would apply there but with some differences.[45] At that time, censorship in Cuba was strict and that may be a reason why the magazine circulated for just six months (Picon Garfield 21). The magazine included many regular sections such as "Revista de Moda" (Fashion Magazine), "Anécdotas" (Anedoctes), "El pensamiento filosófico" (Philosophical Thought), and "Revista de la Quincena" (Quartely Magazine). The first section, or the "Sección Primera," often included a salutation from herself or from a famous guest writer (Fernán Caballero once contributed to this section).[46] Additionally, she would include other articles related to education, philosophy, and letters from the readers. The "Sección Segunda," or the second section, mainly dedicated to literature, conveyed more polemic subjects such as the series of articles "Galería de las Mujeres Célebres" (Gallery of Famous Women). Nevertheless, it is not hard to find intersections with scientific discourse in many of these sections. Although at a different level, and perhaps not as professionally and directly as the Victorian popularizers of science, Gómez de Avellaneda seemed to have found a way to circulate scientific knowledge and promote intellectual debates among her female audience while ensuring she would not transgress the borders of the "canon isabelino."

Throughout the magazine, it is possible to identify an attempt to participate in intellectual debates and revise the scientific models that perpetuated patriarchal standards. Gilbert and Gubar observe there was no space for a woman to become a writer in the nineteenth century because there were only two possibilities according to patriarchal literary standards: either they were figuratively angels or monsters (1–44). Susan Kirkpatrick states that, particularly in Spain, female authorship would be a complex negotiation that involved economic, political, and cultural forces (3). To take part in intellectual conversations in this context was automatically considered a monstrosity—something not appropriate for a woman. To create a space for women to perform intellectual activities, the magazine had to operate within these constraints and forge a space in which such conversations would not explicitly challenge the status quo. The section "Revistas" (Magazines), signed by the well-known Cuban intellectual Enrique Piñeyro (1839–1911),[47] encouraged women's participation in intellectual debates and invited the readers to critically reflect on literature and theater. To make this possible, the author dismantled the idea that intellectual activities would automatically convert women in monsters and created a safe space for such interaction to take place: "Some say women are demons and others that they are all angels: Which of these two opinions should one abide by? That is difficult to solve, especially in the Cuban Album. Let's choose the middle ground and say sometimes they have a little bit of each" (192).[48] Instead of denying the monster stereotype entirely, the author deconstructed this binomial representation by accepting both stereotypical assumptions, therefore placing the magazine within the limits of patriarchal society while transgressing it. Not surprisingly, Gómez de Avellaneda delegated to a well-known male intellectual the task of addressing such debates. Women contributors of "Álbum," nevertheless, had to use caution and operate within more delicate constraints.

One effective way for women writers to engage in intellectual debates was through the use of a more feminized way to address scientific topics. As literary genres such as short stories and poetry were relatively acceptable for women writers, there are several instances in "Álbum" in which its contributors used these genres to participate in intellectual debates taking advantage of the alternate visibility provided by the magazine. One good example is the serial short story "La Cueva de las Brujas" (The Cave of the Witches). Divided into four parts and signed by E. Auber, which is a pseudonym of Virginia Felicia Auber de Noya (1825–1897), the story presented a clever attempt to insert a feminine voice into debates about travel writing and natural history.[49] The story takes place in Tenerife, more precisely, in Aguamansa, a mountain village at the foot of the Teide Mountain, which belongs to the municipality of La Orotava, a place that had been the subject of many travel accounts and naturalist expeditions in the eighteenth and nineteenth centuries. For example, Humboldt's *Personal Narrative of a Journey to the Equinoctial Regions of the New Continent* dedicated sixty pages to his visit to La Orotava when he climbed the Teide Mountain in 1799 at his very first stop in the American continent.[50] Not coincidentally, Auber adopted a narrative similar to the ones found in many accounts about Tenerife. The narrative resembles a travel writing account as she mixed the sublime feelings of her narrator, who was not familiar with the landscape, with observations and the use of scientific names, as well as technical details about the soil of the basaltic mountain. She offered a detailed account of the site, mentioning specific types of vegetation, plants, climate, and particularities about the volcanic terrain. The surveying eye is also present, as the narrator contemplated the landscape from the top on the mountain. However, whereas Humboldt was fascinated by the mountain, which he was eager to climb, and the crater of the volcano, which he precisely measured, Auber offered a rather different rendition of the Teide Mountain. Humboldt's narrative started from the base of the Teide and progressed chronologically until he reached its top, which was the ultimate task he accomplished. He eliminated any vestige of human presence and centered his narrative on the mountain itself, its vegetation, soil, etc. Auber, on the other hand, began her story from the top of the same mountain, descending toward its base, more precisely, to the village of Aguamansa, where her narrator rested her eyes. Her rendition of the volcano contrasted with the village (figure 2.2 shows an engraving of the mountain):

> That sterile and inanimate desert seems nothing else than an immense ossuary of the giants of the past geological times, whose skeletons of granite half unearthed during some convulsion of the globe show their angular forms through the currents of basalt vomited by the dormant volcano. . . . Let's descend again in our wandering march through the pines and brooms and rest our fatigued feet in Agua Mansa, an open place in the forest in which one enjoys an unexplainable wellbeing. How different from the air rarefied by the elevation is the one which one breathes with delight there, fresh and embalmed by the fragrant aroma of lavender and wild oregano. ("Álbum" 216)[51]

As she descended the mountain, her narrative increasingly diverged from Humboldt's. The portrayal of the volcano was in a clear opposition with the village: whereas the former was aligned with darkness, death, and fear, the latter was depicted as alive, green, and inspirational, full of smells and sensations. Establishing a sharp contrast between the volcano, symbolizing death, and the village, symbolizing life, implied that the real source of knowledge was on the people, and not on the volcano itself. It also implied a subtle critique of the fact that Humboldt's accounts rarely referred to the locals and of his tendency to minimize human presence.[52] The story focused on the people

Figure 2.2   Retama Plains.
A voyage in the Sunbeam: Our home on the ocean for eleven months. Annie Allnutt Brassey, 1878, p. 24.

to highlight the importance of their experiences and to offer a more comprehensive understanding of the mountain that would not be revealed by simply measuring it. The dialogue with naturalist accounts becomes even more evident when Auber concluded the first part of the story alluding to a peasant, who offered her some wild strawberries and was about to tell the narrator a story. By allowing the peasant to speak, the narrator literally gave voice to the invisible people often absent in scientific accounts.

The second part of the story transports the reader to the world of the peasants, to a little cottage located in the same spot where the narrator finds herself. The story depicted how the life of these villagers was highly dependent on the volcano and its surroundings. It also reveals their beliefs, superstitions, and explanations of natural phenomena, substituting the measurements and tables offered by Humboldt:

> In 1830, there was in that place a cabin surrounded then as now with a green fence of peaches and quinces. The interior of that humble home corresponded to its rustic exterior. A large carved chestnut table and two or three chairs of the same wood made up all its charm. In the middle there were three large stones, among which the *retama* bushes burned, and by the fire, enjoying the soft heat, a woman of advanced age sat on a stool. . . . ("Álbum" 243)[53]

The cottage was depicted in perfect harmony with the landscape surrounding it, and the elements of nature found outside (i.e., *retama*, a common bush which covers the Teide) were replicated on the inside, as part of the furniture. The old lady's presence was also in perfect harmony with everything around her, suggesting a close connection between human and nature and how their existence interweaved on that specific environment. Immediately after this picturesque description, Maria, the twenty-two-year-old daughter of the unnamed lady mentioned above, entered the cottage. The physical description of Maria, heavily based on nature-related metaphors, once again aligned human and nature: her cheeks were as pink and fresh as the rose in her hair, her lip as red as a coral. Maria and her mother were about to start their meal, when Julián, a young man who was Maria's fiancé, arrived at the cottage. The young man was supposed to be on the mountain cutting wood and his sudden arrival surprised Maria. He reveals that a series of inexplicable events have been happening to him for the last few weeks: his work had been mysteriously done by somebody by the time he arrived at the mountain. The three characters, intrigued by the mystery, which had no logical explanation, immediately resorted to their superstitious beliefs and directed their gaze to the "Cueva de la bruja" (Cave of the Witch), located right above the village. This was precisely when they heard a loud noise, which made them all tremble in terror. The explanation offered by the old lady further unveiled their superstition: "The witch is crying" (243).[54] The voice of the narrator/observer/listener readily transferred to a footnote, clarified: "Phrase still used by those who live in Aguamansa or its surroundings to explain the noise that we have just indicated" (243).[55] This scene indicates how the volcano was embedded in the lives of the people, in how they reacted to the phenomena that were the subject of the scientists' observation. The footnote indicates the presence of a scientific voice, which differed from traditional accounts, as it attempted to incorporate local knowledge to the natural phenomenon that just occurred in the story. In fact, at the end of the narrative, the same scientific voice of the narrator appeared in another footnote clarifying that the noise was, in fact, the sound of the wind hitting the back of the cavern. In other words, the story offered an alternate portrayal of Teide Mountain, which included local knowledge, without denying scientific explanations.

The short story then turned to a fantastic and tragic tale involving the aforementioned witch and the young engaged couple.[56] It can be summarized as follows: Julian climbed the mountain to pick some *Orchillas*, as he would usually do every day. Again, on a footnote, the narrator gave its scientific name and explained the purpose of the plant: "*Rocella tinctoria, liquen*—produced in the Canarias and used to prepare a blue ink" (243). In fact, the *Orchillas* were found on the highest and most dangerous cliffs and were a source of subsistence for the locals, as they were highly desired in Europe to assist in dyeing silk and wool (Meliá 115). Searching for *Orchillas*, Julián fearlessly descended a dangerous cliff only using a rope, alone, and with no other instruments or equipment. Suddenly, the weather changed drastically and the winds became so strong that Julián was about to fall to his death. This was precisely when his life was saved by no one less than the witch so feared by all the locals, who apparently was in love with Julián and wanted him to abandon Maria, threatening to kill her if he did not accept his fate. In the end, Julián, who refused to accept the witch's demands, killed her, who also killed him. Maria found their bodies at the "Cueva de la bruja" and wandered alone for the rest of her life.

The critique to the scientific tropes that dismissed human presence is evident at many levels of the story. First, if Humboldt cited thousands of scientific names on his *Personal Narratives* and described numerous plants, Auber was offering a more comprehensive account of a single plant. Not only did she offer a detailed description and scientific name of the *Orchilla*, she also explained its meaning in the real life of people who actually used, survived from, and almost died because of that plant. When alluding to how difficult and dangerous it was for Julián to collect the plant, she emphasized that he was doing it alone and with his bare hands, as opposed to the naturalists who had all sorts of paraphernalia to assist them. Auber stressed the importance and value of local knowledge, frequently dismissed by European naturalists and explorers. The author also questioned whether the classification and categorization required by scientific models were incapable of predicting and measuring the real power of nature and were, in fact, unable to control it. When describing the torment that almost killed Julian, she noted: "Nature's order becomes chaotic."[57] Finally, including the locals' superstitions and beliefs and how they resorted to that when they could not explain something out of the ordinary could be seen as another way to point out the importance of local knowledge. It highlighted that the naturalists themselves resorted to conjectures when they did not know how to explain a specific phenomenon. When visiting the Carvern of Ice, which probably was "La Cueva de Bruja," portrayed in the story, Humboldt stated: "*Cavern of Ice*, which is at 1728 toises, consequently below the limit of the perennial snows under this zone. It is probable, that the cold which reigns in this cavern is owing to the same causes, which perpetuate the ice in the crevices of Mount Jura, and the Apennines, and on which the opinions of naturalists are still much divided" (*Personal* 135). In this example, he referred to the Alps in an attempt to find an explanation for the fact that somehow the ice perpetuated in the Cavern.[58] However, he admitted that the opinion of the naturalists was also divided and offered no solution to the dilemma. Auber's story offered an opportunity for the magazine's female audience to access information about Tenerife that would not be otherwise available. Moreover, it created a space for a female writer to engage in a debate with important male naturalists and elaborate a response to the scientific accounts about Latin America that were circulating on both sides of the Atlantic. Moreover, her story suggested the need to include local knowledge and insights in the new project of nations that were being elaborated heavily relying on these accounts. Auber reclaimed the importance of hearing the stories of local people and considering their experiences and the impact of the volcano on their lives.[59]

Many articles in the magazine addressed science even more directly, such as "Misterios del aire" (The Mysteries of the Air) and "Los misterios de las flores" (The Mysteries of the Flowers).[60] In "The Mysteries of the Air," signed by a prominent Cuban poet, Juan Clemente Zenea (1832–1871), the author reaffirmed Auber's claims and challenged the naturalist accounts that excluded local knowledge by claiming that there was more to study than natural history (185). Being a famous romantic poet, Zenea challenged the scientific rhetoric, suggesting a more comprehensive approach to botanical studies:

> I have already told you that one needs to study in this part of natural history something more than the character and properties of plants, something more than their organization and vital phenomena, it is good to the lover of nature

to divide the families, to find out the substances that make up the fibers and the juices that sustain them, interrogate the uses of the roots, the development of the stems and determine the time of flowering; It is up to us to feel and set our minds into a simple philosophy that wants to know why a branch of thuja represents a memory . . . and we resort to the myosotia to tell someone we love: Don't forget me! (185)[61]

As much as it was important to classify, measure, and name the plants, it was also important to contextualize the information, and local knowledge played a key role in this process. While admitting the importance of scientific knowledge, the plant's role in its specific culture could offer yet another layer of meaning.[62]

In a similar fashion, "The Mysteries of the Air" delivered another interesting science lesson. The article was intended to address many scientific aspects related to the air, such as gravitational forces, pressure, and atmosphere. The first noteworthy characteristic about the article is that Gómez de Avellaneda also chose a male author to write about the topic. His name was Ramon Zambrana Valdés, a well-respected doctor and professor in Cuba. Zambrana Valdés founded the Real Academia de Ciencias Médicas, Físicas y Naturales de La Habana (1861) and was the most respected authority to discuss any science-related subject on the island at that time. This was a well-calculated move because it automatically gave prestige and authority to her magazine and to the article itself.[63] In fact, Zambrana Valdés created a beautiful scientific piece, outlined as a narrative, a sort of story, whose main character was a young lady called Julia. Undeniably, the article is almost a sensorial experience to help the audience realize the presence, value, and beauty of air. After an almost poetic description of air, the author added that his intent was to explain its mysteries to his audience. Zambrana's language resembles the techniques Lightman describes when analyzing the Victorian popularizers of science. The author explicitly stated the intention of creating a sensorial experience in the audience to attract their attention and translate the scientific subject into a language intelligible to them. This was precisely when the character Julia was introduced. The author then addressed the discourse to her and to the audience as if they were the same as more scientific concepts were unveiled: the weight of air, oxygen, gravitational forces, sound propagation, and colors. After an informative and comprehensive explanation, the author concluded by stating the importance of such knowledge: "Now that Julia is familiar with these accidents of the air, let's take her as a guide. The truth is that she still does not feel the weight of the air on her morbid shoulders, but she already knows it is there . . ." (67).[64] As Lightman emphasizes, the female popularizers of science did not want to compete with their male counterparts; on the contrary, they often created their own way of addressing scientific topics. In Gómez de Avellaneda's case, she used her network to invite a prestigious Cuban scientist to write an article for her female audience, addressing science in a didactic and feminine way, making use of a female guide, and appealing to the senses and to the beauty of nature. Instead of competing with a male writer, she used Zambrana's authority in her favor, ensuring he was using appropriate language to present the subject to her audience. More importantly, making such subjects accessible to women and, therefore, participating in the circulation of knowledge were clearly the goals of her magazine.

Gómez de Avellaneda's periodical writings were evidently not solely devoted to science. At that time, one would expect that a magazine dedicated to women would address subjects such as fashion, cooking, religion, children, and education. Although Goméz de Avellaneda did address these subjects, she reinvented their content, establishing a whole new perspective toward them. For example, in the section "Revista de la Moda" (Fashion Magazine), the author identified only as Felicia surprisingly discussed numerous topics in addition to fashion.[65] In the article "El corsé" (The corset), Felicia discussed women's obsessive pursuit of thinness and beauty. The corset dates from the late medieval period when it was also worn by men. However, in 1795, it reappeared in the fashion world.[66] Kate Haulman observes that "the corset is an undergarment largely identified with mid-nineteenth-century women's fashionable dress, the site of contests over women's health, dress reform, and, for some, an emblem of women's social, economic, and political subjection" (217). It is interesting to draw a parallel between this statement and the fact that Felicia vehemently criticized the corset. She alluded to it as a form of voluntary torture and described it as evil. She strongly discouraged the use of the corset by proving that, besides not making the woman more beautiful, it dictated a model of beauty that did not correspond to reality and that it only tortured women. Haulman also suggests that the corset represents a metaphor of the confinement to which women were subject in patriarchal society (190). In fact, whereas the noun "corset" refers to the tight undergarment, the corresponding verb bears a much more suggestive meaning: to restrict closely, control rigidly. Felicia alluded to this rigidity and admitted her hopes of having "managed to put an end to the abuses of the corset" (189). She suggested that women should have more freedom to move and that the corset was now beginning to be ignored in the fashion world: "Fashion . . . has begun to look at the corset with indifference. The hard and stiff busts that the artifice reveal do not inspire enthusiasm. Now a certain graceful flexibility is demanded in the movements that the rigid, imperious, inflexible corset removes from the best-formed woman" (189).[67] She was also making a sharp critique of the corset as a symbol of the repression women suffered in Spanish society.

Picon Garfield observes that, in general, the articles dedicated to fashion in the Spanish and Cuban periodical publications at the time frequently contradicted the patriarchal agenda proposed by Fray Luis de León regarding women's dress code.[68] They usually encouraged women to buy clothes and accessories and dictated what women should and should not wear. Felicia, however, criticized the excessive materialism and warned her readers regarding the dangers of fashion obsession as opposed to beauty and health. Without adhering to current fashion models, but also not referring to Fray Luis's agenda, her well-written articles encouraged readers to draw conclusions about how the expected behavior of women in relation to fashion was an extension of the roles delegated to them in society and urged her readers to reflect on its impositions: ". . . fashion is the powerful sovereign who dictates the laws; the elegance the right-minded minister who, without making her imprudent opposition, modifies her decrees in such a way that the most absurd order becomes an incontestable benefit" (61).[69] It seems ironic that a section titled "Revista de la Moda," instead of encouraging readers to engage in fashion trends, encouraged them to consider the deeper implications of such choices: "Today, fashion does not recognize a fixed rule in its capricious kingdom. . . . It could be said that in the domains of fashion there are also difficult issues that inspire doubt and which allow everyone to believe in the triumph of one own ideas" (220).[70] Therefore, she was addressing the topics a female magazine was expected to address, but giving them new treatment and reinventing their content, providing an entirely new perspective for her readership. This new perspective, however, had to be subtle to preserve Gómez de Avellaneda's reputation with the queen and with society as a whole. In other words, the idea behind her magazine was to make her readers aware of many subjects and expose them to intellectual debates while ensuring it would remain within patriarchal society's approval.

Because of her relationship with the queen and her commitment to the agenda of the canon isabelino, many of the articles published in "Álbum" were framed within religious arguments. These arguments often had much in common with the ideas of the neo-platonic French philosopher Victor Cousin (Picon Garfield 31). The philosopher established some relations among truth (verdad), beauty (bello), and good (bueno), all subjects of desire and rationality, but somehow related to God (Picon Garfield 31).[71] In fact, as Lightman observes, "Religious themes were noticeably present in science books for children as well as in works by female popularizers of the maternal tradition in the first four decades of the nineteenth century. Elements of the natural theology tradition appeared in many popular science works of this period" (23). The success of the Bridgewater Treatises (1833–1840), a series of conservative and religiously "safe" accounts of science, may have encouraged popularizers to incorporate natural theology themes in their work (Lightman 24). Not surprisingly, religion was a subject embedded in many articles in the magazine. For example, in "La mujer," published in the second issue of the magazine and signed by Gómez de Avellaneda herself, she proposed to discuss the women's position regarding religion, aligning religious discourse with the role she believed they should play in patriarchal society (34). Yet, her rhetorical strategies reveal a manipulation in which Gómez de Avellaneda used the religious argument to deconstruct itself. At the beginning of the article, she reaffirmed the patriarchal belief that men were stronger physically, and even intellectually, and admitted that women reigned in areas related to the emotions (Picon Garfield 41). Gómez de Avellaneda built a sophism in which all the historical achievements she mentioned were the result of emotional decisions and that the stronger heroes were always lead by their hearts (Picon Garfield 41). She turned to the female biblical characters of Maria and Eva to state that both were led by their feelings and had a remarkable role in humanity's destiny. This emotional power, according to the author, was exactly what placed women at the center of society. However, when contextualized, the same discourse almost certainly leads to a completely different interpretation about women's role in society. Thus, this article provides a wealth of material that reveals many aspects of the negotiation and the interrelations among authority and gender.

In fact, the image of women the periodical press in Spain cultivated was that of the "angel of the hearth" or "la mujer virtuosa," rooted in a religious moral code "oriented toward submission, obedience, and resignation before God and the status-quo" (Kirkpatrick 73). However, in many of the articles, Gómez de Avellaneda tried to deconstruct this hegemonic model praising the accomplishments of women famous for their intelligence, strength, and leadership. Geraldine Scanlon observes that the scientific argument supported the belief that women were fragile and unable to practice science. Such argument was based on the idea that women were physically and mentally inferior to men and, for this reason, incapable of performing "masculine tasks" such as public affairs, leadership, and science (170–71). In the magazine, Gómez de Avellaneda not only criticized this generalized idea, but also cited numerous examples of feminine talents with the intent of challenging this assumption with examples from history that proved the exact opposite about female capacities. In a series of articles called "Galería de Mujeres Célebres" she mentioned several women who "managed to force from time to time their entrance [into the sanctuary of science] to steal from the mysterious divinity some of its secrets" (260).[72] First, the word "secrets" here suggests that science was not entirely transparent and objective, as the idea of "secret" automatically implied that something was necessarily hidden. Also, the exceptionally of the women who managed to take away these secrets from this "mysterious divinity" suggests that Gómez de Avellaneda was ironically and subtly opposing women's exclusion from science. Using history, another powerful discourse, to review many examples of women's abilities in scientific matters, she highlighted their talent and competence. In one of her articles, for example, she wrote about Aretha, daughter of Aristipo and author of over forty scientific books, who had an outstanding career as a philosopher and replaced her father after his death.[73] She also drew an explicit parallel between women scientists and women writers who had to pretend to be men to be recognized, ironically praising the "audacity and wisdom of the weaker sex." She mentioned that women who "covered their hairless faces with manly masks to enter, discretely, in the temple of fame" were able to be admitted among the male academics, who could not deny their credentials to be among them, even after they realized they were disguised (262).[74] Gómez de Avellaneda opposed women's inferiority endorsed by scientific arguments and ironically deconstructed this belief with historical examples. In addition, it is possible to interpret the careful selection of examples in her articles as an attempt to rescue women's history and convince her readers that women could be successful beyond the domestic sphere (Albin 173). As a matter of fact, in her articles, she aligned these women with attributes such as reason, medicine, art, truth, logic, and power, to name a few.[75] Gómez de Avellaneda not only anticipated but also contradicted Charles Darwin's argument in *The Descent of Man, and Selection in Relation to Sex* (1871). As Patricia Murphy observes, Darwin's book had serious influence on the literary work produced at the time and thereafter: "Literature penned after Descent's publication reveals a familiarity not only with Darwin's precepts, however, but with an array of gendered scientific suppositions circulating in the culture at large" (3). In fact, scientific discourse and scientific knowledge in the nineteenth century were considered by positivists, such as Augusto Comte, as "the ultimate achievement of human rationality. Science was represented . . . as the value-neutral activity of extracting and abstracting information from the natural world . . . ensuring that the knowledge they generated remained untainted by human influence" (Benjamin 5–6). Therefore, using scientific arguments to delegate women's position in society was a common and unquestionable strategy to perpetuate the patriarchal organization since science became a model of impartiality understood as entirely objective (Benjamin 6). Gómez de Avellaneda's attempt to engage in such debates gave women the opportunity to participate in the discussion. Because sciences became so notorious in the second half of the nineteenth century, "interpreting, and arguing over the social, political, and religious meaning of scientific ideas became the focus of intellectual activity" (Lightman 4). However, engaging in such debates was a delicate enterprise for a woman and Gómez de Avellaneda needed to be strategical not to lose the prestige she had acquired as a writer, or the protection she had from Queen Isabel.

NETWORKS AND AUTHORITY: LAUNCHING A FEMALE MAGAZINE IN CUBA

The epistolary collection available in the archives of the National Library of Madrid from 1859–1861 belonging to Gómez de Avellaneda reveals a complex network underlining the launch of "Álbum" in Cuba. In fact, these letters make it clear that her magazine's publication was only possible because she took advantage of her position as a renowned writer in Spain and because she was married to Domingos Verdugo, an important Spanish colonel who had many privileges with the queen and on the island. In fact, the wedding ceremony took place in the Royal Palace on April 26, 1855, and the monarchs were witnesses of the ceremony (Harper 41). In 1858, five days after the opening of her biblical drama *Baltasar*, colonel Verdugo was stabbed in a street incident that was never fully explained. Following the incident, Gómez de Avellaneda wrote to the queen indicating political reasons for the crime and asking for protection (Harper 43). She publicly accused Antonio Rivera, a man who had previously attacked General O'Donnel, a political associate of Verdugo. On April 15, 1859, the letter in which she urged for justice was published in the magazine *La America*. She appealed to the Queen in order to seek justice for her husband and questioned her influence over the criminal's "powerful protectors." Coincidence or not, soon afterward Verdugo was named governor of the province of Centrifuegos in Cuba and the couple arrived there in November 24, 1859 (Harper 44).

In Cuba, Gómez de Avellaneda received much recognition and homage, and the honors continued "for much of the five years of her stay" (Harper 44). As mentioned above, shortly after she arrived there, she started working on the publication of "Álbum." Her correspondence reveals that she orchestrated her network at many levels to make the project possible. She invited many important men and women from Cuba and Spain to collaborate with "Álbum," either as contributors to the magazine or by playing key roles in making the enterprise viable.[76]

Considering the nature and the nationality of the contributors of "Álbum," both European/and non-European, it is evident that the magazine became a space of interaction, a bridge between two worlds. Gómez de Avellaneda, as the editor, materialized in the magazine her own role as a go-between capable of mediating the dialogue. As Kapil Raj writes, "the go-between is not just a passer-by or a simple agent of cross-cultural diffusion, but someone who articulates relationships between disparate worlds or cultures by being able to translate between them" (xix). There are only a few studies about the years Gómez de Avellaneda spent in Cuba between 1859 and 1864; however, the prestige she had in 1859 is evident in her biography. At this point in her life, she had already published many books and had a successful career in Spain. She used many identities—the writer, the wife, the traveler, the Cuban, or the Spanish—depending on what she was trying to achieve. The fact is that the publication of her magazine was only possible due to the prestige she had both on the island and in Spain, not only to invite impressive contributors but also to surpass the censorship that could have prevented its publication. The unique status she acquired as Cuban/Spanish was projected in her magazine and made the project possible.

Gómez de Avellaneda's travel narratives were fundamental in the formation of the authority that made her literary career possible. By ascertaining herself the unique authority of a transatlantic subject, leveraging her gender constraints, she justified her mobility from the private to the public space and, by extension, her own literary vocation. She employed specific textual strategies to assert her presence within her travel narratives undermining her gendered condition as a woman traveler and writer. Employing the natural history discourse from a literary perspective, the author inscribed her travel accounts and her magazine in a tradition which was in the center of the intellectual activities and discussions in the nineteenth century. Ultimately, the transatlantic subjectivity that emerged from her travel writing allowed Gómez de Avellaneda to create and maintain an authority that allowed her to circulate and disseminate knowledge in Spain and on the island. The notoriety she achieved as a writer allowed her to engage in scientific debates, using "non-professional" genres, such as letters, articles, memoirs, and poetry. After firmly establishing her transatlantic subjectivity and literary authority, Goméz de Avellaneda returned to Cuba determined to be an active disseminator of knowledge and became the editor of her "Álbum," a magazine dedicated to women. As David Turnbull writes, "the processes of knowledge movement, translation, transmission, and the ways in which people, practices, and places are linked and assembled into knowledge spaces, are often hard to discern and bring into visibility" (Turnbull 387). Hence, investigating non-scientific venues, such as magazines, letters, and travel memoirs, is important to expand our understanding of the process of knowledge dissemination. Moreover, it provides the opportunity to evaluate women's participation in this process. Goméz de Avellaneda's initiative is particularly interesting from that perspective because her magazine emerged from the encounter between two different places, cultures, and traditions. This encounter between different knowledge traditions is a key site for investigating knowledge dissemination as such encounters are often somehow problematic and need a mediator (Turnbull 387). Goméz de Avellaneda's travels provided her with the resources to become the perfect mediator, although she had to stay within the boundaries of her gender constraints. Her magazine became a space to discuss and circulate scientific knowledge, providing an alternate visibility to Gómez de Avelleneda as well as to the other contributors, allowing them to take part of an international network of knowledge dissemination.

NOTES

1. The title of this chapter is a reference to Gómez de Avellaneda's poem "El viajero americano" in which she dialogued with the naturalist Alexander von Humboldt. In the poem, she classified the perspective of the traveler encountering American nature as "ilusiones ópticas del alma."

2. "Oda al Niágara" (Ode to Niagara) is a poem by Cuban writer José Maria Heredia. The poem is a romantic rendition of the Niagara Falls in which Heredia exalts Cuba and emphasizes his feelings about his own country while in exile.

3. Gómez de Avellaneda quotes the following passage from the poem: ". . . ví al Océano/Azotado por austro proceloso/ Combatir mi bajel, y ante mis plantas/ Vórtice hirviente abrir, y amé el peligro."

4. In "Las mujeres y el imaginario nacional en el siglo XIX" Mary Louise Pratt offers a useful reading of the gendered nature of the projects of the newly founded nations in the emergent Latin American republics in the nineteenth century.

5. For more details on Gómez de Avellaneda's biography, see Hugh A. Harter, *Gertrudis Gómez de Avellaneda* (1981).

6. It is interesting to compare this picture of Gómez de Avellaneda with the pictures taken by many intellectual celebrities in the nineteenth century. The fact that she is holding a book and marking a page with her finger conveys the idea that she was reading that book and only interrupted the reading to pose for the portrait. This was unusual for a woman's picture. Further, her finger appears to be marking a page toward the end of the book, suggesting, as well, a certain depth of knowledge and seriousness of study.

7. In 1853, she attempted to become a member of the Real Academia Española to occupy the place that belonged to the poet Juan Nicasio Gallego, who had passed away. She tried to convince the Academy that it was his desire that she occupy his chair, but her solicitation was ultimately denied (Scatena Franco 327).

8. I will refer to this account as *Memorias* in my analysis.

9. I would like to thank Stela Maris Scatena Franco for kindly sharing a copy of this rare manuscript with me. In the analysis, I refer to this account as *Mi última*.

10. In fact, these letters were only published for the first time in 1914, more than seventy years after they were written.

11. Desde mi salida de Cuba hasta mi llegada en Sevilla, o sea apuntaciones de mis viajes. Dedicadas a mi amiga y prima Doña Heloysa de Artega y Loinaz.

12. Eran las seis de la tarde cuando saltamos en tierra en el muelle de Polláx, y una multitud de gente se había agrupado allí para esperar a los viajeros. Cada dueño de hotel nos encarecía las ventajas del suyo, *deseoso* de ser preferido; otros nos *perseguían* para que les tomásemos para transportar el equipaje, ya las vendedoras de frutas nos *cercaban* con sus canastos. Esta *ansia* del dinero me chocó de un modo desagradable, porque aún es desconocida en nuestra rica Cuba (emphasis added).

13. Nada tan romántico y encantador como las vistas y perspectivas que ofrecen a los ojos del viajero que hace en el vapor la travesía de Pollax a Bourdeaux en los meses de verano. Yo había visto en Cuba sus soberbios montes, sus campos vírgenes coronados de palmas y caobas; había estendido la vista por sus inmensas sabanas y detenídola en sus ricos plantíos. . . . Sin embargo, me encantaron las campiñas deliciosas que adornan las márgenes soberbias del Garona.

14. My discussion on Gómez de Avellaneda's descriptions of European cultural settings draws from Pratt's analysis of Domingo Faustino Sarmiento's book about his travels to Europe and his role as a *flaneur* (*Imperial* 190).

15. As shown in chapter 1, Maria Graham also uses this strategy when writing about her travels.

16. . . . me veo frecuentemente confundida cuando describo algún objeto por el solo recuerdo que de él conservo, habrá mil inexactitudes y equivocaciones para las cuales reclamo tu indulgencia" I see myself frequently confused when I describe an object merely relying on the memory that I have of it, there will be a thousand inaccuracies and mistakes for which I claim your indulgence.

17. Goméz de Avellaneda refers to her travel accounts as "cuadernillos."

18. Heloysa: alguna vez he ideado formar para ti apuntaciones curiosas de mis viajes, consultar otros viajeros, tomar nociones acerca de la historia, tradiciones y particularidades locales de los sitios de que te hablo; en fin, hermosear estas Memorias que te he ofrecido, haciéndolas instructivas e interesantes, pero no he podido.

19. . . . son los días de Bourdeaux como la línea que divide mis dos existencias: un intermedio entre los sueños dichosos de mi primera edad y las realidades agitadoras de estos últimos días de mi vida.

20. Al llegar a Bourdeaux nuevas emociones de diferente género experimentó mi corazón . . . sentí aquella especie de respeto que inspira una ciudad comercial en toda su opulencia.

21. See chapter 3 for a similar approach employed by the Brazilian writer Nísia Floresta.

22. En el llamado Baluarte de S. Carlos vi la tumba del célebre General Moore, sencilla y elegante, que me agradó mucho. Todos los Ingleses que vienen a la Coruña visitan con respeto la tumba de su malogrado compatriota, yo hice lo mismo sin ser Inglesa y no me retiré de aquel sitio sin decir con emoción este verso de un poema moderno. Grata y blanda esta tierra te sea / Si es que puede serlo nunca jamás / Tierra estrangera.

23. . . . las Americanas pasamos en Galicia por perezosas, holgazanas, y poco aptas para el gobierno domestico; y yo creo que es innegable que bien por efecto del clima, bien por la educación, somos en realidad, las Cubanas por lo menos, más indolentes

que las Gallegas, y que rara mujer en nuestro país se sometería con gusto a ahumarse por la mañana en la cocina . . .

24. *Diario de la Marina* was a conservative Cuban newspaper that circulated between 1844 and 1960.

25. Gómez de Avellaneda's social network will be fully explored below, in the next section of this chapter.

26. She mentioned that her group was formed by French, English, and Spaniards, without giving much detail about its individual members.

27. Madam Roland (1754–1793) was a heroine of the French Revolution who died by the guillotine.

28. El que puede y no visita aquel lugar es un cobarde indigno de llamarse hombre.

29. No esperen, sin embargo, mis amigos, que intente describirles el espectáculo que la naturaleza presentó a mis miradas, no; vayan a contemplarlo si tienen corazón, si sienten vibrar en su alma la cuerda armoniosa que responde a todo lo bello, a lo sublime. Tendrán que afrontar dificultades y fatigas, es cierto; tendrán que seguir angostos desfiladeros, sendas que serpentean por los flancos de la cordillera suspendidos sobre abismos . . . ; palidecerán alguna vez, por valientes que sean, al verse como sepultados bajo inmensas bóvedas de colosales peñascos que amenazan desplomarse sobre sus cabezas. (. . .) Pero en cambio de estos peligros—que no carecen de halago para los espíritus aventureros ¡cuántas impresiones les guardan aquellos lugares *que ningún pincel, que ninguna pluma acertará nunca describir*! (emphasis added.)

30. . . . allí, donde se aglomeran ruinas de los siglos sin alterar el agreste primitivo que aún se ostenta como en el día primero de la creación; allí, a presencia de aquellas cumbres, de aquellos hielos tan antiguos como el mundo, y en el seno de la augusta soledad de que son guardianes, todos observábamos involuntariamente respetuoso silencio.

31. Alexander von Humboldt, *Aspects of Nature, in Different Lands and Different Climates with Scientific Elucidations,* 1850.

32. . . . entusiastas, penetrantes, inteligentes, cosmopolitas por instinto y por educación, y poseedores de ese tacto exquisito que aprecia y comprende todos los caprichos del sentimiento y de la imaginación . . .

33. Scatena Franco contends that the fact that Gómez de Avellaneda places Spain and France in the same side against England might be a consequence of the dichotomy "Anglo-Saxon versus Latin," which was used politically to legitimate French endeavors in Spanish America. Also known as "panlatinismo," this trend believed that Latin people had a "superioridad espiritualista o idealista," as opposed to the spirit "pragmático o empirista," with which Anglo-Saxons were described (325).

34. Tres días hacía apenas que nos hallábamos asociados a los doce o quince personas de la excursión a Gavarnie, y en tan corto número de horas reinaba ya entre todos, no esa intimidad de confianza afectuosa *a que somos propensos los españoles*, pero sí la armonía de gusto, de comunión de impresiones, la recíproca necesidad de agradarnos, que ahuyentando contrariedades contribuían poderosamente a prestar encantos a nuestra expedición, y a hacernos sentir penosamente su término próximo (emphasis added).

35. In fact, the episode with the Englishmen became a joke in the articles. In every piece, she managed to return to the story, satirizing their presence. In her last article, she revisited the subject and suggested they were actually "stalkers" following her group at every step: "Lo que de seguro no sabe nadie—y yo quiero decir hoy a los que hayan tomado la molestia de leer los desaliñados apuntes de viaje cuyas páginas inserta el presente número del Diario de la Marina—es que cuando desembarcamos en las risueñas playas gaditanas, el día 28 del citado mes, vimos, sin poder dudar de la verdad de la visión—que los tres ingleses nos aguardaban en ellas" (46). It is also possible to imagine that Gómez de Avellaneda was responding to many travel narratives written by English travelers who visited the French Pyrenees at that time. For example, see Charles Richard Weld, *The Pyrenees, West and East* (London: Longman, 1859). Weld did not ignore a single opportunity to dismiss the French and Spaniards as travel companions, whom he considered extremely loud and unpleasant throughout his travel narrative.

36. Como si presintiese que había de abandonar próximamente el suelo de la Europa, quise, en mi excursión veraniega del año último, recorrer los sitios más notables de los Pirineos españoles y franceses, tomando notas de las tradiciones que los poetizan.... Revueltos entre fárragos de manuscritos venían conmigo los *ligeros apuntes* tomados en mi indicada excursión, tan *borrosos*, por cierto, y tan *poco inteligibles*, que aun yo misma he necesitado esfuerzos de memoria para descifrarlos, cuando se me ocurrió la idea de que acaso no le vendrían mal a usted para folletines de su apreciable *Diario*.... Pero a falta de bonitas narraciones podía dar a usted ... por *incompletos* y *desaliñados*, lo ganaran acaso por la *sencillez* y *verdad* que caracteriza todo lo que se escribe para mí misma, sin pretensiones de *embellecer* y *abrillantar* las cosas con ropajes de la *fantasía* (emphasis added).

37. The first volume of "Álbum cubano de lo bueno y de lo bello" was published on February 15, 1860. It was a bimonthly magazine especially addressed to the women of Havana. In the poem "A las Cubanas," she salutes her readers: "Respiro entre vosotras, Oh hermanas mias!/Pasados de la ausencia los largos días,/y al blando aliento/De vuestro amor el alma revivir siento.... Mas ay! de las que vengo, tierras lejanas,/Solo una lira traigo, bellas cubanas;/ Solo una lira!/Que al soplo de las auras triste suspira!" (3)

38. She was not new to such an enterprise, however, as she had already been the editor of another periodical in Madrid, "La ilustración de las damas" (The Illumination of the Ladies), in 1845, but was forced to abandon this first project owing to a sick child, and it seemed to be a somewhat unfinished business for her (Picon Garfield 19).

39. Nancy Fraser proposes the term "counterpublic spaces" to refer to the alternative spaces women of different classes created to become part of the public sphere (58–63). Albín also employs this term to refer to the magazine (186).

40. I employ the term "go-between" here in the sense suggested by Simon Schaffer, Lissa Roberts, Kapil Raj, and James Delbourgo in *The Brokered World: Go-Betweens and Global Intelligence, 1770–1820*.

41. Although Lightman's work focuses on the Victorian period and the writers he analyzes effectively wrote about science more explicitly, his model is useful to ana-

lyze Gómez de Avellaneda's periodical writings. Her work has many similarities with the work of the Victorian popularizers of science. Besides, despite the geographical differences, Lightman's analysis is contemporary to Gómez de Avellaneda´s work (1840–1850s).

42. As Sánchez Llama observes, although the Protestant context is different from the Spanish Neocatholicism in many aspects, it is similar in the sense that female authors tried to legitimate the feminine talent by using strong female characters from the Bible (99).

43. Isabel de Borbón (1830–1904) was the Queen of Spain between 1833 and 1868. According to Sanchez Llama, the canon isabelino emphatically rejects the Kantian notion of aesthetic disinterest and associates the notion of artistic beauty with a Christian and anti-liberal commitment, a Lamartinian idealism and, in a general sense, a neo-Catholicism (99).

44. As a matter of fact, Gómez de Avellaneda admitted in her personal correspondence that much of the privilege she received from royalty was because of her "adulation" toward the court members (Scatena Franco 56).

45. Sanchéz Llama also observes that, from 1844, Gómez de Avellaneda had been incorporated in the cultural canon of Spain (93).

46. Fernán Caballero (1796–1877) was the pseudonym of the Spanish writer Cecilia Böhl de Faber.

47. Using the pseudonym Atta Troll.

48. Unos dicen que la mujeres son demonios y otros que todas son angeles: A cual de estas dos opiniones debe uno atenerse? Eso es dificil de resolver y sobre todo en el "Álbum Cubano." Optemos por el termino medio y digamos que tienen a veces lo de uno y de lo otro.

49. Virginia Felicia Auber de Noya (1825–1897) was a Spanish author who was the daughter of a professor at the Universidad de La Habana. She was a well-known writer in the island and contributed to many periodical publications of her time, such as *Diario de la Marina* and *Diario de La Habana* (Picon Garfield 34).

50. Maria Graham dedicated several pages of her travel diary to Tenerife as well.

51. No otra cosa parece aquel deserto estéril e inanimado que un inmenso osario de gigantes de las épocas geológicas pasadas, cuyos esqueletos de granito medio desenterrados durante alguna convulsión del globo muestran sus angulosas formas al través de las corrientes de basalto vomitadas por el inmediato vulcano adormecido. . . . Descendamos de Nuevo en nuestra vagabunda marcha al través de los *pinos y retamas* y fijemos la fatigada planta en Agua Mansa, lugar abierto en el bosque y en que se goza de un bien estar inexplicable. Que distinto del aire enrarecido por la elevación es el que allí con deleite se respira fresco y embalsamado por el fragrante aroma del espliego y el orégano silvestre.

52. Charles Darwin made several hand notes on his copy of Humboldt's *Personal Narratives*. One of these notes reads: "It is however to be regretted, that the want of a thorough knowledge of the Spanish language, and the little care taken to acquire the names of places, rivers, and tribes, have occasioned the most singular mistakes: and it is also afflicting (and the inhabitants of South America have above all to complain) that, in language without taste or dignity, the manners of the natives are described in

the most unjust and disdainful terms." Darwin's notes on volume 7, chapter 29, pp. 468–70 (http://darwin-online.org.uk). Darwin's critique of the fact that Humboldt ignored the inhabitants of South America reveals a flaw that made his work, if not unreliable, at least incomplete.

53. En 1830 había en aquel sitio una cabaña rodeada entonces como ahora de un verde vallado de durazneros y membrillos. El interior de aquella humilde morada, correspondía a su rustico exterior. Una gran mesa de castaño labrada y dos o tres sillas de la misma madera componían todo su ajuar. En el medio veíanse tres grandes piedras, entre las cuales ardían los troncos de *retama*, y junto al fuego disfrutando de su suave calor . . . sentada en un banquillo una mujer de avanzada edad . . .

54. La bruja está llorando.

55. Frase usada aun por los que viven en Aguamansa o sus inmediaciones para explicar el ruido que acabamos de indicar.

56. Many of the stories about witches that circulated in the Canarias derived from the fact that the islands were indeed the site in which many witches were killed during the Spanish inquisition.

57. La naturaleza sale del orden y entra en el caos.

58. Maria Graham also criticized Humboldt's conjectures about facts that he could not explain, as demonstrated in chapter 1.

59. One could infer that claiming that local knowledge needed to be included in these accounts challenged the very same agenda that excluded women's knowledge. It also suggests that, although natural history might be important, there was more than that to consider when analyzing the world.

60. They were both signed by well-known men of science in Cuba and were both published in the first few months of Album's release, and just three numbers apart. However, it is hard to say why this series did not become a consistent section in the magazine, such as the Galería de las mujeres célebres.

61. Ya os he dicho que hay que estudiar en esa parte de la historia natural algo más que el carácter y la propiedades de los vegetales, algo más que su organización y los fenómenos vitales, bien está al pensativo amante de la naturaleza que divida las familias, averigüe las substancias de que se componen las fibras y los jugos que las sostienen, interrogue los usos de las raíces, el desenvolvimiento de los tallos y determine la hora de la florescencia; corresponde a nosotros sentir y lanzar la mente en usa filosofía sencilla que quiere saber por que nos servimos de una rama de thuya para significar un recuerdo . . . y nos valemos de una myosotia para decir a una persona querida:—No me olvides!

62. Thuja is an ornamental tree and myosotia is the scientific name of the flower popularly known as Forget Me Not.

63. Certainly, the effectiveness would not be the same if the author had been a woman or if the article had not been signed.

64. Familiarizada ya Julia con estos accidentes del aire, tomémosla por guía. Verdad es que aún no siente sobre sus mórbidos hombros el peso del aire, pero ya sabe que lo lleva . . .

65. The author is also Virginia Felicia Auber y Noya (1825–1897), cited above.

66. "Middle English, bodice, from Old French, diminutive of corset (corselet), body, from Latin corpus" (Oxford Dictionary).

67. La moda . . . ha empezado a mirar el corsé con indiferencia. Ya los bustos duros y tiesos que revelan el artificio no inspiran ilusión. Exígese ahora cierta fliexibilidad garbosa en los movimientos que el corsé rígido, imperioso, inflexible quita a la mujer mejor formada.

68. Picon Garfield explains that the Spanish hegemonic discourse originated from sixteenth-century treatises that addressed women's behavior, especially *La Perfecta Casada* (1583) by Fray Luis de León. In the nineteenth century, Fray Luis was still an authority to whom many authors referred with regard to women's behavior in society: "Las instruyen y aconsejan sobre la conducta apropiada y virtuosa de la virgen y de la casada" (22). Fray Luis established a clear dichotomy between women and men and their behavior in society: "La perfecta casada debe quedarse en casa, tener pocas visitas, no entablar conversaciones con otras mujeres, y guardar silencio" (23). Fray Luis added that women were not intended to study the sciences, or be in charge of any business or anything that was not related to the domestic sphere (23).

69. . . . la moda es la poderosa soberana que dicta leyes; la elegancia el diestro ministro que sin hacerla imprudente oposición modifica sus decretos de manera que la orden más absurda se convierte en beneficio incontestable.

70. Hoy la moda no reconoce regla fija en su caprichoso reino. . . . Diriase que tambien en los dominios de la Moda se agitan dificiles cuestiones que tienen suspensos los animos y que permiten a cada cual creer seguro el triunfo de sus ideas.

71. Picon Garfield also believes this is the reason Gómez de Avellaneda named her magazine "Álbum cubano de lo bueno y de lo bello" (31).

72. . . . han logrado forzar de vez en cuando la entrada [del santuario de la ciencia] para arrancar a la misteriosa deidad algunos de sus secretos.

73. Arete of Cyrene followed her father to Athens and studied philosophy. It is widely accepted that after her father's death, she headed the Cyreneiac School which he had founded.

74. Pero admirad la audacia y la astucia del sexo débil! Hay ellas que no sé cómo se alzaron súbitamente con borlas de doctores. Otras que cubriendo sus lampiñas caras con máscara varonil se entraron, si más ni más, tan adentro del templo de la fama que cuando vino a conocerse que carecían de barbas y no podían por consiguiente ser admitidas entre las capacidades académicas, ya no había medio hábil de negarles que poseían justos títulos para figurar eternamente entre las capacidades europeas.

75. Until the seventeenth century, science was frequently represented as a feminine entity and these representations were evident in the front pages of many scientific books. As a matter of fact, the feminine icon in science became less prestigious at the end of the eighteenth century (Schiebinger, *Nature* 685). Indeed, the attack that science started on the feminine icon was a turning point on the historiography of science and, in the middle of the nineteenth century, scientists no longer used feminine images to represent science: "As science became more professional, ornamental images disappeared from its texts; at the same time the image of women became more exclusively tied to motherhood" (Schiebinger, *Nature* 687).

76. Besides Fernán Caballero, among the Spanish women who wrote for Álbum cubano are Dolores Gómez de Cadiz, María Verdejo y Durán, María del Pila Sinués de Marco y Angela Grassi. Among the Cuban are Dolores Cabrera y Heredia, Julia Perez y Montes de Oca, Luisa Pérez de Zambrana y Virginia Felicia Auber. (Picon Garfield 29)

Chapter Three

Nísia Floresta Voyages through Europe
Transatlantic Perspectives on Nature, Progress, and Women's Education

"That day ... I cast one last look, veiled with tears, towards that magnificent bay, to those majestic mountains beautifully covered by eternal vegetation, those two cities, Rio de Janeiro and Niterói ..." (*Itália* 85).[1] This quote, extracted from Nísia Floresta's (1810–1885) diary of her travels to Italy, makes use of the sublime to convey her feelings of sadness and longing when she left Brazil for the first time. The scene she was leaving behind, and which resonated throughout her travel writing, was the same one that impressed so many European travelers who arrived in America in the naturalist expeditions in the nineteenth century: "That land covered with the most splendid magnificence of nature disappeared behind me: part of everything that I most loved on earth stayed there with it" (*Itália* 85).[2] In the same way, Humboldt and other travelers made use of the rhetoric of the sublime such as that present in these two passages to aggrandize this exotic and unknown place and emphasize its importance in validating the authority of the explorer who had been there and conquered it. Floresta, however, used this landscape that had made Humboldt and others famous to forge her voice as a travel writer. Unlike the men, she had to leave this landscape behind and travel elsewhere. Had she stayed in Brazil, she would have merely remained part of the exotic backdrop. Hence, at least in part, the act of leaving was key to the construction of the authority as a writer that she would achieve overseas. Nísia Floresta, I argue, employed the natural history discourse to approach both Brazilian and European nature and to participate in debates related to the situation of women, politics, and education on both sides of the Atlantic. She became famous for being the only Brazilian writer, male or female, to go overseas and publish travel accounts abroad in the nineteenth century. Moreover, these travel accounts, written in French, demonstrate that she contributed to shaping and propagating information both in Europe and in Brazil and therefore participated in the construction of knowledge that was being disseminated in the contact zones. Following a chronological order to discuss a selection of texts by Floresta, first, I analyze her writings about education produced before leaving Brazil, and then, I examine the travel accounts she wrote when living in Europe accompanied by her daughter, Lívia Augusta (1830–1912), to demonstrate how Floresta benefited from the social leverage offered by the transatlantic voyage to achieve recognition as a writer. Unable to implement her educational and political ideals in Brazil, she traveled to Europe and engaged in travel narratives. By employing the scientific discourse of natural history, she contested and challenged the accounts produced by her male counterparts about Latin America, which largely served as means to validate the establishment of its newly established nations. Furthermore, she forged a counter space to discuss women's education, carving a unique authority to advocate for the role of women in society.

FROM BRAZILIAN EDUCATOR AND WRITER TO TRANSATLANTIC TRAVELER

Nísia Floresta was born on October 12, 1810 in the state of Rio Grande do Norte, in the northeast of Brazil (figure 3.1).[3] She was the daughter of a Portuguese lawyer named Dionísio Gonçalves Pinto Lisboa and a Brazilian woman named Antônia Clara Freire. Born on a little farm called Floresta, she was baptized as Dionísia Gonçalves Pinto Lisboa. From the time of her first publication, however, she adopted the pseudonym of Nísia Floresta Brasileira Augusta: Floresta after her birth place, Brasileira to state her nationality, and Augusta as homage to the father of her children, as Cláudia Luna explains (506–7). Charlotte Hammond Matthews claims that her pseudonym, rather than an attempt to achieve literary anonymity, was an act of self-construction (1). In fact, Floresta used many pseudonyms throughout her life: Mme. Floresta A. Brasileira, Nísia Floresta, Brasileira Augusta, Telesilla, B. A., B. Augusta, "Une Brésilienne," F. Brasileira Augusta, and Mme. Brasileira Augusta. By doing that, she highlighted a changeable identity which surpassed gender limitations. In other words, she created a rather versatile and intricate literary persona who would be difficult to classify under any label. Although she might not have done so for anonymity, her many pseudonyms do make it more difficult to locate her texts in the archives around the world.

In 1823, when she was only thirteen years old, Floresta married Manuel Alexandre Seabra de Melo, but the marriage only lasted a few months. At this point, Brazil had just become independent from Portugal, in September of the previous year. Floresta, along with her father, mother, and brother, moved to the northeastern state of Pernambuco. In 1828, her father was assassinated and Floresta moved in with the man who would later become the father of her children, Manuel Augusto de Faria Rocha (Lima Duarte, *Vida* 48). The couple never formalized the relationship as she was still married to her first husband and divorce was not allowed in Brazil at that time. She had her first daughter, Lívia Augusta, in 1830. In 1832, because of the negative gossip that their relationship created, the couple relocated over 2,000 miles south, to the city of Porto Alegre, in the extreme south of Brazil, and their son Augusto Américo was born there in 1833. Shortly after the child was born, at the age of twenty-five, her partner unexpectedly died of cardiac arrest, and she was left alone with two young children to look after (Lima Duarte, *Vida* 48). At

Figure 3.1. Watercolor of Nísia Floresta.
Reproduced with the consent of Gabriela Motta.

this point, her first book, *Direitos das mulheres e injustiça dos homens* (1832) (Women's Rights and Men's Injustice), had been just published in Porto Alegre. After living a few more years in that city, teaching and writing, she decided to move to Rio de Janeiro, the capital of the country at the time, to open the school that she would direct for the next several years.

In 1838, she announced in the newspapers of Rio de Janeiro the inauguration of her Colégio Augusto (Augusto School). Her method of education for girls, which included languages and geography among other subjects, was severely criticized by many Brazilian newspapers: ". . . language-related activities were not lacking; those related to the needle were left in the dark. Husbands need a wife who works more and speaks less" (quoted in Lima Duarte, *Primeira Feminista* 26).[4] Teaching did not consume all of her time, however, and by 1847, she was already a professional author with several published works. She traveled to Europe with her children in 1849 and stayed there for two years, where she took part in various intellectual circles. She settled with her children in Paris, where she enrolled herself in several courses at French education institutions, such as the Collège de France and the Museu de Historie Naturalle. She traveled back to Brazil in 1852 with Lívia and Américo and remained in the country for three years, returning to Europe again with Lívia in 1855. She would once again travel to Brazil, this time alone, in 1872 and stay there for another three years. The nature of her stays is obscure, and her biographers attribute that to business related to her inheritance. In 1875, she departed to Europe and never again returned to Brazil.

During the thirty-six years in which she lived in Europe, Floresta traveled throughout the continent mostly accompanied by her daughter, Lívia Augusta. Among the countries they visited were Portugal, England, Italy, Germany, Greece, and France. She published several works in Europe between 1857 and 1878 in French, English, and Italian. Among her most important publications are *Itinéraire d'un voyage en Allemagne* (1857) (Itinerary of a Voyage to Germany), *Consigli a mia figlia* (1858) (Advice to my Daughter), and *Scintille d'un'anima brasiliana* (1858) (Sparks of a Brazilian Soul). From 1858 to 1861, Floresta traveled throughout Italy and Greece and, in 1864, she published *Trois ans en Italie, suivis d'un voyage en Grèce* (Three Years in Italy Followed by a Voyage to Greece). In 1867, her daughter translated *Scintille* to English and the work was published in London. In April 24, 1885, Nísia Floresta died of pneumonia in her home in France, but her body was not repatriated to Brazil until September 12, 1954. Her remains were taken to her hometown, Papari, in the Brazilian state of Rio Grande do Norte, where she now rests. Her hometown was renamed after her and as such, it is now called Nísia Floresta. Such an impressive career as a writer for a woman who is still largely ignored by the Brazilian canon.

EDUCATING GIRLS IN NINETEENTH-CENTURY BRAZIL

The political situation of Brazil after its independence in 1822, which made the country the only empire in Latin America, had a great impact on Floresta's career, both as a writer and an educator, and influenced her decision to move to Europe and engage in travel writing. In the years that followed the independence, the Emperor D. Pedro I (1798–1834) increasingly lost both military and civil endorsement within the country. On April 7, 1831, less than ten years after the Emperor had proclaimed Brazil independent from Portugal, D. Pedro was no longer able to resist the pressure to step down from office. Because military and public opinions were decidedly against him and there was growing ferment in favor of Brazil becoming a republic, he decided to abdicate the throne in favor of his son, D. Pedro II, who was born in Brazil and was only five years old. For the next twelve years, José Bonifácio de Andrada[5] (1763–1838) would be the tutor of young Pedro and Brazil would undergo the period known as the regency era. It was not until December 2, 1843, that Pedro's son would personally exercise his power as a monarch. Roderick J. Barman divides the years before D. Pedro II reached the age of majority into two periods: from 1831–1837, the liberal experiment; and from 1837–1842, the triumph of tradition (*Brazil* 160). According to the author, the first six years consisted of a time of "failed ideas and frustrated innovations" in which the liberals tried to decentralize power and create states that were more independent (*Brazil* 187). The six years that followed consisted of the triumph of traditionalism, which recentralized power in the hands of the national government. During these years of uncertainty, Brazil went through many regional rebellions and by 1838 the liberal movement was losing its power because of the many defeats in failed rebellions, most notably the Farroupilhas in Rio Grande do Sul. Hence, when Floresta opened her school for girls in Rio de Janeiro in 1838, the political situation in Brazil was very unstable, and the conservatives were still recovering their political power. The years that preceded her first voyage to Europe in 1849 were therefore marked by the triumph of tradition and the empire over the liberal experiment.[6]

This period marked the need to forge a Brazilian national identity and the nationalist discourse was one of the most pronounced characteristics of the work of many writers of the literature from that period, among them the romantic writers Gonçalves Dias (1823–1864) and José de Alencar (1829–1877).[7] Gonçalves Dias was perhaps one of the authors who best addressed the problem of national identity in Brazilian literature. His famous poem, "Canção do Exílio" (Song of Exile), written in 1846, dealt specifically with the feelings of love for his nation, making an explicit opposition between Brazil and Portugal (lá e cá) (here and there): "The birds that sing here, do not sing as they do there" (Dias 103).[8] In line with René de Chateaubriand's *Atala*, the romantic trope of the native Indian was broadly adopted by Dias with the purpose of forging a national hero to endorse a new project of nation, and although it was not necessarily a new literary aesthetics in Brazil, Dias's approach to this aesthetic was groundbreaking (Nunes 40).[9] In fact, Indianist literature contributed to the establishment of the values and beliefs related to the national imaginary. For example, Iracema and Martin, a Brazilian native woman and a Portuguese settler, the heroes of José de Alencar's novel *Iracema* (1847), personified representations of docility and the capacity of self-sacrifice for love. As Sommer observes, the interracial romance portrayed by the protagonist couple has been widely accepted and replicated in Brazilian popular culture for more than a century (141). The urgency of rescuing the past and promoting a reconciliation with the colonizer was evident in this discourse. Sommer also points out that Latin American foundational novels such as *Iracema* presented a clear message on the key issue of Brazilian national identity: racial miscegenation. For Sommer, ". . . Brazilians are a coherent race produced long ago from the mutual love between native noble and the best Portuguese" (161). The novel, in spite of all the losses that Iracema suffers, ends in conciliation represented by the son she leaves, which represents the new race as the solution for the national identity dilemma (Sommer 161). Not surprisingly, writers of this period, Gonçalves Dias and Alencar included, relied on financial support from the Emperor.[10] In fact, the crown financed not only the writers but also the publication of their works.[11] D. Pedro II was, thus, the main sponsor of Brazilian intellectuals and this is a strong evidence that these male writers, at least on the surface, supported the imperialist project of the nation (Torquato Lima 45). The project of nation proposed by this literature not only promoted miscegenation and the mystification of the *bon savage*, but it also relegated women to a secondary role in Brazilian society, in which she was represented as a savage who had to sacrifice herself to give birth to her baby, the future of Brazil. To guarantee the success of this project, it was fundamental that Brazilian women assumed their role in the new nation, a role that Floresta vehemently opposed as a writer and as an educator.[12]

In fact, women's education, or lack thereof, played a major role in maintaining the power of the monarchy and the status quo in Brazil. Men were raised to become the leaders of the new nation whereas women were supposed to fully embrace their roles as mothers, and this family model was at the center of the Brazilian imperial project. As an educator and writer, Floresta had to negotiate with these discourses to avoid being dismissed. Her first work dealing with the subject was *Direitos das mulheres e injustiça dos homens* (Women's Rights and Men's Injustice), published in 1830. Initially identified as a translation of Mary Wollstonecraft's *A Vindication of the Rights of Women* (1792), this work has been the subject of much scholarly discussions since the 1990s. In fact, despite these controversies, Floresta became moderately famous in Brazil because of this translation and this sudden reputation ironically assisted her project to become an educator.[13] In *Direitos*, she advocated for equal rights for women and defended that they should be allowed to participate in the public sphere: "Why is science useless to us? Because we are excluded from public office positions; and why are we excluded from public office positions? Because we do not know science. I say further, there is no science, nor public office position, which women are not able to fulfill as well as men" (*Direitos* 52).[14] This passage also reveals Floresta's engagement with the scientific discourse of her time, which labeled women as not talented for scientific subjects. She believed that women were trapped in the domestic sphere precisely because they lacked the education which would provide them the skills to participate in the public sphere. With that in mind, she envisioned a model of education for girls that would go beyond the traditional cooking classes: they would also be taught more erudite (and therefore useful) subjects and finally have the skills to participate in the public sphere on par with men. It is important to highlight, though, that when she published *Direitos*, in 1832, hope for the creation of a more liberal Brazilian society was at its peak.

Floresta's school, Colégio Augusto, opened its doors in 1838 in Rio de Janeiro, eight years after the publication of *Direitos*, and inaugurated this new educational project for girls in which they would learn subjects not necessarily designed to support the imperial project of the nation, which exposed Floresta to criticism and retaliation. Floresta's pedagogical approach was still framed within the patriarchal standards and domestic education was the main goal of her teaching philosophy, which was an evident form of negotiation with the prevailing social norms. In fact, Hammond Matthews points out that the curriculum of the school was more comprehensive than advertised and that she offered "a genuine broadening of intellectual, abstract knowledge for her own pupils" (35). Despite the criticism and the highly conservative values held by the Brazilian society at the time, by 1842, Floresta's school was well established and she took advantage of the good moment to write a second book addressing women's education, but now using a more traditionalist discourse. Whereas it was acceptable for a woman to teach, writing was a more problematic activity that would require some more negotiation. To enter the public sphere as a writer needed a careful strategy, which becomes very evident considering the choices she made in order to publish her work. Addressing *Conselhos à minha filha* (Advice to My Daughter) directly to her daughter, Lívia, who was also a student at her school, Floresta somewhat blurred the line between the public and the private, creating a safe space to write and participate in the dialogues about women's education. Historically, women writers on education and science often benefited from not challenging the accepted bounds of femininity (Benjamin 40). By remaining within these bounds, Floresta pioneered the initiative to educate girls in Brazil and expanded the curriculum beyond the domestic realm, which, notwithstanding its conservative premise, was in clear opposition with the belief that girls' education was not useful and relevant to the progress of the nation.

Shortly after these publications, Floresta advertised the performance of sixteen of her students who graduated in 1846 in the newspaper Jornal do Comércio, with her daughter's name appearing on the top of the list. Although she received some praise from the press, the achievements of her students also inflamed negative comments and her curriculum was harshly criticized by several newspapers in Rio de Janeiro a month later (Hammond Matthews 36):

> And why not Greek and Hebrew? Poor principal! She is so satisfied with herself and her school; she is so intimately persuaded that it is the first establishment of instruction of the empire that, in fact, one feels pitiful to destroy such sweet delusion! . . . It is natural that Dona Nisia, who never saw anything but her own school, should set it above the others. There is in her opinion more naivety than vanity. We note only to D. Floresta that she somewhat forgets the true purpose of education, which is to acquire useful knowledge and not to overcome difficulties, with no real use. (O Mercantil, 17 de janeiro de 1847 quoted in Martins Castro 251)[15]

Floresta's school and her educational project were severely mocked and ridiculed by the press. Moreover, several articles challenged Floresta's own expertise and her credentials to educate girls. The criticism she received indicates that when she attempted to make her students' achievements public, transgressing the limits of the domestic sphere, the situation escalated, despite the apparent conservative nature of her philosophy of teaching. Coincidently or not, only two years after the publication of the aforementioned article, Floresta embarked to Europe hoping to educate herself and speak from a more authoritative standpoint upon her return. Not surprisingly, she chose to establish residence in Paris.

FLORESTA'S FIRST TRAVEL TO EUROPE: EDUCATION, NETWORKS, AND THE PUBLIC SPHERE

Floresta embarked on her first voyage to Europe accompanied by her son and daughter in 1849. Although they first traveled to Portugal and England, she decided to establish their residence in Paris. It is noteworthy to consider her choice in detriment of the other European countries she visited, including Portugal, a more logical choice considering her native language, although she spoke French fluently. Barman explains that the connections between France and Brazil were uniquely remarkable and that France was the preferred choice of the majority of the Brazilians that ventured abroad in the fifty years following the independence of the country ("Brazilians" 24). The author observes that, for the Brazilian elite, France represented the model of an ideal society and culture and that many Brazilians sought to benefit from this experience. The main reason Brazilians would travel to France was to pursue education, which was considered highly prestigious and desirable. Besides, their educational system was very inclusive and had a tradition of being accommodating to the needs to foreigners ("Brazilians" 25). Upon fixing residence in Paris, in 1849, Floresta immediately started to attend classes at the Collège de France. The Collège offered a wide range of courses, which were free and open to the public, although no formal degrees were conferred. Among the courses offered in the 1849–1850 academic year were Astronomy, Physics, Comparative Embriology, Archeology, etc. (figure 3.2). It is difficult to determine precisely how many classes Floresta took, but her correspondence shows that she attended the Histoires Naturales Des Corps Organisés (Natural History of the Organized Bodies) in the same year taught by the French naturalist George-Louis Duvernoy (1777–1855), a disciple and successor of Georges Cuvier.[16] Duvernoy was the chair of the Department of Natural History of the Collège between 1837 and 1855 and Floresta developed a close friendship with him, evidenced by the letters they exchanged as well as on her first travel account. She also attended a series of philosophic lectures on the General History of Humanity in the Palais Cardinal, in Paris, where she became acquainted with the French philosopher Augusto Comte.[17] The friendship with these two men opened the doors for Floresta in the European intellectual circles and she was invited to take part in many evening conversations (*soir*ées) with other intellectuals (Souza Maia 126).

After spending two years studying in Europe, Floresta traveled back to Brazil with her children, arriving in Rio de Janeiro in February of 1852. Several Brazilian newspapers announced her return, emphasizing her educational enterprise in Europe and her role as an educator in Brazil (Souza Maia 128). In fact, Brazilians who had the opportunity to live in France, given the prestige granted by this experience, would often benefit once they returned to the country. As Barman explains, "Brazilians who went to France gained . . . what Pierre Bourdieu has termed 'cultural capital.' They acquired cultural and social attributes that allowed them, on returning to Brazil, to exert considerable influence over other groups" ("Brazilians" 25). Leveraging her stay

Figure 3.2. Courses offered at the Collège de France in 1849–1850.
Collège de France. Reproduced with Permission.

in France, Floresta resumed the direction of her school and published another work on education, now addressing a considerably larger audience: *Opúsculo Humanitário* (1853) (Humanitarian Opuscule). As mentioned, Floresta had attended Duvernoy's lectures in Natural History at the Collège de France and took part in intellectual discussions during her stay in Paris, an experience that must have opened her horizons about the debates regarding women's education.[18] Her correspondence with her mentor and friend endorses this claim. Right before publishing *Opúsculo*, in a letter addressed to Duvernoy in August of 1852, she admitted that the experience in Paris had changed the way she saw the world around her: "Since I returned to Brazil, I can't ignore the interest I have for our insects and the strong desire to study them . . ." (Letter to Duvernoy, 1852). She praised his mentorship and affirmed that his dedication to science inspired her to do the same for the education in Brazil:[19]

> I wish I could scold you, my genius friend, for so much abnegation that threatens to take you away from your friends, but still, I am dying to imitate you in the narrow sphere of my intelligence, by dedicating myself to the study of education in my country, where is still so hard to reach the level of perfection that I hope for. The people that work on an arid land are often happier when they get results than the ones that work on a fertile land. (Letter to Duvernoy, 1852)

Floresta not only revealed her admiration for Duvernoy's work, but also aligned his contributions to science to her attempt to contribute to women's education in Brazil. Whereas she stressed that her duty as a propagator of ideas about education was important, she employed the rhetoric of modesty by stating that she would stay within the boundaries of her "narrow intelligence." She also admitted that the level of perfection she envisioned was virtually unreachable in Brazil at that point and would most likely fail to succeed. Moreover, by describing her country as an arid land, she also acknowledged that any small progress would be a great achievement. A more attentive reader could also infer that she was proposing to act as a scientist of her own expertise. Whereas Duvernoy was sacrificing himself and his personal life to dedicate himself to science, he inspired her to study education with the same level of sacrifice and dedication (Souza Maia 144). She envisioned a great future for Brazil as a nation but recognized that a great civilization emerging in America was still centuries away. She added: "In the meantime, each of us must carry a little stone to the base of this edifice and even myself, in my literary incapacity, have been compelled to contribute to it with my *Humanitarian Opuscule* that I have just published and which I would love to translate into your beautiful language and offer it to you" (Letter to Duvernoy, 1852). She emphasized the fact that her book was an attempt to contribute to knowledge, while recognizing that her contribution was a small, yet important, piece of a much larger and more ambitious project. In a sense, her claim could explain the fact that this work is often considered more conservative by her critics, if compared with *Direitos*. I contend, however, that, well aware of her gender constraints, Floresta chose to adhere to a more conservative approach, advocating for education within the domestic sphere, and hoping that it would be the foundation of an educational project that would allow women to enter the public sphere in a fairly distant future. Although more conservative in terms of ideas, *Opúsculo* was very well argued, when compared to her previous publications.

Opúsculo also served as an opportunity for Floresta to respond to the critics who had challenged her expertise. The work was organized in sixty-two essays dedicated to several aspects of education, employing numerous authoritative discourses that evidenced Floresta's extensive knowledge of history, literature, statistics, and science. The seventeen first essays trace the evolution of women's conditions from the earliest times in Egypt, Persia, India, Babylon, Greece, and Rome, and to the nineteenth century in Germany, France, England, and the United States. She portrayed European women as useful members of society, as magnificent educators of young people, both at home and in schools, as well as intelligent companions of their husbands (Sharpe-Valadares xxxii). In contrast, Brazilian women were victims of the oppression of a cloistered existence, of illiteracy, serving only for procreation and could not be compared, either in strength of character or morality, with their American and European counterparts. Moreover, in *Opúsculo*, the lessons she took in Paris would start to resonate on her writings. The work was far more elaborated than both *Direitos* and *Conselhos* in terms of language and content, but also due to its engagement with the scientific debates of her time. Floresta argued against biologically determinist arguments appealing to science itself, similarly to what many feminists still do nowadays (Birke 246):

> Physical weakness is one of the excuses that certain sophists use to justify depriving a woman from education, which they consider improper for her. It is not his physical characteristics, according to Helvetius claims, that makes man superior, but his intelligence. Voltaire, Racine, Pascal, and many others, all of which had an overly delicate complexion, prove this fact. And intelligence, which has no sex, may be equally superior in woman, except for the opinion of some materialists whose weak spirits relate, forgive our expression, with the scalpel that reveals the organization of the animals, rather than inspiring them by the sublime thoughts of Duvernoy, Schoenlein, Orfila, and the eloquent Serres. (*Opúsculo*, 62–63)[20]

As Lynda Birke explains, the belief on the fixity of gender was well established among the scientific community by the nineteenth century (247). She adds: "The biological arguments took roughly two forms; women were either alleged to be weak or inferior because of the peculiar features of her anatomy and physiology, or their physiology was itself inherently so weak that it was easily disrupted. At a time when women were struggling to enter higher education, a major source of such disruption was held to be education itself"

(247). On the above passage Floresta intertwined an argument against this biological determinism, which prevented women from receiving education. Her belief was that women were not biologically inferior to men, and citing the names of several male philosophers, such as Helvetius and Voltaire, she supported her claim that the real cause of women's inferiority was their lack of education.[21] She also made a sharp critique of eighteenth-century naturalists, particularly comparative anatomists, who proposed a scheme of animal organization solely based on inherent physical distinctions, mainly related to gender and sex. By referring to their use of a sharp scalpel, she criticized their practices and, by extension, their conclusions solely based on an idealized male body, which delegated females to an intrinsic inferiority, regardless of their race (Schiebinger, *Nature* 160). Precisely, according to Schiebinger, these studies in anatomy further validated racial and gender inequalities, which generated the new body politics in Europe in the nineteenth century. This has ultimately prevented women from receiving education and confined them to the domestic sphere (*Nature* 172). By evoking the name of her mentor Duvernoy, among others, she implicitly referred to the debate between functional and philosophical anatomy lead by Cuvier and Geoffroy in 1830, mainly instigating the need of discussing scientific methods and practices, which determined women's inferiority. Moreover, the passage above evidences that Floresta was aware that the scientific discourse was legitimizing the exclusion of women from the educational system and from the public sphere.

Similar to *Conselhos*, her main goal now was to advocate for the primary right of education for girls, and her intent was aligned with the metaphor she used on her letter to Duvernoy: a small brick on the base of the building. The problem Floresta was trying to solve was far more complicated than it appears to the modern reader. As the passage above indicates, Floresta was primarily challenging the scientific debates of her time, which endorsed the biological determinism that prevented women to receive education. The patriarchal society in fact took advantage of this determinism to inscribe women in the domestic sphere, however, "gender as a product of social learning was much less evident than it is today" (Birke 246). To propose a change in the education system would take a lot more than words and Floresta realized that she would not be able to take advantage of these changes herself. It was a project for the future generations:

> The hope that the future generations of Brazil will assume their responsibility can only console us about their present condition. In the meantime, let's continue to follow the example of the poor and courageous explorer of our virgin forests, exposed here and there to the bite of poisonous reptiles, to survey a field that others will have to seed and harvest its tasty fruits. We would be fortunate

if we could collect the result of this work to offer to our compatriots as a token of the true interest that has inspired us. (*Opúsculo* 45–46)²²

It is notable in the passage that Floresta was employing a natural history metaphor to describe her project as she was putting herself in the position of an explorer who was consciously performing a self-sacrifice in the name of a greater goal. She paired herself with a traveler exploring the unknown, not only surveying virgin forests but also exposed to the danger of being bit by poisonous reptiles. In other words, as the explorers and scientists, who often had their findings and conclusions challenged and dismissed, she elevated her educational project to the status of science: an attempt to propose new knowledge capable of creating new practices. It is inevitable to refer back to the aforementioned newspaper article, in which she was severely attacked for the curriculum of her school (O Mercantil, 17 de janeiro de 1847).

Floresta had arrived back in Rio de Janeiro in 1852 with the goal of promoting an educational reform in Brazil, leveraging the knowledge and prestige she acquired in her stay in France. Although her project was not revolutionary, given the fact that she operated within the patriarchal constraints, as she had predicted in her letter to Duvernoy, it still failed to provoke significant changes or discussions in the Brazilian society. On March 24, 1855, she wrote another letter to him, which corroborates the fact that she was not feeling accomplished: "In my native country, the cultural life is at its infancy and not enough—not yet—in order to give the joy that I have been craving since my tender youth. So far, the financial improvement and the infrastructures are my country's main concerns. Some of my important projects have been completed. I am still waiting for intellectual and artistic development. . . . So far, I was able to publish a couple of articles on the topic of education . . . I am sending you a copy with this letter" (Letter to Duvernoy, 1855). Comparing the passage above with the letter she wrote to him in 1852 when she had just returned from Europe, it is evident that she seemed discouraged about her ability to impact the intellectual development of her own country. While she was aware that, in 1852, her *Opúsculo* was a project for the future, she was still hopeful that her ideas would impact her society. If leveraging her experience as a traveler to France granted prestige to the white upper-class male upon their return to Brazil, it was not enough for Floresta to overcome the gender biases and the traditional ideas regarding women's education she faced in her country. Besides, she admitted that she craved to satisfy her intellectual needs in Brazil, a need she could only fully fulfill in France: "I would so much like to be in Paris now, with you, learning about your admiration for life's creations. That would be the best remedy against the worries of the world! Since I left Paris and your company, my life runs empty. This emptiness and boredom makes me realize how lucky I was to have met you. It is only after Paris that I started appreciating the existence that your knowledge opened to me" (Letter to Duvernoy, 1855). Her discouragement and the fact that her mother passed away in 1855 seemed to have motivated Floresta to abandon the direction of her school in Rio de Janeiro in the same year. Floresta's previous stay in Paris had changed her profoundly and she no longer found a place for herself in Brazil. Not surprisingly, she once again returned to Paris in 1856, taking her daughter Lívia, who was then twenty-three years old, with her. There, she rejoined the Parisian intellectual circles and started her career as a travel writer. She then implemented an individualized educational plan for her daughter in Europe, which would transform her life and provide her a unique education for a woman of her time. This education would be based on the experience of traveling and learning, a project that Floresta would have found impossible to undertake had she stayed in Brazil.

NÍSIA FLORESTA'S TRAVEL ACCOUNTS OF HER VOYAGES TO EUROPE: AUTHORITY, ALTERNATE VISIBILITY, AND TRANSATLANTIC SUBJECTIVITY

By the time Floresta left Brazil for the second time in 1856, she had already published a few works on education, despite her reputation as a writer being heavily biased by her gender. When she decided to move to Europe, it was not her intention to abandon her educational project or her career as a writer, but she had to carve the authority needed to be able to resume her endeavors abroad. Although at that point of her career the majority of her publications in Brazil were concerned with women's education, to address this subject to the European audience, she first needed to build a reputation as a writer. In the second half of the nineteenth century, travel narratives were very popular and it is not surprising that Floresta resorted to this literary genre to publish her first work in Europe. Floresta was a well-traveled woman and had an extensive knowledge about travel writing, as she indicated in *Opúsculo*, where she cited numerous travel accounts about Brazil. Even though the genre was relatively open for women, as discussed in the introduction of this book, the act of traveling itself always required negotiation in terms of race, class, and gender (Foster and Mills 9). Although these variables might be shared with male travelers, for women, it was always more problematic because their departure from the domestic sphere necessarily required some level of defense (Foster and Mills 9). It was common for women to have to rationalize their travel plans "simply because their departure from the interiority of the domestic sphere involved greater justification and management, both ideologically and practically" (Foster and Mills 9). Publishing a travel account for the first time, Floresta had to simultaneously negotiate her authority as well as her gender constraints. Seeking to create a space for her as a traveler and a writer, although preserving her intent of propagating her ideas on women education, she constructed her narratives as quests for intellectual knowledge, leveraging on her nationality, and preserving her femininity. However, ". . . women travelers had a lot at stake; they needed to establish some narrative credibility while, at the same time, countering attacks against their femininity prompted by their so called unnatural an inappropriate behavior" (Siegel 3). As Monica Szurmuk and Claudia Torre write, "the space from which they wrote was heterogeneous and often contradictory. The tensions between public and private inform the writing of these women" (115). It is evident from her career that Floresta wanted to become a more knowledgeable woman, participate in intellectual debates, and provide her daughter with the opportunity to educate and transform herself, but she mediated this desire by negotiating her position as a traveler, a woman, and as a writer.

Noticeably, Floresta wrote her travel accounts as a Brazilian woman author and foreign traveler addressing the European audience. As Méndez Rodenas puts it, "by shifting from the Americas to Europe, nineteenth-century Latin American women upset the presumption that 'travelers' are, by definition, European and not Latin American, assimilating a dominant paradigm of male-authored travel, while forging their own writerly vocations" (10).[23] Upper-class Brazilians often traveled to Europe and sent their children there to pursue an education, but they rarely wrote about their travel experiences: "One might suggest that as colonial subjects they lacked the authority or a legitimate position of speech from which to represent Europe" (Pratt, *Imperial* 189).[24] If colonial subjects lacked the authority to write about Europe to their compatriots, Floresta's first strategy was to take advantage of her own exotic identity to forge this authority to write and to attract the interest of European publishers and readership. Writing in French, she also asserted her erudition and intellectual capability to communicate in a non-native language. Seeking to carve a space for her travel writing, Floresta signed her first travel account with the pseudonym Mme. Floresta A. Brasileira. This choice, besides emphasizing her nationality, also highlighted her gender and marital status, indicating that she was either married or widowed. Travel writing was a highly competitive market and both the author and the publisher had to find ways to make the work distinguishable and desirable. As Thompson puts it, ". . . women travel writers were undoubtedly often received and treated differently by editors, publishers, reviewers and readers. Frequently pigeonholed under the patronizing label of 'lady traveler,' women faced satire or outright censure if they appeared to overstep the norms of contemporary femininity" ("Journeys" 132). Some authors, such as Isabella Bird, in fact used their gender as a unique characteristic when advertising their work (Bird 41). In the same vein, Floresta took advantage of both her gender and nationality. Women travelers from the nineteenth century often were able to leverage their presence in a foreign country to take a position of authority, taking advantage of a unique perspective as eyewitness. However, these women often used this strategy to gain authority when addressing their writing back home, since the necessity to report what they were seeing could be justified as urgent and therefore overcome their gender limitations (Bird 39). In Floresta's particular case, her condition as eyewitness was undermined by the fact that everything she was seeing and describing was not new to her audience, as several accounts of travels to European countries were available on the market. Instead, she proposed to explore her unique perspective as a Brazilian woman as the urgency she needed to legitimize her writings. However, she still needed to negotiate with her gender expectations, and instead of directly addressing the European audience, she wrote an epistolary travel account to narrate her travels.

Floresta's first travel account, *Itinéraire d'un voyage en Allemagne* (Itinerary of a Voyage to Germany), printed in France in 1857, was written in form of letters to her family in Brazil, the epistolary being an acceptable vehicle for women to reveal their interior selves and to write about their travels (Mills, *Discourses* 71).[25] The preference of women travelers for diaries and letters is, at least in part, strategic since "the epistolary genre is strongly linked to the feminine, the domestic and the affective. The choice of this form sends a strong signal to the reading public: though the travel writer may wander into the public sphere, her moral compass is firmly pointed towards home" (Bird 41). She wrote thirty-four daily letters, from August 26 to September 30 of 1856, addressing her family in Brazil. Nevertheless, the fact that she wrote these letters in French makes it obviously questionable that her intention was to reach only her family and not to publish her accounts. Although French was a language widely spoken by the Brazilian upper class, it was doubtful that it would be her preferable language choice to write personal letters to her family. Her itinerary was carefully prepared and her intentions as well: "I preferred to enter in Germany through Belgium and leave through Kehl, to go from Strasbourg to Montbéliard . . ." (38).[26] Her itinerary included twenty-three cities between Belgium and Germany, and back to France. Although the letters do inscribe a more intimate tone to her prose, by staying within more acceptable forms of writing for women, Floresta had more freedom to explore the possibilities of travel writing and discuss more scientific subjects. Although claiming that her letters and observations were not professional and that she had the sole intention of sharing her travel experiences with her family, her narrative reveals method and consistency, both characteristics of more professional travel writing: "I have no time to write the history of Brussels . . . or of the cities to which I am going to travel; I will indicate only what most interests me, and at night I will communicate my impressions of the day" (*Itinerário* 43).[27] Floresta indicated a clear method to organize her memoirs and wrote a letter about each city she visited, always at night after a long day of explorations. However, instead of her mere impressions, and her promise of not mentioning historical facts, her lavish narrative sounded more like a history lesson embedded in the natural history discourse of travel writing.

As Míseres observes, scholarship on Latin American women travelers often focus on the autobiographical nature of their writings. Scatena Franco and Szurmuk have also emphasized these women's intention to dispute and counter Latin American nationalist discourses. Míseres proposes that to analyze the direct dialogue of these writings with the male cannon of travel writing represents an innovative and more fruitful discussion (116). Drawing from this premise, Floresta's diary offers a possibility to analyze how she dialogued with her male counterparts and created a unique way to write about her travels. In her analysis of *Viaje de Recreo* (1909) by Clorinda Matto de Turner, Míseres contends that the traveler synthetized and transformed the image of the Latin American intellectual traveler in Europe by placing her own work in a direct dialogue with the male canon (122). But while Matto de Turner wrote in Spanish targeting a Latin American audience, Floresta addressed both the European and Latin American readerships, therefore reassessing the role of Latin American intellectuals on both sides of the Atlantic. Such an ambitious project, then, required an ability to present her perspective as valid to both audiences. In order to do that, she needed to reassert both her presence and mobility within her narrative. She resorted to the tropes of natural history discourse to establish a direct dialogue with her male counterparts, an effective tool to ensure the credibility of the narrator of a travel account.

Foster and Mills observe that even though a woman travel writer might not be explicitly adopting a scientific posture, she might still be "attempting to situate herself within a scholarly discursive tradition which foregrounds knowledge rather than personal response" (89). Thus, nineteenth-century women travelers who engaged in travel writing with the purpose of acquiring and disseminating knowledge often employed the rhetoric of natural history to describe the places they visited. Interested in natural history debates, Floresta was aware of the conventions imposed by the writings of other male travelers and often employed the discourse of aesthetics, mainly seeking to achieve "a common ground of evaluation drawing on previously authorized high status discourses" (Foster and Mills 91). Humboldt, for example, as Poole argues, proposed a typological discourse of visual experience which attributed to each place its own "physiognomy," allowing the observer to create an "overall impression" of particular regions (70). For Humboldt, the reliability of this overall impression depended on the choice of observing the right elements. For example, he considered rock formations to be not appropriate because "rocks evoked powerful memories that Humboldt feared could obstruct the scientific task of deciphering the physiognomy or visual character of a place" (Poole 71). Plants, in Humboldt's opinion, were the perfect stable element to achieve this goal. But a reliable impression was only possible to be achieved if the observer could combine both the senses and the intellect, in which the latter controls the former tendency to sentimentalism and imagination (Poole 71). Similar to Gómez de Avellaneda, Floresta rejected Humboldt's method and aligned nature, civilization, and history in her travel narrative. On her excursion to the mountains surrounding the Reno river, she wrote:

> The mountains' tops crowned with ruins of castles, belvederes, houses, chapels; the rocks' tips, lost in space, bearing the memory of a grand past; the towns, the burgs, the villages, this variety of natural and artistic objects, continued without interruption from one side to the other. My ardent imagination lent more charm to the aspect of these portentous landscapes, they speak more eloquently to the meditative spirit than all the great pages that have been written about them. (*Itinerário* 95)[28]

Her rendition of the European landscape then, rather than an attempt to establish the physiognomic overall impression proposed by Humboldt, was a clear manifestation of her own opinions and feelings. The aesthetic vocabulary of the sublime provided women travelers the opportunity to combine this high-status discourse with a more feminized emotional response to the landscape. However, while the sublime landscape was, for most travelers, a pristine one, with no signs of civilization, Floresta subverted this rhetoric. Instead, she employed the discourse of aesthetics, mainly seeking "to put her work in conversation with these high status discourses" (Smith 9). In this panoramic portrayal of the landscape, she resorted to the rhetoric of the Monarch-of-All-I-Survey, as Pratt explains, "the relation of mastery predicated between the seer and the seen" (*Imperial* 204). Rather than possessing, her seeing eye imagined a possibility of being part of a backdrop in which nature, history, and civilization coexisted to form a spectacle to her eyes. Employing a painting analogy, her aesthetic representation was a transcendental experience, in which all her knowledge started to come alive before her eyes. The alignment of traveling with knowledge acquisition through experience was embedded in the narrative, as Floresta reminded the reader that the books were never capable of teaching her at the same level as the possibility of imagining, seeing, and feeling could.

As opposed to the male travelers who employed this rhetoric, instead of merely possessing the landscape, her travel narrative reflected her belief that the experience of traveling could offer a unique learning opportunity to the traveler: "It is very beautiful to contemplate from a single altitude, one by one, three different nations . . . I make sure to register this image in my memory, like a magnificent dream . . . there where the most beautiful and picturesque landscapes unfolded before my eyes as in a living geographic map, under an immense horizon embellished by the last rays of the sunset" (189).[29] Her depiction of the landscape as alive, once again, disrupted the static rhetoric of the Monarch-of-All-I-Survey, as well as the idea of possession and dominance. Instead, a geographical map came alive before her eyes, and the fantasy of possessing three nations at once became knowledge stored in her memory. By disrupting this rhetoric of imperial superiority, as a colonial subject, the fantasy of domination became a form of empowerment materialized in the possibility of knowledge acquisition. However, the intellectual quest was not a narrative trope easily available to a woman, and her newly forged authority still needed to avoid more controversial forms of knowing, relying on "attitudes to the acquirement, display, and transference of knowledge that were consistent with the ideal of womanliness" (Benjamin 44). To fully validate her authority as a writer, she resorted to the narrative of pilgrimage to describe her visit to the tomb of her mentor, Duvernoy, who could metaphorically grant her permission to undertake her quest.

ITINÉRAIRE D'UN VOYAGE EN ALLEMAGNE: A PILGRIMAGE TO LEGITIMATE HER INTELLECTUAL QUEST

As other women travel writers, Floresta always felt the need to defend her travel plans in terms of health needs. She decided to travel in August, claiming she felt ill and depressed because of the loss of both her mother and husband in that month. She needed to go somewhere else, since Paris was "monotonous and almost unbearable" (*Itinerário* 37): "It was necessary for me to go through new countries, and there draw new impressions. To be under a broader horizon and a freer atmosphere, consequently more in line with my preferences . . . you can naturally see that I chose the old and poetic Germany, the honored homeland of Leibnitz and Kant" (*Itinerário* 38).[30] She implied that traveling reflected the possibility of learning, a need for freedom, which would allow her to transcend her gender constraints. She mentioned Leibnitz and Kant, two of the most important German philosophers whose work advocated for the necessity of empirical learning and external experience

(Nachtomy 954). Simply justifying her travel plan in terms of heath needs would not be sufficiently convincing to her readership and paying homage to the tomb of her male mentor seemed to be a better excuse. Then, she opened her account "proposing to make a pilgrimage to the tomb of my venerable friend, the wise and good Duvernoy" (*Itinerário* 38).[31] Pilgrimage narratives became popular in the middle ages, and usually had a religious connotation, reporting a journey to a holy place or some sort of spiritual quest, which lead to a ritual of purification and cleansing at the holy site (Smith 11).[32] These pilgrimage narratives were often justified by the spiritual need of the pilgrim to evolve, a rite of passage and redemption. For women, the urgent nature of the pilgrimage also served to justify their wanders (Denegri 349). In other words, Pilgrimage narratives written by female authors are often presented as spiritually necessary and serve as a strategy to negotiate and justify the movement of the female body and offset its transgression (Nenzi 223). As Francesca Denegri points out, "travel narrative was a difficult genre for women writers in the nineteenth century, given, first of all, the absence of a female tradition of travel-writing, and secondly, the fact that travel-writing represented the imperial thrust of the century of progress and science, from which women were largely excluded" (352). Floresta appropriated the trope of the pilgrimage, establishing the visit to her mentor's tomb as the holy place she would visit at the end of her journey. By forging a sacred value to her enterprise, she attempted to validate her intellectual quest and create a space to authorize the subversion of her limited learning opportunities. Floresta also used this narrative of pilgrimage to justify yet another transgression: her own engagement with travel writing and her intellectual quest, and, in that sense, her pilgrimage becomes a feminized way to approach travel writing.

In this narrative space, in which traveling was the best way to educate oneself, she corroborated and enabled her own beliefs on women's education. However, "the archetypal nineteenth-century traveler was represented as an active, commanding, privileged man in search of wealth and knowledge. In contrast, classic iconography depicts a pilgrim as a selfless, humble traveler who undertakes a materially unproductive journey, who disavows any claims to earthly power, and who accepts his or her position" (Denegri 353). Floresta, however, subverted this classic depiction of the pilgrimage; her quest was intellectual. As Floresta observed an Italian teacher on a field trip with her pupils in Germany, she recollected her own teaching experience back in Brazil. The moment became an opportunity for her to reaffirm and further validate her need for an intellectual quest. By comparing herself with the Italian teacher, she reflected on the reasons that prevented her educational project from being carried out in Brazil. As the Italian teacher and her pupils admired the same flowers she was admiring with her daughter on a garden, Floresta observed:

> It reminded me of a teacher whose heart and spirit harmonized to instruct the youth; she limited herself to ministering her lectures among the walls of an organization in a country where the full relevance of a general education, which forms both the moral and the physical, is not yet understood. In contrast, the woman who was there before me, traveling, instructing her students, whose parents know how to appreciate the advantages of this method, which would make the old-fashioned spirits laugh. . . . Thus two foreign teachers met on German soil: one disappointed by her hopes of twenty years of devotion and work; the other intoxicated by the promising perspective offered by this beginning of a life that is just starting. (*Itinerário* 162)[33]

The autobiographical digression triggered by this encounter brought back the memories of her past as a teacher and of an education project which was ostracized in her own country. Her remark confirmed her prediction when she had written to Duvernoy a few years later: her country was not ready to receive her educational project. The Italian teacher, on the other hand, found in traveling the means to teach her pupils and had the support of the parents and of her country. By celebrating the importance of travel experience as an educational strategy, despite her disappointment after twenty years of devotion to her career, this encounter foreshadowed the agenda of her career as a travel writer, and her intent to use travel narratives as a space to discuss women's education. It also further validated her own educational mission and her necessity of traveling. Right after this encounter with the Italian teacher, Floresta proceeded to receive the blessing from her mentor, undermining the very premise of the unproductive journey of the pilgrim.

If one could say that Floresta's *Itinerário* has a plot, then her pilgrimage to Duvernoy's tomb would be the resolution as there was no better way to end her narrative than paying a last homage to the men who inspired her to pursue her intellectual endeavor: "It is time to pay the debt of the blessed friendship at the grave of the venerable wise man who honored me with a particular regard and whose death caused me an immense inner emptiness when I was in France" (186).[34] The pilgrimage to Duvernoy's tomb served to place herself firmly as his former student and close friend, which granted her a certain degree of authority: to place herself under a calculated shield of protection from a male mentor, and, ultimately, to justify her own need to travel to implement her educational project. Moreover, it served to corroborate her claims that female intellectual pursuits were legitimate and that her quest for knowledge acquisition had the approval of her mentor. In that sense, her peregrination was crafted in the narrative as a rite of passage, and as something that she had to do alone. Leaving her daughter behind, she started a journey of 200 miles to enact the culminating moment of triumph of her travel narrative.

After narrating a journey of physical trial, she finally arrived at Duvernoy's tomb, where she almost fainted of emotion. Despite her physical and emotional fatigue, after a dramatic description of her feelings before her ceased mentor, she still walked for one hour to visit Duvernoy's daughter's house. After an enduring and difficult walk through an arduous terrain, she arrived at the house, where she was welcomed and invited to spend the night. There, the rite of passage was finally completed when she was offered Duvernoy's own bedroom to spend the night. Absorbed by a moment of spiritual conjunction with her mentor, she wrote the last passage of her diary from his own desk: "I am writing from this precious office, surrounded by all these moving memoirs" (201).[35] The memories triggered by the objects that belonged to him, provoked a reflection:

> Tomorrow, when the sun reaches the Vosges Peak, I will no longer have before my eyes this precious office, where you spent so much time venerable Duvernoy, where you worked so hard for your love for science. . . . This furniture . . . these trees, these hills . . . all of that will disappear before my eyes. But I will carry the memory deeply registered in my heart. My head is weakened, and my exhausted body will rest in the bed that used to be yours . . . (*Itinerário* 203)[36]

The transcendental experience of her pilgrimage could not end more poetically. Using a similar rhetoric she employed when describing the landscapes, she contemplated throughout her journey, Floresta replaced the narrative of possession and domination by the possibility of knowledge acquisition. As she took control of her memories, she took control of her learning and her own future. Her fantasy was not a fantasy of possession and mastering, it was a fantasy of transcending her role as a woman and contributing to the construction of knowledge. After sleeping in Duvernoy's own bed, she was now ready to undertake her second journey, this time to Italy and Greece.

Trois ans en Italie, suivis d'un voyage en Grèce: The Discourse of Natural History Aligned with the Progress of the Cities

Floresta's second travel account, *Trois ans en Italie, suivis d'un voyage en Grèce* (Three Years in Italy Followed by a Voyage to Greece), was published in two volumes in 1864 and 1872.[37] Instead of an epistolary account, she resorted to a diary to narrate her voyage, which was considerably longer than the first one, covering three years and encompassing a significantly larger territory. As women's travel narratives often had to indicate their proximity to home, she opened the diary with a letter to her son in Brazil, pointing to an intention to address the account to her own country: "May the talisman of this holy love, passed on from the old to the new world, lead you always through the noble path of duty, bringing to your heart the last *elan* and the last hopes of your tender mother" (*Itália* 5).[38] By dedicating the diary to her son, she reinstated her role as a mother and used her gendered maternal role as a shield to protect herself from her own transgression. Maternal duty also justified the need for her trip, as she hoped her son would benefit from her experience. Instead of competing with more masculine forms of knowledge, she feminized her intention by aligning this knowledge with maternal love. Moreover, she reaffirmed her condition as a transatlantic subject intending to circulate knowledge between two worlds. The diary was organized chronologically, but instead of systematically dated entries, the chapters are titled, for the most part, after the name of the cities she was visiting. Resembling a travel guide, Floresta displayed more confidence and authority to write her impressions and dialogued with the works of other travelers who had made equivalent journeys before her own. She also made historical observations and displayed her opinions about the society as well as the political situation of Italy.

In this narrative, Floresta leveraged her unique perspective as a transatlantic subject to create a new model to narrate her experience: the transatlantic eyewitness. To establish herself as an authentic transatlantic eyewitness, she engaged in the scientific rhetoric of natural history when describing the landscapes, and established a marked comparison between Brazil and the countries she visited. By doing that, she validated the perspective of someone who, belonging to the other side of the Atlantic, could offer a more authentic account of both places, replacing the unfamiliar gaze of the European male traveler about Latin America at the same time she projected her own unfamiliar gaze on the familiar European scenarios for her audience. By contrasting and comparing Brazilian and European nature and civilization, she established firmly both her presence and mobility within the narrative and proposed a debate that disrupted the sharp dichotomy permeating many travel narratives about Latin America, which oftentimes focused solely on the grandiosity and barbaric character of its nature. By making such comparisons, she inserted her presence firmly on both sides of the Atlantic, and defied the immobility imposed on her because of her gender. In that sense, Floresta's travel writing seems to present an alternate possibility and an intent to inscribe women's perspectives as another source of knowledge for the new emerging Latin American nations.

As a matter of fact, the majority of travelers in the nineteenth century often associated America with nature on their accounts. Regina Horta Duarte, in her analysis of the accounts of four male travelers about Brazil in the first half of the nineteenth century, observes that these narratives focused mainly on its exotic and impenetrable forests, its indigenous habitants, presented as savage and uncivilized, as well as the commercial possibilities in the region. Horta Duarte contends that all the travelers she analyzed, Robert Avé-Lallemant (1812–1884), Alexander Maximilian (1762–1867), Auguste de Saint-Hilaire (1779–1853), and Johann Tschudi (1818–1889), visited many Brazilian cities from 1818 to 1859, but preferred to portray them as backwards and disorganized (267–88). As stated in the introduction of this book, the Latin America represented in these kinds of narratives was mistreated and ready to receive European intervention. The overt emphasis on the lack of civilization endorsed the discourse of civilization versus barbarism that ultimately validated the nation building projects in the continent. In fact, as Cañizares-Esguerra argues, these travel narratives became "utopian patriotic accounts of the landscape and nature" (13). Nevertheless, instead of simply strengthening the empire, they became the means to legitimize these new projects of nation. Such projects, as previously mentioned, asserted the male, white, and Creole elite as the sole agent capable of bringing civilization to the continent. These racialized conceptions of nation were, to a great extent, shaped by notions of gender and sexuality: ". . . elites often linked political authority to masculine authority and racial eugenics to the control of sexuality and reproduction" (Appelbaum, Macpherson, and Rosemblatt 15). The metaphors of nation that emerged from these narratives relied on the notion of family as the only institution capable of securing racial purity: ". . . the metaphor of nation as a product of a unifying heterosexual embrace projected the patriarchal power of the family onto the nation" (Appelbaum, Macpherson, and Rosemblatt 15). This project however, was only possible by asserting masculine control over "their" women. Then, women's role in the new Latin American nations was confined to the private sphere, as mothers of the sons who would become the new leaders of these nations. To some extent, Floresta's travel writing seemed to validate these new projects of nation. However, her narrative displays some ambiguities and inconsistencies. As mentioned above, by comparing Brazilian and European nature, she established her presence on both sides of the Atlantic. Nevertheless, whereas she endorsed the very rhetoric used by the Brazilian and Creole elites to exclude women as active participants on their project of nations, she still used her travel narrative to advocate for their education.

Her travel writing then, served as a space in which she could participate in such debates, and while reinforcing some of the tropes and stereotypes perpetuated by her male counterparts, she could also find a space to present her own idea of nation. Floresta compared European and Brazilian nature and established a clear opposition between the two. By resorting to her childhood memories, she placed herself firmly as an authority to state that Brazilian nature was in fact superior, more impressive and vigorous than its European counterpart. Returning to the quote which opened this chapter: ". . . that magnificent bay, to those majestic mountains beautifully covered by eternal vegetation, those two cities, Rio de Janeiro and Niterói, disappearing, little by little, behind those gigantic daughters of the earth that surrounds them . . . in the most beautiful bay of the world, which separates them" (*Itália* 227).[39] Floresta employed grandiose expressions such as "magnificent bay" and "majestic mountains beautifully dressed of eternal vegetation," which were key elements of Humboldtian tropes for representing American nature, emphasizing the striking beauties of Brazilian nature and geography. The image she was depicting was a projection of her memory, a mere recollection of a landscape she was no longer contemplating. But evoking these memories, on Floresta's narrative, rather than possessing the landscape, represented her willingness to share her knowledge with her audience. The use of lavish phrases and splendid descriptions of sublime landscapes allowed her to put herself on par with other travelers, such as Humboldt, reaffirming her own merit and, consequently, reinforcing her narrative presence. When remembering another Brazilian landscape, she mentioned: ". . . according to the celebrated Humboldt, tall palm trees swaying their superb plumes, dominate the surrounding trees, and form, in long colonnades, a forest above the forest" (*Itália* 24).[40] Interesting, nevertheless, is the fact that she was referring to Humboldt's description of the palm trees he saw in Mexico and Venezuela, since he had never visited Brazil: "Of all vegetable forms," says Humboldt, "the palm is that to which the prize of beauty has been assigned by the concurrent voice of nations in all ages" (*Aspects of Nature* 20). Floresta appropriated Humboldt's description of the palm tree to align the Brazilian landscape with the rest of America, which further validated her authority as someone who shared Humboldt's experiences and opinions. Moreover, this rhetoric would certainly meet the expectations of her readership, accustomed to read similar accounts about the continent. Akin to Humboldt, Floresta described Brazilian nature as magnificent and sublime and exalted the physical dimension of the country, she also emphasized its potential in terms of progress (Scatena Franco 227): "And those mountain ranges, those virgin forests, those rich meadows, those prodigious waterfalls, those rivers, those birds, all those natural masterpieces of the land where I was born returned lively to my spirit . . . under a foreign sky, no matter how seductive it may be, can it ever be compared to yours [Brazil]? (*Itália* 163).[41] By employing the expression "natural masterpieces" she elevated Brazilian nature to the status of art and tried to grant Brazil a natural superiority in relation to Europe, at the same time she was repeating the rhetoric about the grandiosity of Latin American nature employed by earlier travelers.

The marked dialogue with previous travelers emphasized her knowledge about the literature and her intent to dialogue with their accounts, revealing her need to elaborate on the knowledge circulating about the places she was visiting. For example, when she described her journey to the Vesuvius Volcano, she noted that she had Chateaubriand's impressions in mind (Scatena Franco 135). However, she highlighted the fact that the landscape had changed because of previous volcanic eruptions: "Chateaubriand was right to exclaim, observing, from here, the magnificence of Naples and its surroundings: 'It is paradise seen from hell.' The shape of the crater was different from what it is today, for with each eruption it changes. . . . Thus, of all the descriptions of the various forms of the Vesuvius crater I saw, none had given me the idea of the present (*Itália* 218).[42] By pointing out changes that had taken place in the landscape, as Maria Graham had also done, more than simply showing that she was a knowledgeable traveler who was familiar with the most important works, Floresta was validating her position as a transatlantic eyewitness. However, although she made it clear that Chateaubriand's descriptions were outdated, unlike Graham, she did not try to update the descriptions of her precursor. Instead, she implied that describing the crater was an impossible undertaking.[43] In fact, although Floresta echoed natural history tropes when she tried to portray the European landscape, she sometimes found this rhetoric insufficient when reflecting on the experience of traveling. When she climbed Mount Vesuvius, she employed a rhetoric similar to that used by Gómez de Avellaneda when climbing the Pyrenees to convey the idea that the sublime experience was impossible to be described using any kind of language (Scatena Franco 230)[44]:

> The curious crowd, the numerous torches stirred by the night breeze, the torrents of lava hurling themselves down the mountain, a part of which, chilling in some places, slid making slight clicking sounds, overlapping into layers and forming incandescent hills: the flames coming out of the new craters and dyeing with a reddish color all that incandescent portrayal, to the point that the sky which serves as a vault seems to be on fire as well . . . the clicking of the lava; the roar of the repeated detonations of the volcano that now has several craters . . . all that horrible, comic confusion presented a beautiful and terrifying picture, which would be truly impossible for a painter to reproduce. The genius of man is insufficient to properly account for such scenes of nature. Only those who saw them are capable of understanding, admiring, and assimilating them in their spirit. The most skillful artist, however, can never represent them on canvas. (*Itália* 266)[45]

Floresta's description of her experience at the volcano emphasized the power of nature and the paradoxical feelings it raised in the traveler (i.e., beautiful and terrifying). However, the use of expressions to convey the movement of the scene as opposed to the static nature of aesthetic representations underscored her argument that some experiences were impossible to be reproduced by a painter or a traveler. Once again, she subverted the rhetoric of the Monarch-of-All-Survey by suggesting that the relationship between the seer and the seeing was not static and monolithic, but an exchange of experiences and knowledge. She reinstated the unique opportunity provided by experience, which afforded a memory impossible to be translated by any artist. Then, this possibility of knowledge acquisition and exchange created a space of intellectual debate in her narrative, refuting previous travelers' attempts to represent their experiences.

Notwithstanding the fact that European nature was not comparable to its Brazilian counterpart, Floresta's admiration for European civilization is very evident in her travel account. In fact, although Floresta many times repeated the rhetoric of the sublime used by other European travelers such as Humboldt to portray nature, at the same time she admired the progress of the European cities. Nature and progress always had a dialectical relationship fueled by the idea that human mastery over nature was a necessary condition for civilization. The environment should be controlled and the means to achieve such control was through science and technology (Leiss 101). Floresta deconstructed this dichotomy by aligning nature and progress and showing that they were equally important and not necessarily opposites. In her descriptions of Europe, she showed nature, people, and cities in a symbiotic relation in which these elements were equally important (Scatena Franco 244). For example, on her way to Tivoli, Italy, she stated: ". . . this vegetation that covers these immense remains of so many works of art and luxury" (*Itália* 161).[46] She frequently echoed the dichotomy "here and there" used by Gonçalves Dias when comparing European and Brazilian nature in his poem "Canção do exílio" mentioned above. Unlike Dias, however, she was not using this contrast to show how Brazil was better than Europe. Instead, she was doing almost the opposite. She showed that Brazil was the raw material with an exuberant nature, whereas Europe, despite its relatively inferior nature, was able to explore its full potential by means of human intervention, and the final product ended up being superior. As she saw Brazilian nature as superior to that of Europe, she predicted that a similar project of progress would make Brazil a magnificent nation in the future. In order to validate her claim, she used her travel writing as a space to praise European progress while highlighting that it still failed as a civilized model of modernity for Latin America. Although her appreciation of progress aligned her with many male writers of her time, both

European and Latin American, she did not portray nature as something that needed to be controlled or eliminated, but as an integral element of progress.[47] By emphasizing the striking contrasts of Brazilian and European nature, she indicated that if properly cultivated, the country could eventually be transformed into a model of economic and cultural superiority.

Evidently, Floresta was not a professional scientist, although the rhetoric of the sublime and the scientific discourse of natural history were widespread in her travel writing and became instruments to assist her in the process of creating her literary authority. She dialogued with her predecessors and displayed a distinctive way of depicting European nature and civilization. By comparing Europe with Brazil, she assumed the unique position of someone who had been on both sides of the Atlantic and, for this reason, had authority to speak about both places. On a time when the scientific discourse of natural history was being widely used to shape new Latin American nations and often employed to normalize dichotomies such as nature/civilization, public/private, she took part in these discussions and offered another possibility. By aligning nature, progress, and civilization as an ideal and possible undertaking, she transformed her narrative on a counter space to discuss women's education. Her ultimate goal was to propose a new educational model for girls which would include the necessity of traveling and having natural history and science lessons. This educational model would challenge the then prevailing scientific discourse, which considered women inferior to men, and therefore, prevented them from receiving proper education.

A New Educational Project for Girls: Feminizing the Grand Tour

Motivated to pursue her intellectual quest, Floresta departed with her daughter Lívia to Italy and Greece on a journey that lasted three years. She made it clear that the entire trip was planned by herself and that she had her own preferences regarding the itinerary, indicating her preoccupation in carefully selecting the places she would visit and in which sequence: "I had fixed my departure for March 19 and, wishing to be in Rome during holy week, I gave up entering Italy by the long route of the Cornice, proposing to visit it later" (*Itália* 24).[48] From the beginning, she displayed not only her knowledge about the common and preferred routes but also the willingness to make a route on her own, disregarding common sense about the "beaten track." The fact that she intended to arrive in Rome during the holy week demonstrates that she was anticipating the climax of her narrative, leveraging the fundamental pillars of the Grand Tour when describing her itinerary. Besides this carefully prepared itinerary, the narrative structure of her tour also included the traversal of boundaries, literary mediation, pleasure, and cultural benefit.

The Grand Tour was a tradition that started at the end of the sixteenth century and lasted well into the nineteenth century. Thomas Nugent, in his influential volume *The Grand Tour* (1749), defined it as "a custom to enrich the mind with knowledge, to rectify judgment, to remove the prejudices of education, to compose the outward manners, and in a word form the complete gentleman" (quoted in Buzard 98). Eighteenth-century British grand tourists to Italy generally followed a standardized itinerary from London to Rome and Naples. From London, travelers crossed the English Channel to Calais, and continued across France, usually with a lengthy stop in Paris. There were two options for crossing into Italy. One could either cross the Alps or book a sea voyage from southern France to Leghorn. On their return to England, they often traveled through Germany and the Low Countries. European tours of this sort typically lasted a year or more. The eighteenth-century itinerary remained popular well into the nineteenth century and was later the model for nineteenth-century American tourism to Europe. In general, as Chloe Chard suggests, a traveler undertaking the Grand Tour "should locate the point of his or her journey somewhere in the northern Europe, should aim to travel to the southern side of the Alps . . . and should register a desire or intent to visit Rome . . ." (15). That is to say, the itinerary of the Grand Tour was fairly fixed: "Texts decreed which sights should be viewed. Many travelers took guide books or other travel books which listed the most important, worthwhile sights, and rated them for the traveler before the traveler had even arrived, the site was thus categorized" (Mills, *Discourses* 84). However fixed the itinerary had to be, travelers often planned and mapped their own routes, according to the sites they sought to see and according to the demands of their own narrative, in which the excitement would increase gradually from place to place. But if in the seventeenth century the Tour was specially designed to confirm the travelers' masculinity, by the middle nineteenth century, the practice involved the acceptance of a more feminized way of travel that entailed sophistication, emotional response to art, and ability to observe foreign society and manners, as opposed to the hardships of the adventure quests. Even so, travel accounts of the Grand Tour written by women authors often established an authority through their position as eyewitness rather than the authority of a classical scholar (Chard 35–36).

In that sense, Floresta's narrative of the Grand Tour resembled the one practiced by upper- and, to a lesser extent, middle-class young men, whose main goal was to educate themselves, and return to their homelands prepared to assume their responsibilities as men. Throughout the journey, these wealthy young men were mentored by their tutors, known as "bearleaders." The bearleader was always a man who was knowledgeable about the itineraries, the most important buildings, paintings, views, and historical sites, which would be important to educate the young men. Famous bearleaders, Thomas Hobbes (1588–1679), John Locke (1632–1704), and Adam Smith (1723–1790), all became influential scholars later in their lives, and all left their diaries and letters that detailed their experiences. Floresta, however, subverted this tradition by impersonating the bearleader position herself and replacing the young men with her daughter. By establishing her position as a mentor of her daughter, she aligned herself with these famous bearleaders, and forged an authority which was not common for a woman of her time. Relying on her duty as a mother, she outweighed her transgression since the experience of traveling was the perfect opportunity to provide her daughter the "educational tour" to broaden her knowledge through experience. In addition, writing about their travel experience would serve as a model for all the mothers and daughters out there who could learn and benefit from their experience.

However, while the grand tourists were inclined to confirm prior observations and repeat the same itineraries, enforcing the tour as a cultural norm, Floresta often disregarded the opinions of previous travelers, privileging her own perspectives of the places she visited and employing an authoritative and confident tone in her descriptions (Smith 5). As demonstrated above, she rebutted many of the preconceived ideas and descriptions of the places she visited, giving her own perspective, many times criticizing previous travelers. Moreover, she explicitly manifested her enthusiasm with the fact that she had freedom to express her own opinions about her experiences: "Among the advantages and amusements offered by travel, there is that of being able to gather freely in front of the objects of art and nature that affect you the most, and that of hearing the reflections or reasoning often discordant among other travelers with whom you find yourself in contact" (*Trois* 11–12).[49] The nature of the places they visited endorsed the educational nature of her Grand Tour, evidenced by their interest in sites such as natural history museums, art museums, universities, libraries, etc. They also took part in active learning opportunities and, in Florence, attended classes at the university along with other foreign women:

> We find it fascinating to attend the botany classes of the great Parlatore. . . . Many women, almost all of them of foreign origin, attend here, as they do in Paris, the classes offered to the general public. This course is another attraction in Florence, and I can enjoy here, as I did in Paris, the useful recreation of studying, which, in the past, has strongly connected me to the College of France and to the Natural History Museum. Mr. Parlatore, who used to work with the great Humboldt, published some studies on Botany. . . . He teaches his classes with great accuracy and fine taste, meeting with dignity all the demands for teaching the beautiful science to which he dedicates himself. (100)[50]

Floresta reaffirmed her interest in educating herself and her daughter under the mentorship of a renowned botanist, a disciple of Humboldt and her mention of the classes she took with Duvernoy in Paris further emphasized her attempts to construct a cohesive narrative of knowledge pursuit.[51] By labeling their activity as a useful pleasure, she was still within the limits of her own femininity and the demands of the Tour as a narrative of pleasure and education. By mentioning the presence of other women, she established the classes as a feminine space to knowledge exchange and interaction.

However, her Grand Tour was also an irreplaceable opportunity for adventure, and her itinerary was not limited to the libraries, museums, and the appreciation of works of art. It also included field experience and the possibility to offer her daughter the opportunity of being exposed to more than the limited information available in the books. Referring back to the passage above, in which she encountered the Italian teacher in Germany, Floresta was convinced that the walls of the classroom offered limited opportunities in terms of education. In her excursion to the Vesuvius volcano, she stated: "Of all the descriptions of the various forms of the Vesuvius crater I read, none had given me the impression of the current one" (*Itália* 218).[52] She subverted the pillars of the Grand Tour aligning the experience with more adventurous and not so sophisticated accounts of travel writing, referring back to the rhetoric of the sublime and the Humboldtian tropes mentioned above. The details she offered about the excursion further validate this claim: "Just as the pilgrim of the vast deserts of Africa, after long walks under the scorched sky, rests happily in the benign oasis that covers the fountain that quenches his thirst, so I felt happy, magnetized by the ponderous influence of that magical spectacle" (210).[53] By aligning her account with male African journeys, she exoticized her experience and added a taste of adventure to her narrative of the Grand Tour.

Moreover, if throughout the narrative she remained within the limits of her femininity, when climbing the Vesuvius, she transgressed gender boundaries as she chose to undertake the experience by foot, refusing to be carried by men on a chair provided to the tourists. At the same time, she did not allow her daughter to do the same, making sure she had a chair for herself. By "protecting" her daughter, she guaranteed that her transgression would not be perceived as offensive to her audience:

> . . . climbing alone, as best I could on the lava, I followed the vehicle of my daughter, who stopped her carriers, from moment to moment, to stay within the reach of my vision. With each step, the difficulty increased, the lava threatened to slide and crush my feet, already injured despite the "ad hoc" shoes that we wore for the ascension. But every time, when I stopped to rest, I turned to the horizon that widened as I climbed the elevation, my soul was elevated by that

perspective, which was constantly changing, and all my worries about dangers vanished. (*Itália* 216)⁵⁴

By choosing to climb the mountain by foot, Floresta destabilized her narrative and undermined the feminized subject she had carefully crafted, that is, she became "the other to her ordinary, unheroic, 'feminized' self" (Smith 32). By subjecting herself to the endurance of the climbing, she enabled the possibility of a heroic act of resistance. However, on the course of climbing the mountain, her perspective was gradually amplified and outweighed the danger of her actions. This can be understood as a metaphor of her entire enterprise in the sense that she was exposing herself to the danger of being scrutinized by society by undertaking her voyage but at the same time offering her daughter, and other women by extension, safely seated on the chair, the opportunity to receive the unique education provided by their traveling experience. In other words, she was consciously risking her own reputation, but her actions would benefit other women in the future. Moreover, the image of an educated woman climbing a mountain conveyed the idea of the possibility of overcoming gender constraints: ". . . so I performed the ascension of the Vesuvius as slowly as I used to climb the green peaks of the hills in my homeland on days that are already far behind me" (*Itália* 216).⁵⁵ Metaphorically, climbing Vesuvio slowly, steadily, but persistently, she would complete her quest for intellectual knowledge. By aligning the mountain with the Brazilian mountains she climbed in her youth, she hoped that her ideas would eventually reach on her own country.

Floresta's greatest "twist" to the Grand Tour, however, was to embed on the narrative of the intellectual quest the recurring notion that both nature and civilization were in a symbiotic relationship, thereby aligning the traditional humanistic nature of the educational tour with a novel view that included a more scientific/naturalist perspective. Her interest in the landscape, geography, and population, among other factors, conformed to the scientific voyages made by other professional travelers. Moreover, Floresta tried to grant to her travel observations the status of science: ". . . the most magnificent paintings attract my attention, and the enchanting nature of Italy exhibits its most gracious smiles. . . . Observing the world is a great science" (*Itália* 256).⁵⁶ As opposed to the social explorers described by Pratt, such as Flora Tristán, she did not present herself as someone solely interested in the aspects of the European society (*Imperial* 155). She looked at society as an inherent part of nature, history, and geography: "Several times . . . when my daughter and I left a church or gallery with our eyes tired of examining the beauties they kept, we would ask the coachman to drive us to Capena and wandered on that road, where every day a new object attracted our attention and refreshed our memory, outdoors, in the most eloquent and solemn meadow of all deserted meadows" (*Itália* 92).[57] Their experience as travelers was only complete if, as they discovered marvelous objects of arts, they could also discover a new object in nature too, displaying an inseparable perspective of nature and civilization. In other words, her narrative revealed a world in which civilization and nature could not exist separately, in which they were equally important and fundamental: "Where can we find in Italy a piece of land uncultivated or cultivated that has not been marked by a historical fact, glorious or dark? . . . Italy is an immense living book . . ." (*Itália* 194).[58] The Italian livingbook she was studying was equally rich in history, despite being cultivated or raw. If when describing Brazilian nature Floresta many times replicated the rhetoric that reduced Latin America to pure nature employed by travelers such as Humboldt, eliminating its history and any traces of human presence, when describing the European landscapes, she also revealed the impossibility of separating nature from civilization:

> When, by sunset, we returned from our climbing of the promontory of Pausilipa, after wandering through modern villages, where cactuses, orange trees, pink laurel trees proliferate. . . . In one of the elevations that dominate the city and all the magnificence of its surroundings, rises, gloomy and towering, with the memory of the illustrious victims who it saw moaning among its blackened walls, the infamous Castle Saint-Elmo. (*Itália* 264)[59]

In her description of the Castle Saint-Elmo she placed the building as part of nature, as if it were emerging from the mountain. In a symbiotic relationship between nature and civilization, the walls of the building reveal its history. By presenting nature and civilization as harmoniously coexisting entities, Floresta deconstructed the antithetical relationship between them, which was repeatedly forged on the descriptions of an uncivilized America. In fact, as she praised Brazilian nature, she saw in progress, without eliminating nature, a possible grand future.

Rita Felski has demonstrated how evolutionary narratives, specially toward the end of the nineteenth century, have often associated pre-modernity with women. However, narratives portraying women as antagonists to the demands of civilization were widespread since the beginning of the century (51). Therefore, Floresta's insistence on presenting nature and civilization in a symbiotic relation, where one fueled the other, exemplified by the constant comparisons between Europe and Brazil, can be read as an attempt to deconstruct these narratives, laying out the theoretical groundwork which would support her educational project for girls. In other words, her parallel alignment of nature and civilization countered the same discourses which prevented women from receiving education. Floresta demonstrated in her narrative that women could be part of civilization and cited the impact of their participation in the Italian society. Although her educational project was still conservative, she envisioned that women needed to be educated and that it would impact society as a whole: "the undeniable influence of women's moral education on the happiness and well-being of nations" (*Itália* 143).[60] She cited the philosopher Jules Michelet, who defended women's education as a fundamental pillar of the progress of civilization:

> Let us have faith in the future. The attention of the blind civilizations will awaken to their most urgent interests, hopefully they will appreciate, they will know how to practice the eloquent reflection of the progressive spirit of a celebrated French writer: "Philosophers, biologists, economists, statesmen, we all know that the excellence of a race, the power of the people, is due mainly to the woman." (*Itália* 270)[61]

Just like nature and progress could coexist, a model she repeatedly defended as ideal, civilization would overcome its flaws only by educating women. In other words, women could also be part of civilization, but only if they were educated. She therefore deconstructed the antagonist relationship between women and civilization at the same time she validated the possibility of women's education. In that sense, her travel narrative brought to the forefront questions of nature, progress, civilization, and women's education, countering the exclusion of women from the Latin American projects of nation.

Floresta's Reputation After Her Travels: Alternate Visibility

Nísia Floresta was able to present herself as a traveler and an educator, leveraging her role as a woman and a mother and her own condition as a transatlantic subject in Europe. After a frustrated attempt to be an educator and participate in the intellectual circles in Rio de Janeiro, she decided to depart her home country and lived in Europe for more than thirty-six years. There she took botany and natural history classes in France and Italy and managed to inscribe herself in the intellectual world. Using the discourse of natural history was a strategy she successfully employed to align herself with her male counterparts and apply her knowledge to compare and contrast Europe and Brazil and propose an alignment between nature and civilization. Nísia Floresta also inscribed herself in the Grand Tour tradition, the travel ritual English men of the upper classes engaged in during the 1800s, and as a result, created a feminine perspective of this practice. She not only followed the same itineraries but also made her travels seem like an intellectual quest that would define herself while also providing a complete educational experience for her daughter who accompanied her.

She often eulogized Brazilian nature and European progress by contrasting and comparing both, aligning Europe and Latin America. Floresta at first used this rhetoric to imitate Humboldt's romantic gestures with regard to the Brazilian landscape. Her strategy of exoticizing Brazilian nature assisted her in creating her identity as an exotic subject herself, who was above gender limitations.[62] Later, she also used this authority to refute other naturalists and travelers and criticize them with respect to their depiction of Brazil.

In fact, after the publication of Floresta's travel journals, her involvement with the intellectual circles in Europe only grew and she was able to publish several of her works in France, Italy, and England. Because of the authority she was able to forge in Europe, she had the opportunity to associate with prominent men and women there and participate in intellectual debates at that time which would eventually reach Brazil. She adopted a new pen name, "Une Brésilienne" (A Brazilian Lady), reinforcing the argument that she fully embraced her foreign gaze as a unique asset of her work. This newly acquired identity offered her the opportunity to address her European audience, and challenge previous travel accounts of her own country. Perhaps this alternate visibility which could only be offered by her transatlantic gaze was what attracted so many admirers to her work in Europe. In 1871, she published *Le Brésil* (Brazil), in which she presented her own perspective of Brazilian natural history dialoguing with several travel writers who had visited that country, such as the French botanist Auguste de Saint-Hilaire (1779–1853), who was there between 1816 and 1822. She also dialogued with Johann Moritz Rugendas (1802–1858) who became famous for his *Voyage Pittoresque dans le Brésil*. In *Le Brésil*, addressed to a European audience, Floresta praised not only Brazilian nature, but its people, and defended the idea that the country was promising in terms of civilization. In her descriptions, she presented Brazilian nature and civilization as interconnected. Her goal was to correct some misconceptions about the country, which according to her, were widespread in Europe as she defended the idea that Brazil was indeed a nation with potential to become what she had envisioned years before. Whereas in her travel accounts she had compared Brazilian and European nature, portraying the Brazilian one as superior, she now had the purpose of clarifying previous accounts about the country, as she brought out several examples of Brazil progressing as a nation in areas such as science, arts, industry, etc. (Scatena Franco 237). One could infer that she was able to take advantage of the status and reputation she acquired as a traveler to write this more authoritative text in which she updated previous accounts about Brazil and offered a more reliable description of the country.

Eventually her success in Europe started to resonate in Brazil as well. In particular, Floresta was deeply involved with Comte's positivist movement and they exchanged several letters in which he expressed his hope that she would become his disciple.[63] Although she never fully subscribed to be

Comte's discipline, she did support some positivist ideals, and her relationship with him gave her some prestige back home.[64] Marcela Varejão observes that her positivist ideas were disseminated in Brazil in several newspapers (162). Hence, the fact that Floresta traveled to Europe allowed her to not only form a network of intellectuals but also gave her authority to write to the same newspapers which had ridiculed her a few decades earlier. Among the Brazilian newspapers to which she contributed were *Jornal do Comércio*, the *Mercantil*, the *Diário do Rio de Janeiro*, *O Liberal*, *Brasil Ilustrado*, and several newspapers of Paris and Florence (Varejão 162). Floresta's biography was published in the Brazilian newspaper *O Novo Mundo* (The New World), in 1872, which had published biographies of other prominent men before, such as Victor Hugo, Louis Agassiz, and Beethoven, and her biography was the only one belonging to a woman published by that venue. By the time her biography was published in Brazil, Floresta was a well established writer in the European intellectual circles and this is a strong indication that she had to have her work recognized abroad before she would be acknowledged in her own country.

According to Said, most travel writing makes a clear separation between the race of which the narrator is representative, and that of the country being described (55). As Mills observes, ". . . this Othering process is essential for Europe to regard European behavior as the norm and hence to assert itself as a superior race" (*Discourses* 88). Although Floresta lacked this European superiority, she managed to use this same mechanism to place Brazil, and by extension herself, in a superior position. Unable to achieve a reputation as a writer or as an educator in Brazil, Floresta traveled to Europe and wrote her travel narratives, achieving a remarkable reputation. Carving her name as a writer there, she found a space to achieve the alternate visibility she needed to address the subject of women education, collaborate to the construction of knowledge, and ultimately, gain prominence as an intellectual woman on both sides of the Atlantic.

NOTES

1. Naquele dia . . . lancei um último olhar, velado de lágrimas, na direção daquela magnífica baía, daquelas majestosas montanhas pomposamente vestidas de eterna vegetação, daquelas duas cidades, Rio de Janeiro e Niterói . . .

2. Desaparecia atrás de mim aquele chão revestido das mais soberbas magnificências da natureza: nele ficava parte de tudo que mais amei na terra.

3. For more details on Nísia Floresta's biography, see Constância Lima Duarte, a Brazilian scholar who has done extensive research on her. *A primeira feminista do Brasil* (2008).

4. . . . trabalhos de língua não faltaram; os de agulha ficaram no escuro. Os maridos precisam de mulher que trabalhe mais e fale menos. *O Mercantil*, January 2, 1847.

5. For more details about Jose Bonifácio de Andrada and his role on the Brazilian empire, see chapter 1 on Maria Graham.

6. It is important to notice that although Brazil was the only Latin American country which did not become a Republic, its Independence was also shaped by the interests of an elite very similar to the Creoles in the rest of Latin America. For more about the details surrounding the Brazilian Independence, see Barman, Roderick J. *Brazil: The Forging of a Nation*, 1798–1852. Stanford: Stanford University Press, 1988.

7. Antônio Gonçalves Dias was a Brazilian Romantic poet, naturalist, ethnographer, lawyer, and linguist. A major exponent of the Brazilian Romanticism and Indianism, he was also an avid researcher of the Brazilian indigenous languages and folklore. José Martiniano de Alencar was a Brazilian lawyer, politician, orator, and novelist. He is considered one of the most famous and influential Brazilian Romantic novelists of the nineteenth century, and a major exponent of the literary tradition known as Indianism.

8. As aves que aqui gorjeiam, não gorjeiam como lá.

9. Following the European tradition inaugurated by French writer François-René de Chateaubriand (1768–1848), Indianist discourse, and the idea of the Indian as the *bon savage* was a tradition that Brazilian romanticism broadly adopted and was widely propagated, especially by prominent writers such as Gonçalves Dias and José de Alencar.

10. Charlotte Hammond Matthews observes that the Emperor was the president of the Instituto Histórico e Geográfico Brasileiro (Brazilian Historical and Geographical Institute) and often furnished the authors and researchers with monetary incentives.

11. Dias himself participated in the first expedition to the North of Brazil, sponsored by the Emperor. For more details on the Brazilian scientific expeditions, see *Comissão Científica do Império: 1859–1861* (2009) edited by Lorelai Kury. This comprehensive study brings together images and archival documents about the expedition, which had Gonçalves Dias as one of its members.

12. In 1849, Floresta published an Indianist poem, "Lágrima de um Caeté" (Tear of a Caeté), and this poem can be read as her response to the failure of the liberalists. In the poem, Floresta aligned the collapse of the liberalist mission with the project of the nation proposed by romantic writers, such as Gonçalves Dias (1823–1864) and José de Alencar (1829–1877).

13. Her reputation as a translator of Wollstonecraft lead many literary critics to label Floresta as the first Brazilian feminist. By comparing the two works, nevertheless, it was possible to find remarkable differences between them and Lima Duarte concluded that Floresta was not translating the work literally, but adding her own perspectives. However, a study carried out by Maria Lúcia Garcia Palhares-Burke in 1995 revealed that she had indeed translated another text: *Woman not Inferior to Men: a Short and Modest Vindication*, written in 1739 by Sophia, A Person of Quality. About the dispute, Hammond Matthews suggests that it is possible that Floresta

actually thought that the text she was translating was Wollstonecraft's *Vindication*, which is a plausible theory given the conditions that foreign books arrived in Brazil, many times without the front cover (13). Although this discussion is not relevant to this study, the fact that Floresta's first work was a translation of a treatise on women's rights and education suggests that she endorsed the ideas she was spreading, despite of its authorship.

14. Por que a ciência nos é inútil? Porque somos excluídas dos cargos públicos; e por que somos excluídas dos cargos públicos? Porque não temos ciência. Eu digo mais, não há ciência, nem cargo público no Estado, que as mulheres não sejam naturalmente próprias a preenchê-los tanto quanto os homens.

15. E porque não grego e hebraico? Pobre diretora! Está tão satisfeita de si mesma e de seu colégio; está tão intimamente persuadida que é o primeiro estabelecimento de instrução do império, que, em verdade causa dó arrancar-lhe tão suave ilusão! . . . É pois natural que D. Nísia que nunca viu senão o próprio colégio o ponha acima dos demais. Há mais nesta opinião mais ingenuidade do que vaidade. Notaremos apenas a D. Floresta que se esquece um tanto do verdadeiro fim da educação, que é o de adquirir conhecimentos úteis e não vencer dificuldades, sem nenhuma utilidade real (*O Mercantil*, 17 de janeiro de 1847).

16. Georges Cuvier (1769–1832) was a well-known French naturalist and zoologist who mentored Duvernoy and prepared him to continue his work on the field of comparative anatomy. Georges Louis Duvernoy assisted Cuvier in his *Iconographie du règne animal* and replaced him as a professor of natural history at the Collège de France, in 1837. *Dictionary of Biography, Past and Present*, 156. For more information, see *The Cuvier-Geoffrey Debate: French Biology in the Decades before Darwin* by Toby A. Appel, 1987.

17. Comte's ideas deeply influenced Brazilian intellectual thought and approaches to science and the social sciences (Rhodes Gollo 153). In Brazil, the first public manifestations of positivist ideas started around 1844, although the real positivist influence flourished only around 1874 (Varejão 160). There were four types of positivism: French, British, Latin American, and logical positivism. French positivism was based on the ideas of Comte, who believed human knowledge had progressed from a mythical mode to a metaphysical mode and would embrace a final positivist model, a scientific model of knowledge based on the observable world (Gilson 14). Comte argued that according to a universal law of history, a culture advances through each of the three stages, culminating in the final positive stage. The first stage, the theological one, is the stage of superstition. The metaphysical state is the period of belief in the individual rights. For Comte, his theory of stages was able to reconcile order and progress: "Science replaces superstition, and elite specialists replace the tendency of liberal systems to mob rule" (Cologero 85). In Latin America, positivist ideas developed in Argentina, Mexico, Chile, and Brazil and started to be popularized around 1860. As Latin America was still struggling to define itself as independent, positivism seemed like a promising path to progress: "Positivism was anticlerical at a time when Catholicism was seen as an impediment to progress, and was authoritarian at a time when enlightenment ideals of democracy and individual rights seems romantic and impractical. Positivism promoted utilitarianism, science (or scientism),

an emphasis on material; progress, and Social Darwinism" (Cologero 83). Comte envisioned a society based entirely on knowledge gained from the application of the scientific method. From his perspective, nature and society were a closed system where scientists would determine the laws of society as they did with physics: "Auguste Comte created positivism within an altogether different paradigm, one which emphasized the emancipation of the intellect from the superstition and myth present among institutionalized religious orders of the time" (Rhodes Gollo 154). For Brazil, relying on Comte's doctrine was an opportunity to extricate the government from the influence of the Catholic Church. Brazilian positivism took on the characteristics of Comte's *A General View of Positivism* (1848). Frequently, Brazilian positivism is associated with the abolition of slavery and the establishment of the republic. The Brazilian flag's inscription, "Ordem e Progresso," refers to the two main words from the positivist movement: "Positivism was introduced to Brazil to bridge the philosophical gap between that nation and Europe and by doing, to synchronize Brazil with the contemporary capitalist world" (Rhodes Gollo 155). The positivist movement in Brazil gained force after the triple alliance made by Brazil, Argentina, and Uruguay won the war over Paraguay (1864–1870). Despite the victory, the Brazilian economy was devastated after the war, and, due to the lack of money, the emperor D. Pedro II ignored the military requests for modernization. The positivist movement in the military gained incredible support after the war. Led by Colonel Benjamin Constant, at the military college of Rio de Janeiro, positivist thinking became part of the curriculum: "All of it, except the ideas of getting rid of the men in uniform" (Rose 134). As D. Pedro II refused to listen to the military, Constant became an enthusiastic republican and advocate for positivist ideas. He was the founder of the Positivist Society of Rio de Janeiro, in 1876. He advocated for positivism as the religion of humanity and in several letters written by Constant to his wife Maria Joaquina, he tried to convert her to positivism (Rose 135). After the end of slavery on May 13, 1889, the monarchal regime became even weaker and on November 15, 1889, Brazil became a republic after a military coup. In fact, between 1889 and 1894 Brazil was under the rule of a military dictatorship. Therefore, the movement that lead the Brazilian republic to be born started around 1870.

18. Souza Maia also points out that Floresta's stay in Europe opened her horizons upon her return. Hammond Matthews also observes a marked change on her writings.

19. There are two letters at the Bibliothèque Central–Muséum National d'Histoire Naturelle, Paris addressed to Duvernoy. Ludmila Souza Maia located the letters and brought them to light.

20. A fraqueza física é um dos pretextos de que se prevalecem certos sofistas para subtraírem a mulher ao estudo, para o qual a julgam imprópria. Não é a natureza física, como pretende Helvécio, que faz a superioridade do homem, mas sim a inteligência. Voltaire, Racine, Pascal e outros muitos, de uma compleição demasiadamente delicada, comprovam esta verdade. E a inteligência, que não tem sexo, pode ser igualmente superior na mulher, salvo a opinião de alguns materialistas cujo espírito fraco identificou-se, permita-se-nos a expressão, com o escalpelo afeito a revelar-lhes a organização animal, que não a inspirar-lhes os sublimes pensamentos de Duvernoy, Schoenlein, Orfila e do eloquente Serres, quando, na indagação dessa nobre ciência

que reclamam as dores físicas da humanidade, eles elevam a alma de seus admiradores por suas filosóficas considerações.

François-Marie d'Arouet (1694–1778), better known by his pen name Voltaire, was a French writer and public activist who played a singular role in defining the eighteenth-century movement called the Enlightenment. Jean-Baptiste Racine (1639–699) was a French dramatic poet and historiographer renowned for his mastery of French classical tragedy whose work has influenced Voltaire. On his historical and mythological plays, Racine destabilizes gender dynamics to create powerful female protagonists, that is, "Iphigenia" depicts a princess' absolute submission to her father's will, despite his determination to sacrifice her to gain divine favor before going to war, "Phaedra" shows a woman's struggle to overcome her overwhelming passion for her stepson, "Athalia" portrays a pagan queen, who defies Jehovah in her desperate attempt to keep the throne of Jerusalem from its legitimate heir. See "Gender Reversal in Racine's Historical and Mythological Tragedies" by Richard E. Goodkin. Claude Adrien Helvétius (1715–1771) was a French philosopher who believed that natural equality applied to all men in all nations, and thus the differences in national characteristics were not the result of innate differences between the people therein, but rather a byproduct of the system education and government. Blaise Pascal (1623–1662) was a French philosopher, mathematician, scientist, inventor, and theologian. Etienne Reynard Augustin Serres (1786–1868) challenged Cuvier's theories about the development of the brain. Johann Lukas Schönlein (1793–1864) was a German naturalist. Mathieu Joseph Bonaventure Orfila (1787–1853) was a Spanish naturalist who introduced forensic medicine.

21. By mentioning notorious women such as Sappho and Hypatia, emphasizing their intelligence and achievements, Floresta dismissed the assumed intellectual inferiority of women and attributed their apparent inferiority to their lack of education.

22. A esperança de que, nas gerações futuras do Brasil, ele assumirá a posição que lhe compete nos pode somente consolar de sua sorte presente. Entretanto, sigamos o exemplo do pobre e corajoso explorador de nossas virgens florestas, exposto aqui e ali a mordedura de venenosos répteis, para rotear um campo que outros terão de semear e de colher-se saborosos frutos. Felizes nós se pudéssemos conseguir o primeiro resultado desse trabalho, que muito nos lisonjearíamos de oferecer as nossas conterrâneas como penhor do verdadeiro interesse que elas nos inspiram.

23. Méndez Rodenas also observes the use of a more specific terminology to refer to the Latin American travelers in Europe. She adds that the term "Strange pilgrimages" has been proposed to refer to the Latin American intellectuals who settled in Europe, expanding from its religious connotation. Besides, the term "haunted journeys," has been proposed by Denis Porter: "this term implies a transatlantic encounter in another direction, a reverse movement from the New World to the Old, a pattern traced in new studies of the genre" (10).

24. Pratt observes that Creole Spanish Americans also traveled to Europe to study, but never wrote about their experiences until 1850, when Domingos Fausto Sarmiento published the first travel account of this sort, *Imperial* 189.

25. For an analysis pertaining to Floresta's inner feelings through the narrative, see the Constancia Lima Duarte, *Vida e Obra*.

26. ... preferi entrar na Alemanha pela Bélgica e sair por Kehl, para ir de Estraburgo a Montbéliard. ...

27. Não tenho tempo disponível para lhes escrever a historia de Bruxelas ... nem das cidades que vou percorrer; indicarei apenas o que mais me atraia a atenção e, a noite, lhes comunicarei minhas impressões do dia.

28. Os cimos das montanhas coroadas de ruinas de castelos, belvederes, de casas, de capelas; as pontas de rochedos, perdendo-os no espaço, portando a lembrança de um passado grandioso; as cidades, os burgos, as aldeias, toda essa variedade de objetos naturais e artísticos sucedia-se, sem interrupção, de uma a outra margem. Minha ardente imaginação emprestava um encanto a mais ao aspecto dessas paisagens portentosas, a falarem mais eloquentemente ao espirito meditativo do que todas as grandes páginas que se escreveram sobre elas.

29. É muito bonito contemplar assim, de uma única altitude, uma a uma, três nações diferentes. ... Faço questão essencial de guardar na minha memória, como um sonho grandioso ... ali onde as paisagens mais belas e pitorescas, como em um mapa geográfico vivo, desenrolaram-se ante meus olhos, sob imenso horizonte embelezado pelos últimos raios do sol poente.

30. Era-me necessário percorrer novos países. Neles haurir novas impressões. Sob um horizonte mais amplo, em atmosfera mais livre e, consequentemente, mais consentâneas com minhas preferências ... vocês veem naturalmente que me decidi pela velha e poética Germânia, a digna pátria de Leibnitz e Kant.

31. Propondo-me realizar uma peregrinação ao túmulo de venerável amigo, o sábio e bom Duvernoy. ...

32. Méndez Rodenas points out that women's travel writing has a hybrid nature that upsets the binary European paradigm of travel writing as either romantic or scientific and suggests the use of the term "pilgrimage narratives" to define their journeys. For Méndez Rodenas, they are pilgrims because "treading on a route whose end goal may be either deferred or never fully realized (10)."

33. Fez-me lembrar uma professora cujo coração e espirito se harmonizavam para instruir a juventude; apenas, limitava-se a ministrar lições entre os muros de um estabelecimento e em um país onde não se compreende ainda toda a relevância de uma educação geral, que forme ao mesmo tempo o moral e o físico. Em contraste, a mulher que ali estava diante de mim, viajando, instruía seus alunos, cujos pais sabem apreciar as vantagens desse método que fará rir os espíritos ainda antiquados. Palestramos alguns instantes juntas e nos separamos; ela muito feliz de haver visto as belas paisagens que percorrera com suas jovens alunas, cercada de todas as vantagens e diante de um belo future que ainda esperava. E eu, entregue as minhas meditações e recordações! Assim, as duas professoras estrangeiras encontramo-nos no solo alemão: uma decepcionada com suas esperanças de vinte anos de devotamento e trabalho; a outra embriagada pela perspectiva risonha que oferece este começo na vida que apenas inicia.

34. É tempo de pagar a dívida da santa amizade, no túmulo do venerável sábio que me honrou com particular estima e de cuja morte me resultou, na França, em um imenso vazio.

35. Estou escrevendo desse bureau precioso, cercado de todas essas remiscências tão tocantes.

36. Amanhã quando o sol clarear o cume dos Vosges . . . não mais terei sob os meus olhos este bureau precioso junto ao qual tanto velaste, venerável Duvernoy, tanto trabalhaste por amor a ciência. . . . Estes móveis . . . estas árvores, estas colinas . . . tudo isso vai desaparecer ante meus olhos. Mas eu levarei a lembrança profundamente gravada em meu coração. Minha cabeça está enfraquecida e meu corpo alquebrado vai repousar no leito em que dormias . . .

37. The versions I refer to in this chapter are the Portuguese translations *Itinerário de uma viagem à Alemanha* (1982) and *Três anos na Itália seguidos de uma viagem a Grécia* (1999).

38. Possa o talismã deste santo amor, passando do velho ao novo mundo, conduzir-te sempre pelo nobre caminho do dever, levando ao teu coração os últimos elãs e as ultimas esperanças de tua terna mãe.

39. . . . naquela magnífica baía, daquelas majestosas montanhas pomposamente vestidas de eterna vegetação, daquelas duas cidades, Rio de Janeiro e Niterói, desaparecendo, pouco a pouco, por detrás daquelas gigantescas filhas da terra que as cerca . . . na mais bela baía do mundo, que as separa.

40. . . . segundo dizia o célebre Humboldt, altos caules de palmeiras agitando seus soberbos penachos, dominam as árvores circunstantes, e formam, em longas colunatas, uma floresta sobre a floresta.

41. E aquelas cadeias de montanhas, aquelas florestas virgens, aquelas ricas campinas, aquelas prodigiosas quedas d'agua, aqueles rios, aqueles pássaros, todas aquelas obras-primas naturais do solo que me viu nascer, voltavam vivamente ao meu espírito. . . . Que encanto sob o céu estrangeiro, por mais sedutor que seja, jamais vos poderá ser comparado?

42. Chateaubriand tinha razão ao exclamar, observando, daqui a magnificência de Nápoles e de seus arredores: "É o paraíso visto do inferno." A forma da cratera era então diferente da que se apresenta hoje, pois a cada erupção ela muda. . . . Assim, de todas as descrições das diversas formas da cratera do Vesúvio que vi, nenhuma me dera a ideia da atual.

43. See chapter 2 for a similar strategy employed by Gomez de Avellaneda.

44. See chapter 2 for more details on Gómez de Avellaneda climbing the French Pyrenees.

45. A multidão compacta de curiosos, as numerosas tochas agitadas pela brisa da noite, as torrentes de lavas a se arrojarem de alto a baixo da montanha, uma parte das quais, resfriando-se em alguns lugares, deslizava com leve estalido, superpondo-se e formando colinas incandescentes: as chamas saindo das novas crateras e tingindo de uma cor avermelhada todo aquele recinto incandescente, a ponto que o céu que lhe serve de abóbada parecer também em fogo. . . . o estalido da lava; o fragor das detonações repetidas do vulcão que agora tem várias bocas. . . . O gênio do homem é insuficiente para dar conta apropriadamente de tais cenas da natureza. Quem as viu e é capaz de compreendê-las, senti-las e admirá-las, daguerreotipá-las-á em seu espírito. Os artistas mais hábeis, porém, jamais poderão representá-las na tela.

46. . . . esta vegetação que cobre esses imensos restos de tantas obras de arte e luxo.

47. For example, see *Facundo: Civilización y Barbarie* (1845) by the Argentinian writer Domingo Faustino Sarmiento. For great examples of Floresta's descriptions of nature and progress in a harmonious relationship, see her depictions of Rio de Janeiro in "Passeio ao Aqueduto da Carioca," published in the newspaper *O Brasil Ilustrado* in 1855.

48. Havia fixado minha saída para o dia 19 de março e, desejando encontrar-me em Roma durante a Semana Santa, renunciei entrar na Itália pela longa rota da Cornija, propondo-me a recorrê-la mais tarde.

49. Parmi les avantages et les amusements qu'offrent les voyages, il y a celui de pouvoir se recueillir en liberté devant les objets d'art et de nature qui vous touchent le plus, et celui d'entendre les réflexions ou les raisonnements souvent discordants entre eux qu'en font les voyageurs avec lesquels vous trouvez en contact.

50. Encontramos um novo encanto assistindo o curso de botânica do sábio Parlatori. . . . Muitas mulheres, quase todas estrangeiras, seguem aqui, como em Paris, os cursos públicos, este curso é uma atração a mais de Florença, pois encontro aqui, como em Paris, a útil recreação do estudo que outrora me ligou tão fortemente ao Colégio de França, e ao Museu de História Natural. O Sr. Parlatori, que trabalhou com o grande sábio Humboldt, publicou alguns estudos de Botânica. . . . Ele expõe suas aulas com grande correção e muito gosto, cumprindo dignamente todos os deveres exigidos para o ensino da bela ciência a que se dedica.

51. Filippo Parlatore (1816–1877) was a famous Italian botanist who has published several books on the Italian flora. In 1840, Parlatore traveled to Paris where he was mentored by Alexander Von Humboldt. In 1844 he founded the Botanical Institute of Florence.

52. De todas as descrições das diversas formas da cratera do Vesúvio que li, nenhuma me dera a ideia da atual.

53. Tal qual o peregrino dos vastos desertos d'Africa, após longas caminhadas sob o céu abrasado, repousa feliz no benfazejo oásis que recobre a fonte que lhe matou a sede, assim eu me sentia feliz, magnetizada pela ponderosa influencia daquele espetáculo magico.

54. . . . subindo sozinha, da melhor maneira que pude faze-lo sobre a lava, segui o veiculo da minha filha, que detinha seus carregadores, de momento em momento, para ficar ao alcance da minha visão. A cada passo, a dificuldade aumentava, as lavas ameaçavam deslizar e esmagar-me os pés, já machucados apesar do calcado "ad hoc" de que nos munimos para a ascensão. Mas todas as vezes que, parando para repousar, me voltava para o horizonte que se ampliava à medida que eu escalava a elevação, minh'alma elevava-se ante sua perspectiva, cuja mudança ia sucedendo sempre, e toda preocupação de perigo desaparecia.

55. . . . assim, realizei a ascensão do Vesuvio tao lentamente como escalava os cumes verdejantes de minhas Colinas natais em dias que já estão bem longe.

56. . . . os mais magníficos quadros de arte atraem minha atenção, e a encantadora natureza da Itália exibe seus mais graciosos sorrisos. . . . Observar o mundo é uma grande ciência.

57. Muitas vezes . . . quando minha filha e eu saíamos de uma igreja ou galeria com os olhos cansados de examinar as belezas que elas guardam, mandávamos o

cocheiro nos conduzir à porta Capena e nos encontrávamos nessa estrada, onde cada dia um novo objeto atraía nossa atenção e refrescava nossa memória, ao ar livre, na campina mais eloqüente e mais solene de todas as campinas desertas.

58. Onde encontramos na Itália um pedaço de terra inculto ou cultivado que não seja marcado por um fato histórico, glorioso ou tenebroso? . . . A Itália é um imenso livro vivo . . .

59. Quando, pelo ocaso, voltamos do passeio que escala o promontório de Pausilipa, contornando-o por entre vilas modernas, em que os cáctus, as laranjeiras, os loureiros-rosa proliferam. . . . Em umas das elevações que dominam a cidade e todas as magnificências de suas circunvizinhanças, ergue-se, sombrio e altaneiro, com a recordação das ilustres vítimas que viu gemerem entre suas muralhas enegrecidas, o famoso Castelo Santo-Elmo.

60. . . . a inegável influência da educação moral da mulher para a felicidade e bem estar das nações.

61. Tenhamos fé no futuro. A atenção dos povos cegos despertará para seus interesses mais palpitantes, eles apreciarão, eles saberão por em prática, esperemos, a eloqüente reflexão do espírito progressista de um célebre escritor francês: "Filósofos, biólogos, economistas, homens de Estado, todos nós sabemos que a excelência da raça, a força do povo, deve-se sobretudo à mulher."

62. As opposed to Gómez de Avellaneda who criticized the Humboldtian tropes.

63. See *Cartas de Nísia Floresta e Auguste Comte* Editora Mulheres, Florianópolis, 2002.

64. In her house in France, she promoted weekly conversations and these meetings were called the "salão positivista." It is possible to find evidence of these positivist discussions in the correspondence of people who had the opportunity to participate in these debates (Lins 21–22). She received, among others, Alexandre Dumas (1802–1870), Victor Hugo (1802–1885), and Augusto Comte (1798–1857).

Chapter Four

Beyond the Laboratory Walls

Doris Cochran's Strategies to Build a Reputation as a Scientist in the Early Twentieth Century

In the twentieth century women continued to face barriers to engage in the production of knowledge and establish themselves as professional scientists, despite that fact that an increasing number of women scientists started to achieve a professional status in their fields.[1] By 1921, as Rossiter explains, although women had accomplished much progress if compared to the previous century, their professional opportunities were still very limited and their gender continued to pose barriers to the advancement of their careers as scientists. In the first two decades of the century women scientists employed many strategies to expand their professional opportunities. Many of them addressed specific research topics in fields such as anthropology and psychology with the objective of dismantling patriarchal beliefs that defined them as inferior. Others engaged in politics and participated in feminist movements, such as the suffrage. However, these initiatives ultimately failed to offer them equal professional opportunities, and although women's participation in the public sphere had improved significantly in the first decades of the century, they were still discriminated and segregated (Rossiter 128). Thus, although women finally could pursue higher education and become professional scientists, to be able to advance in their careers, they needed new strategies: ". . . many doors to the house of science had been unlocked for them, but women were still on the first floor and still faced many obstacles to their further acceptance" (Rossiter 128). Considering this context, this chapter analyses the intercontinental collaborations between the American scientist Doris Mable Cochran (1898–1968) and her Brazilian counterpart Bertha Maria Júlia Lutz (1894–1976) to further understand how transatlantic travels continued to be an effective tool for women to successfully engage in scientific discussions and construction of knowledge, even if they were professional scientists.

Highly educated, both women were naturalists working in respected institutions, eager to participate in the circuits of knowledge production of their times. Nevertheless, they were still largely prevented from doing so due to the exclusively male world that was well established among scientists. By analyzing travel diaries, letters, and some unpublished manuscripts of Cochran and Lutz, I confirm that although women's participation in scientific enterprises continued to be challenging well into the twentieth century, travel and mobility still facilitated their contributions to the construction of knowledge.

The modernization and industrialization that took place in the second half of the nineteenth century promoted new ways of traveling around the globe. The early twentieth century, especially in the inter-war years, propelled a renovation of modes of transportation and fostered new ways of documenting the world (Farley 278). Although travel writing lost some of the prestige and status it enjoyed in the previous centuries, it remained very popular, and new travelogue formats indicated the genre's capacity of reinventing itself to attend the demands of industrialization and technology (Korte 182). Nevertheless, in the early twentieth century, travel writing was, to a great extent, still endorsed by European and U.S. expansionism and the imperial enterprises (Thompson 196). A close reading of Cochran's unpublished travel account of her scientific expedition to Brazil, "Just a Minute, Miss," demonstrates that she employed the hegemonic rhetoric of discovery and exploration, while still preserving her femininity. Taking advantage of her transatlantic subjectivity, she ultimately managed to transcend the gender boundaries which prevented her from taking part in the construction of knowledge.

CROSSED PATHS IN THE SCIENTIFIC WORLD: BERTHA LUTZ AND DORIS COCHRAN

The biographical information about Doris Mable Cochran is very scattered and most of the material available derives from her personal archives at the Smithsonian Institution, where she worked from 1919 to 1968. According to the historical note provided by these archives, Cochran was born in Pennsylvania in 1898, and moved to Washington, D.C., when her father was assigned to a government position in 1908. The comprehensive collection of Cochran's personal papers, organized by herself, offers a glimpse of her early life as well as of her many talents. She was a very skilled painter and illustrator and her ability to draw accurate pictures of very small creatures and animals as well as landscapes opened the doors for her scientific career (Child, A-16). When asked why she started to work at the museum when she was only twenty-one years old, she replied: "Because I could draw" (Shelton,

F-7). Despite describing herself as a city girl, she reported that her interest for the natural sciences started at a very young age: "From the time she was a small girl, Dr. Cochran has had an overwhelming interest in natural history. She attributes much of this to childhood walks with her parents, observing plants and animal life near her home. As soon as she could read she delved into natural history. By the time she went to college she had selected natural history as her main area of interest ("Frog Lady," *The American Magazine*). Indeed, she pursued a very successful career as a scientist. She was an only child, never married, and very little is known about her family or personal life. A few correspondences to an aunt and cousin in Minnesota and to her friends show that she lived with her mother until at least 1935 and that she always had many pets, loved to read, to knit, to take care of her garden, and to cook.

Her first appointment at the Smithsonian Museum of Natural History was as an aide to Dr. Leonhard Stejneger in the Division of Reptiles and Amphibians, where she worked until her retirement in April of 1968.[2] In 1933, after being employed by the museum for fourteen years, she received her PhD from the University of Maryland. Her principal areas of interest were the reptiles and amphibians of Central and South America, and she dedicated her life to building her reputation as a herpetologist. The fact that Cochran worked for the museum, more specifically in zoology, was a rare privilege for women at her time. Her appointment was instrumental to her scientific career and her correspondences reveal that she wanted to collect new specimens and engage in field work but faced much resistance at the Smithsonian Institution. Over the course of her career, she published several books, more than ninety articles, and named over one hundred new species and six new genera of amphibians and reptiles.[3] At the Smithsonian, she overlooked a collection of over 150,000 specimens (figure 4.1). Besides her scientific publications and contributions, she dedicated much of her time to writing popular books of science, such as *Living Amphibians of the World* (1961), which has been translated into six languages. She also gave a number of radio talks and newspaper interviews about reptiles and amphibians. Impressive feats for a woman who is hardly known today. As Rossiter observes, women had to create means to insert themselves in the professional world. Instead of hopelessly trying to compete in more popular and hostile fields, women's magazines of the 30s recommended they to "try to turn a unique hobby or an unusual interest into a satisfying position. For women scientists this generally meant ... practicing an exotic specialty (herpetology, perhaps) at a traditional institution (such as a zoo or museum)" (265).[4] This was the strategy that Cochran employed when she built her entire career around her unusual interest in frogs and snakes. And in doing so she found an ally on the opposite side of the American

Figure 4.1. Doris Cochran at her desk at the Smithsonian, 1934.
Smithsonian Institution Archives Image #96-955. Reproduced with permission.

continent: another woman who also had an unusual interest for reptiles, the Brazilian scientist, feminist, and politician Bertha Lutz.

Bertha Lutz was born in São Paulo, Brazil, in 1894 and was the daughter of an English nurse, Amy Fowler, and the Swiss-Brazilian microbiologist and scientist Adolfo Lutz. Given the limited opportunities for women to pursue an education in Brazil, her privileged economic status and the support of her parents allowed Lutz to study in France and graduate with a major in natural sciences in 1918 from the University of Sorbonne, in Paris. Soon after she graduated, in 1919, she became the second woman to be employed by the public service in Brazil as a secretary in the National Museum of Rio de Janeiro. Her involvement with her father's work, her qualification as a botanist and a zoologist, and some political maneuvers gave her the opportunity to be promoted to naturalist at the same institution a few years later.

Besides her extensive work as a scientist, Lutz was also a prominent feminist and politician and is mostly remembered as the leader of the suffrage movement in Brazil from 1920 to 1930. Inspired by her European experience, her involvement with the feminist movement started in 1919, when she founded the League for the Intellectual Emancipation of Women (Liga pela Emancipação Intelectual da Mulher) in Rio de Janeiro. In 1922, Lutz went to Baltimore to participate in the Pan-American Conference and, upon her return, she officially formed the Brazilian Federation for Feminine Progress (Federação Brasileira pelo Progresso Femenino), which was affiliated with the International Women's Suffrage Alliance. The main goal of the federation was to increase the cultural and educational level of women with the purpose of improving their conditions in every aspect of their lives: domestic, public, political, and intellectual. She earned a law degree in 1933 and joined the Brazilian congress soon after that, being the second woman to occupy that position in the country. Her fight for the rights of women was especially concerned with their professional and educational situation, and she was able to secure many rights for them, including the right to vote, which was incorporated into the Brazilian constitution in 1934. In the politics she quickly achieved the reputation she would never have inside of her laboratory, and her personal correspondences reveal that she felt frustrated with the fact that her political responsibilities would take her away from her scientific career (Letter to Cochran, 1930).[5] Lutz never married or had children, and besides the feminist cause, she dedicated her life to continue her father's scientific research and to preserve his legacy after his death, in 1940. With her father, she learned how to perform field work (figure 4.2). As a secretary of the Brazilian National Museum and a politician, Bertha Lutz had the opportunity to travel to many countries representing the interests of the museum and the Brazilian government. She took advantage of her privileges to build a strong network with scientists around the globe and to help other women pursue their intel-

Figure 4.2. Bertha Lutz and Adolpho Lutz during field work in Rio de Janeiro, 1935. Museu Nacional (Brasil). Seção de Memória e Arquivo. *Fundo Bertha Lutz*, 1927–1968. Reproduced with permission.

lectual endeavors.[6] Only three years before she died, in 1973, Lutz was finally able to have her lifetime project, *Brazilian Species of Hyla*, published by the University of Texas Press, her most prominent contribution to the field of zoology.[7] The fact that the work was written in English and published in the United States suggests that her work as a scientist was recognized abroad long before it was at home. She was never admitted to the Brazilian Academy of Sciences, the main venue related to scientific development at Brazil at that time.[8] She worked for the National Museum for forty-six years and had an impressive career as a scientist, although she is hardly remembered for her participation in the history of sciences of Brazil.

MUTUAL INTERESTS AND FRIENDSHIP: EXCHANGING KNOWLEDGE IN THE SCIENTIFIC COMMUNITY

A recently discovered collection of letters archived at the National Museum of Rio de Janeiro sheds new light on the details about how exactly the relationship between Cochran and Lutz started and how they built a network of collaborators that lasted more than forty years.[9] It is evident from the letters that the connection between them began many years before Cochran traveled to Brazil, in 1935. In fact, according to the documentation found on the Brazilian National Archives, the collaboration between Lutz and Cochran might have started as early as 1919.[10] At that point, both women were just starting their careers in their respective museums and this archival information indicates that they were probably beginning to establish a channel to exchange materials and knowledge between their institutions. By 1926, however, their collaboration was already very well established, and their correspondences indicate that an active and efficient mechanism of scientific exchange was in place. For example, several pieces of correspondence from that year mention that Lutz was consistently sending frogs, turtles, and scientific catalogues to Cochran. These letters also indicate a very close relationship, in which both women shared several aspects of their personal lives, common friends, and interests. The network of contacts both women had constructed also becomes evident in these correspondences, as they mention names such as Maynard Mayo Metcalf and Waldo Schmitt, the former an important collaborator and the latter a senior curator of the Smithsonian Institution.[11] In November 30, 1926, a letter from Cochran to Lutz mentioned superficial matters such as a package that was returned and the compliments she heard from Metcalf about his recent trip to Brazil and the materials he collected there. She also commended the book *Jungle Peace* from Charles William Beebe and his work at the English Guiana with great enthusiasm.[12] As time passed, the correspondence became increasingly more personal and, on February 1, 1928, in a letter to Lutz's father, Cochran wrote:

> Dr Stejneger and I feel that our collection of Brazilian amphibians is far from representative . . . Dr. Stejneger is particularly eager to secure representatives of genera which we do not have and he will deeply appreciate anything you may do to help us to fill out our series. Dr. Remington Kellogg who is now working on the Mexican amphibians desires me to ask if you will send him a copy of your "Observations on the Brazilian Batrachians" . . . and says he in return will send you his work on Mexican amphibians when it is published. The separate may be sent in my care. I am glad to know you have recovered from your illness sufficiently to take up your work on Brazilian frogs again. Please accept my sincerest regards for yourself and give my love to Bertha and tell her I will write to her soon. Sincerely yours, [signed]. (Letter to Adolpho Lutz)

This letter is remarkable because it evidences that the Smithsonian Institution lacked and was very interested in pursuing many specimens of Brazilian amphibians, indicating the importance of the collaboration with the Brazilian museum. It also reveals that Cochran had a well-established channel of communication with Lutz and the Brazilian institution, and that she was working under the supervision and the endorsement of both Stejneger and Kellogg, two of her senior curators at the Smithsonian.[13] From one side, the fact that she was writing on behalf of both men indicates that she was subjected to becoming an "invisible associate," a trap to which most women scientists were exposed, due to the fact that, between the 20s and the 30s, most of them occupied subordinated positions in relation to their male counterparts, regardless of their competence and credentials (Rossiter 268). On the other hand, one could infer that the fact that she positioned herself as an intermediary in the exchanges taking place between the institutions allowed her to become the bridge between Brazil and the United States, a unique position of authority that would allow her to travel there in order to secure the specimens her museum needed just a few years later. In fact, the few women who were able to overcome the trap of remaining mere "invisible associates" often used some sort of "extrascientific assets": "Chief among these additional factors was the enthusiastic backing of powerful and politically astute male colleagues, without whose support even the most meritorious work would go unrewarded" (Rossiter 268). The letter also demonstrates a level of intimacy between Cochran, Adolpho, and Bertha Lutz, evidenced by Cochran's concern with his health and her request to send Bertha "love," promising to write to her soon. The letter corroborates the solid collaboration and exchange of knowledge that took place between Cochran and the Brazilian scientific community in the previous years, suggesting that her scientific expedition to Brazil in 1935 began to be crafted many years earlier.

In 1932 Bertha Lutz received a grant from the Carnegie Corporation and the Endowment for International Peace to travel to the United States and visit fifty-eight museums in twenty different cities in the Midwest and the East Coast. Her purpose was to investigate the educational role of the museums in the country. As a secretary of the National Museum of Rio de Janeiro, Lutz dedicated herself to revise the policies of the institution, instead of performing exclusively administrative tasks. As a result of this trip, she wrote a detailed report in which she analyzed the organization of the institutions she visited, their collections, and educational activities.[14] Curiously, the report of the trip reveals the first evidence of a physical encounter between Lutz and Cochran. She mentioned that she visited Cochran's herpetology lab at the Smithsonian, where they worked together after hours (Função Educativa 75).[15] She also emphasized Cochran's role as a herpetologist at the institution and her position as an assistant curator. The letters also indicate a close friendship evidenced by their discussion of more personal matters. By 1933, the relationship between them was already very personal. For example, in December of that year Cochran wrote to Lutz congratulating her on her law degree, and discussing personal and even frivolous matters, such as her pets and the weather in Washington (Letter to Lutz, 1933). Among the subjects mentioned were Carrie Chapman Catt, the American leader of the feminist suffrage movement and Lutz's involvement with the cause. Lutz often complained about the limited time she had to work on her "hobby" of catching frogs due to the amount of time her political activities required from her (i.e., Letter to Lutz, 1930).

More than merely documenting an increasing exchange of scientific knowledge and specimens and the development of a very personal relationship, the letters provide further details on how Cochran's travel to Brazil was carefully planned and articulated by both women over the course of several years. In fact, Cochran's field expedition to Brazil was a product of their close relationship and mutual interests. Lutz not only used her political influence with the Brazilian government to authorize Cochran's expedition but also persuaded her father to assist Cochran on her enterprise. A letter Cochran wrote to Lutz in June of 1934 discloses many details about the arrangements of her trip to Brazil:

> Your note on May 4 sent by airmail reached me on the 12, but so far I have not yet had your father's note. Dr Stejneger insists upon settling everything to the minutest details before he even discusses the trip with Dr. Wetmore and the other authorities who control the museum's funds. So you can see I am eagerly awaiting the mail which will bring me the plan of the book and the work to be done upon it by me, as outlined by your father. . . . Indeed, I do really think that if you can manage to get that note from your father we have a very good chance to get approval for it. (Letter to Lutz, 1934)

The letter also reveals the several layers of negotiation that made the trip possible and the strategies both women used to overcome the barriers they faced in the scientific community. That is not to say that male scientists did not have to plan and negotiate their field travels with other male scientists. What makes their collaboration remarkable though is the fact that women had rare opportunities to engage in this type of activity, especially at the highly institutional level that Cochran's visit took place. Cochran and Lutz orchestrated the trip to Brazil together, which would only be possible with the agreement and endorsement of an entire male scientific network, which they sought to convince. The letter indicates that Cochran and Lutz relied on Lutz's father's invitation for Cochran to collaborate with him, without which Stejneger would not even consider discussing the subject. Although Cochran was almost certain that she would be able to receive permission to go to Brazil in possession of Lutz's note, she also articulated an extra layer of support. In the same letter, she wrote:

> Dr. Thomas Barbour stopped here in Washington a few weeks ago, just after your letter came and I told him about our plan and he was greatly interested. . . . He is sailing for an inspection of the zoos in South Africa on June 24th and he has plans to stop in Rio on the way. He promised to see you and your father, so please show him the colored plates and tell him just what you plan in regard to having me work with you. I know Dr. Barbour's words carry great weight with both Dr. Wetmore and Dr. Stejneger, so if you get his full cooperation your plan is sure to be carried out. (Letter to Lutz, 1934)[16]

This complicated negotiation exposes the dynamics of power relations implicated in making Cochran's collecting trip possible and how both women conspired to navigate the limitations of their gender to overcome the barriers they had to face. It also confirms Rossiter's argument that women relied on the approval of their male counterparts to be able to overcome the trap of invisibility (268). The letter shows their awareness of their condition as women and that they were complying with what Rossiter calls the realist approach to pursue their endeavors. Rather than protesting and confronting their male counterparts, they patiently conspired to get their compliance to their plan (Rossiter 265).

Cochran's letter also suggests her understanding of the gendered perception of scientific travels and field work: "Mrs. Gaige wrote that she would be very glad to see me to take the trip to Brazil. . . . As you said, being married certainly is a bar to many plans and she certainly does not care to go away without her husband" (Letter to Lutz, 1934).[17] Her remark indicates that remaining single was a subject previously discussed with Lutz, and that they agreed that "being married" imposed a direct limitation to a woman scientist.

Single women had a better chance to excel on their scientific careers and, in fact, discrimination against married women was widely and oftentimes overtly practiced among several academic and government institutions (Rossiter 142). If being single was an advantage for Cochran, she still imagined a field expedition to Brazil as a very masculinized activity, and replicated many of the stereotypes about Latin America previously produced by the travel accounts of her male counterparts:

> Do you think it will be desirable for me to learn how to swim, to shoot, to ride horseback and to speak a few words of Portuguese? I am totally ignorant of all those things and a trip to Brazil seems unthinkable without some of those things. You see, I am speaking as if the trip were already agreed to by the museum. . . . Please give me all the suggestions you can think about preparing myself to do the very most I can to help your father during the short time I shall have to work in Brazil. I shall certainly appreciate every hint you may make as to equipment, both mental and physical, as soon as a definite decision is reached for me to go. I shall familiarize myself with the literature. (Letter to Lutz, 1934)

First, her remarks demonstrate that she imagined Brazil as an exotic and uncivilized place in which not being able to shoot or swim would make survival almost impossible. Second, Cochran's preoccupation with her level of preparation for the trip replicated the gender stereotypes and expectations that prevented most women from taking part in scientific travels and collecting activities. The abilities she listed, which she considered indispensable, were highly masculinized and pointed back to the idea of the male naturalist explorer permeating the travel narratives of the nineteenth century. She seemed not to believe that she was about to have an opportunity to pursue a more independent status as a researcher and even feared her own ignorance. As a woman scientist, she was never trained and, one can infer, never expected to be able to go to the field. Such perception might sound somewhat anachronist considering that she was traveling to Rio de Janeiro, the capital of Brazil at the time of her trip. As Terry Caesar observes, North American travel texts about South America in the twentieth century still reinforced stereotypes of the continent as degraded, exotic, and even romanticized, a blank slate awaiting to be discovered (184).[18] Nonetheless, she knew that the opportunity would be unique, and she was ready to transcend her own gendered condition and beliefs and relied on her friend's advice to do so. While she was replicating some of the gendered stereotypes and expectations of her profession, by implying that she would be able to acquire such skills in a short period of time, she hinted that she did not feel that her condition as a woman would prevent her from performing what she clearly considered more masculine tasks. Thus, her remarks uncovered an instability in the gendered perceptions presented by the difficult position occupied by a woman scientist.

Ultimately, their meticulously designed plan was successful, and in January of 1935, only six months after the aforementioned letter was written, Cochran traveled to Brazil to carry out her first field expedition. This voyage marked the consolidation of a lifetime collaboration that made it possible for Cochran and Lutz to build their careers as scientists in the early twentieth century. Their subsequent correspondences show an exchange of knowledge and a friendship that resulted in several personal and scientific achievements for both women, particularly Cochran, who returned to the United States completely transformed after her voyage. Cochran's travel diary, "Just a Minute, Miss," documented very well her scientific expedition and the transformation she went through in her journey.[19] From her diary, it is possible to further understand the gendered context in which she was ascribed and how her beliefs and experiences shaped and informed her narrative. Similar to the other women travelers analyzed in this book, the complex negotiation that took place in her quest for scientific authority reveals that her travels to Latin America presented an opportunity for her to achieve a transatlantic subjectivity and to attain authority to challenge the limits of her gender.[20] She established both her mobility and narrative presence firmly in her travel account by employing several textual mechanisms in order to ascertain her authority as a traveler and as a scientist.

DORIS COCHRAN'S SCIENTIFIC TRAVELS AND EXPLORATIONS IN BRAZIL

In December of 1935, Cochran received authorization to embark on her first scientific enterprise: a field exploration trip to Brazil. She stayed in the country from January 18 to May 23, 1935, and traveled over one thousand miles through the states of Rio de Janeiro, São Paulo, and Minas Gerais, indicating her willingness to cover as much territory as possible while she was there. The opportunity to go to South America represented a watershed in Cochran's scientific career since it provided her with the chance to leave the laboratory to collect enough material for a lifetime of research on amphibians. But why did she write a diary to document her trip in the first place? Traveling as a scientist of the Smithsonian Institution, her primary goal was to collect specimens and make observations about her field work. Yet, she decided to engage in travel writing to record her experience. As Monica Anderson observes, travel narratives in the nineteenth century were the mediators between scientific enterprises and the general public (36). In the imperial context, travelers published their accounts describing discoveries and revealing new information: "Blank spaces existed not only on the maps of the geographers, but also on the maps or systems of all sciences" (Anderson 36). Although travel narratives did become less popular in the twentieth century, Thompson observes that they could still be used as means to make important contributions to multiple fields of knowledge (*Routledge* 198). Moreover, they still conferred visibility and acknowledgment to the traveler and offered a unique opportunity to textually mark these blank spaces (Anderson 37). Cochran's goal was to inscribe her enterprise on the tradition of travel writing with the intent of propagating her experience beyond the walls of the museum and the scientific community, which would eventually have access to her discoveries through her scientific publications. Moreover, her travel account provided her an opportunity to establish her narrative presence as a traveler. She was looking for the general public's acknowledgment to make sure her enterprise would be remembered in the years to come. She also emphasized that Latin America was a still a blank space to her North American audience: "[Traveling to Brazil] offered me the chance to observe living examples of many perplexing species, as well as to collect material in other groups from a region that was scantly represented in North American Museums" (Intro). Cochran indicated the need to fill a blank space at the Smithsonian museum, considering that its collections lacked the specimens she intended to pursue. At the same time, filling this gap would grant her a place in history beyond the scientific community. By bringing a significant collection to the museum, Cochran attempted to claim a physical space in the male territory of science. By engaging in travel writing, she was claiming a place in the public sphere as a writer of travel narratives: "Because travel narrative is commonly addressed to readers at home, it marks a return, even if it is not officially returned to the sending culture" (Smith XII). However, as a woman, Cochran had to carve her authority as a traveler and a scientist, and her narrative uncovered inconsistencies in her discourse, which were inevitable when one tried to occupy such paradoxical spaces. Her travel diary was a mediator of her roles as a woman, a traveler, and a scientist. As a herpetologist, Cochran was interested in finding new specimens to examine, classify, compare, and name. As a traveler, she wanted to document her experience, record her observations, and "mark the blank spaces." As a woman, she still had to comply with textual parameters and paradigms set by earlier female travel writers: ". . . twentieth-century women travel writers still have to negotiate a world in which certain kinds of knowledge are considered more 'manly' and 'womanly'" (Foster and Mills 88). Similar to women travelers, as Schiebinger explains, women scientists "often live in two worlds—the world of science and the world of womanhood—with very different expectations and outcomes. Strategies to success learned in one world can be lethal in the other" (*Has Feminism* 68). Although women had always been traveling, their travels had always been gendered and situated within complex social, cultural, and historical forces (Smith XIII). In that sense, Cochran's narrative displayed the negotiations and tensions of a woman trying to combine the paradoxical roles of woman, traveler, and scientist.

The title of her diary, "Just a Minute, Miss," presents a perfect example of these paradoxical conflictive discourses that permeated Cochran's narrative: "The clash of feminine and colonial discourses construct texts which are at one and the same time presenting a self which transgresses and which conforms both to patriarchal and colonial discourses" (Mills, *Discourses* 106). Her title alluded to the fact that in the tropics things took much longer to happen than in other places of the world. This rhetoric frequently appeared in earlier travel accounts written by white male Europeans in which the delays in the tropics were repeatedly portrayed as unbearably long, a language often used to represent Latin America as backward and primitive and ultimately meant to justify the necessity of a civilizing mission since the colonial times (Pratt, *Imperial* 144). Adhering to the conventions of travel writing, Cochran explained her intent on writing the diary and her choice of title:

> And so my journal came to be written . . . as a slight reminder in years to come of the luxuriant aspect of tropical nature unrolled before the eyes accustomed to the more restrained beauties of the north temperate zones. That the energies of the punctual Anglo-Saxon temperament contrasted to the calm Latin-American indifferences to the passage of time may finally prove amusing to the reader, thereby alleviating the ponderous effect of too much description and rendering the perusal of this book something more than a mere exercise of will power. (Intro)

A woman traveler and a scientist were roles still unconceivable to her audience in the United States. In an attempt to downplay her transgression, she resorted to the use of a more humorous, feminine narrative voice. By evoking her image as a woman on her title, "Just a Minute, Miss," she deviated the attention of the reader from her use of the masculine scientific discourse or, more precisely, her intention to contribute to the construction of knowledge. Then, although she was writing as a woman scientist performing field work, Cochran managed to justify her use of the prevailing masculine discourse about the tropics as an attempt to simply amuse her readers and make the process of reading her painful scientific writing more pleasant.[21] As she established a position of superiority over the observed, a perspective shared with her readers, she reaffirmed the parameters of cultural supremacy, which often framed travel narratives and conferred credibility to the narrator. Therefore, as Cochran attempted to create her authority as a woman scientist and a traveler, her narrative displayed the residue of imperialist tropes of discovery, based on a sharp contrast between herself and the other: "Women travel writers, like their male counterparts, seek out narrative strategies that allow them to negotiate the pitfalls of reader expectations and contemporary gender norms, often at the expense of cultural sensitivity or solidarity" (Bird 37). Besides, adopting a scientific voice associates women with high-status discourses situating them within a hegemonic scientific tradition. This tradition includes mentioning scientific names, detailing the logistics of collecting specimens, all elements present on Cochran's narrative (Foster and Mills 90). This hegemonic scientific tradition required an authority not necessarily available to a woman traveler, even if she was a scientist herself. Similar to Maria Graham and other colonial travelers of the nineteenth century, aligning herself with imperialist forces was, at least on the surface, an effective way to establish a superiority that could undermine the gender stereotypes that threatened her authority as a narrator and a scientist.

Discoverers and explorers reproduced the cartographies and myths perpetrated by their predecessors (Smethurst 228). Cochran was convinced that Brazil was an exotic place in which she would discover many new species, an unexplored paradise. Although her diary was written in 1935, her travel writing was an open dialogue with similar narratives produced by other travelers, men and women, in the previous century and her travel account reinforced her own expectations as well as the anticipations of her readership. As Hayward observes, with the industrialization that occurred in both the United States and Europe in the twentieth century, Latin America was often represented in travel accounts as "an Edenic retreat from the pressures of civilization," conforming with the prevailing tropes of discovery, which dominated the narratives of the nineteenth century (*Routledge* 367). In fact, the American frontier myth was redeployed in the Latin American context to produce images of empty spaces and childish people inept of economic development (Caesar 181). As a matter of fact, the hegemonic representation of her enterprise becomes very clear from the following passage:

> Since 1838, when the United States Exploring Expedition stopped in Rio bay on its journey around the Horn of the South Pacific, no general collections had been received from that region by my museum. . . . Knowing how very important this general material would be, not only to collect, but also to study in the various departments of the museum, I prepared to take a plant press, seines for fish, traps for small mammals, cotton for stuffing birds, large and small containers for anything from a mosquito to a monkey, and in short, collecting materials of all kinds. (Intro)

The expedition she referred to was nothing less than the most prominent scientific expedition conducted in the nineteenth century, the United States Exploring Expedition, or simply the U.S. Ex., which explored the coast of the

Pacific from 1838 to 1842. The expedition covered more than 80,000 miles and its purpose was to broaden the nation's visibility and foster the development of scientific knowledge. The materials acquired by the U.S. Ex. assisted in the creation of the first collections at the newly founded Smithsonian and many other scientific institutions in the United States.[22] By aligning her own enterprise with the U.S. Ex., Cochran conferred her initiative the same level of importance and implied that she would be able to accomplish similar achievements. She also stressed that she was prepared to collect for all the departments of the museum, as the largest and most prestigious expedition the country ever conducted before had done in 1838. Cochran impersonated a hegemonic scientific authority capable of collecting every specimen, plant or animal, and performing all the tasks that were performed by at least nine scientists and artists on the previous expedition. The grandiosity of her mission, which replicated the imperialist rhetoric of benign possession and domination, was in clear opposition with the fact that she was a woman traveling alone and with considerably limited resources. Establishing her racial and cultural superiority was fundamental to allow her to carry out her ambitious plan to accomplish as much as the U.S. Expedition as well as to meet the expectations of her readership.

Throughout her travel account, Cochran asserted her nationality, the color of her skin, and her networks as powerful assets which allowed her explorations: ". . . as women write home from abroad, they presume to remake the world in the image of the United States, which is to say in the image of the white, Protestant, middle-class values. Women's texts of travel are often arms of nationalism, classicism, racism, the practice of 'othering' in patriarchal definitions of Woman reinforced even if they are sometimes contested" (Schriber 9). In other words, the hegemonic nature of her project relied on the establishment of a racial superiority and the participation on certain Orientalist tropes that authenticated travel narratives (Mills, *Discourses* 139–40). The hierarchy between herself and the Brazilians was in clear alignment with that between Brazil and the United States. Not surprisingly, her renditions of Brazilian people and Brazilian cultural manifestations were often evaluative and served as a textual device to establish her superiority and authority as a narrator. When representing the other as uncivilized and exotic the observer establishes a position of superiority which assimilates the other to her own cultural paradigms (Mills and Foster 94). As a result, Cochran's narrative often depicted Brazilian people in severely homogenized terms and subjected to a collective "they" (Pratt, *Imperial*, 64):

> The crowd is *very* mixed, and in most of the faces negroid influences show up clearly, and probably Indian, although I am less familiar with that racial type, and many of the faces have a hawk-like boldness about the eyes which is found

in southern Europeans. They are not at all a happy-looking race, in spite of the suffusion of negro-blood . . . and do not seem to be able to understand the art of "kidding" at all . . . (23)

It is noteworthy to mention that she emphasized the word "very," referring to the high degree of miscegenation among Brazilians. She was clear to confine the mixture among indigenous people, African, and Southern Europeans, replicating the marginalization of the South of Europe by the North.[23] This association only reinforced the racial inferiority of the Brazilians, and a corresponding inherent cultural and moral inferiority (Anderson 50–51). Besides, their lack of sense of humor dehumanized them, further highlighting their intrinsic inferiority. She compared the people on the streets with the animals of the market, often placing the animals at a higher position: "The market people are a miserable-looking lot. There were plenty of beggars. But all the mules—and there are many—are quite fat and handsome, while each team has its merry jangling bells, which add much to the gayety of the streets" (21). However racist such comments might sound, it is necessary to situate Cochran's text as a "reflection and mediation of the society which has produced it" (Foster and Mills 97). By clearly marking her racial superiority, which situates women travel writers within class and race, rather than gender parameters, she was also setting herself firmly within her own culture, "with all the privileges which that position entailed" (Foster and Mills 94–96).

Cochran often represented the Brazilian people and their culture as aesthetic objects, another form of discourse which also served to align women with the imperial project. By employing the high-status discourse of aesthetics, women travelers showed their erudition and capacity of observation, placing themselves on par with male travelers (Foster and Mills 91). Exoticizing or idealizing the other in terms of painting metaphors entailed a position of superiority to the observer, who assumed the authoritative position of eyewitness. For example, on one occasion, while having dinner with her travel companions, she wrote:

> The meal was excellent and quite clean. . . . But the faces lit by candlelight as we sat around the table suggested those of "Fra Lippo Lippi" by Browning, and I wished I had had the gift and the materials to record what I saw. The mysterious darkness of the kitchen, illuminated only by the queer, banked stove in which our food was cooking, watched by an old, old negro woman,—the smiling little native girl in a red dress and bare feet moving noiselessly to serve us,—the candle stuck in the top of a Caxambu bottle lighting the face of Joaquin intent on his beans, with the owner of the armazem and Dr. M.L.'s chauffer next to him, both of them talking endlessly, then Dr. D. next to me, very gallant and smiling and entirely sweet . . . and me in my corner not saying much and wishing violently for a cup of hot tea. (91–92)

Although Cochran implied lacking the skills to describe the scene, she proceeded with a meticulous rendition of the dinner table. Her representation, introduced by her mention of "Fra Lippo Lippi" by Robert Browning (1812–1889), replicated his discussion about the role of the artist when representing reality. On this dramatic monologue written in 1855, Lippo Lippi, a painter and narrator of the poem, struggles between his desire to represent the real world and his master's contend that he should improve reality in his art. He ended the poem revealing a plan to please both him and his master: he decided to portray a religious scene, but to include a picture of himself watching the scene (Corson 248–60). By employing the high-class discourse of aesthetic to describe the dinner table, although apparently replicating the hegemonic rhetoric of racial superiority, she was challenging the very authenticity of such representations. The lavish details, including elements of local color such as the "caxambu bottle," a famous brand of bottled water founded in Minas Gerais in 1714, and her mention of the word "armazem," small businesses common in the countryside of Brazil where travelers often found food and other supplies, confer a strong sense of reality to her rendition. The conflict between the painter's own desires and the demands of the world replicate, to a great extent, Cochran's own situation as a woman scientist, confirmed by her representation of herself, at the corner, observing the scene. However, just as Lippo Lippi ended up being discovered by his master, she was also subjected to being uncovered. Then, even if the representation could suggest her appreciation of the difference rather than criticism, by revealing her violent wish for a cup of tea, she reinforced the superiority of her own culture and, by extension, her presence on her narrative.

However, the racial and cultural superiority Cochran tried to establish in her travel account was often betrayed by her disposition to understand and accept the other. As Foster and Mills observe, "details of unfamiliar dishes and willingness to try, even to enjoy, them may express a challenge to cultural hegemonies" (95): "To pass time before our friends were due to arrive, the Botanist suggested getting a water-ice from the street-vendor. I was not much in favor of it, as he looked very dirty, but she got the ices in small flower-pot-shaped cones . . . and they really were quite refreshing" ("Just a Minute" 60). Her representations of the domestic realm also may offer an opportunity for cultural exchange as well as a destabilization of the hegemonic superiority Cochran sought to reproduce:

> Dr. L. introduced me to my first tropical mango, which was delicious, but which one must devour in rather primitive but efficient methods, by slicing with a knife on either side of the enormous pit, turning these slices inside out and sucking the pulp from them, then sucking the pit itself until the two or three tablespoonful of turpentine-flavored juice are extracted. Dr. L. remarked that the best way

to eat a mango is in a bathing suit in a bathtub, and I am nearly ready to agree with him! (20)

The depiction of the mango as a strange fruit and the detailed primitive ritual needed to consume it makes it sound like they were at some sort of exotic indigenous tribe. By taking part in the ritual, she challenged her own hegemonic superiority. However, the destabilization of her narrative was strategic because it also served as part of a broader project meant to confer a more feminized tone to her account.

When describing her routine at the Brazilian laboratory, besides including details about the scientific work she was performing there, Cochran insisted on balancing what would otherwise be a highly masculinized space with more feminized tropes. To normalize her presence among the male scientists at the museum, she included details about the daily meals they served and her observations about the menu:

> At twelve o'clock he [Dr. Lutz] took me to lunch in a little unscreened summer house. . . . About fifty or sixty doctors and their assistants clad in white smocks were already seated at the little tables. . . . A little waiter brought in a plate of rice and some black bean soup which is ladled out onto the rice, the beans then mashed, the whole mixture sprinkled with a spoonful of "farinha" which absorbs the bean soup and makes it into a paste that can be eaten with a fork and which is amazingly good! (19)[24]

Besides offering details about the menu, and remarking her appreciation and willingness to try it, she placed herself side by side with "about fifty or sixty doctors and their assistants" (19). This scene represents a microcosm of her experience in Rio, and how her interactions with the Brazilian male scientific community took place. Instead of trying to compete with them, she kept herself within the boundaries of her gender by inserting a more feminine perspective, whereas she was still sitting at their table and taking part in their scientific conversations. In other words, by employing the feminized trope of domesticity in a highly masculinized public space, she destabilized the public and private dichotomy and challenged gender boundaries. Moreover, she established a narrative presence able to occupy very paradoxical spaces at once. By using these strategies, then, Cochran was able to assert her presence within her narrative of mobility, which eventually would set the ground for the transformation of herself upon her return to the United States. Although in many instances her diary replicated the hegemonic rhetoric of racial superiority, her heterogeneous narrative also reveals a complex negotiation of her gendered roles.

CATCHING FROGS AFTER DINNER: TRANSCENDING THE LIMITS OF GENDER

Cochran's engagement with various travel writing traditions resonates with her difficulty to find a place for herself, and her narrative strategies reveal her awareness of her condition as a woman scientist and traveler. Motivated by her scientific enterprise, her intent was to collect specimens for her museum, going back to the natural historian task of locating species, extracting them from their surroundings, naming them, and placing them in their appropriate spot, in this case, the Smithsonian (Pratt, *Imperial* 31). Presenting herself as an explorer, Cochran's diary is full of scientific nomenclatures, and Linnaean italics pervade her narrative. She acted as a Linnaean emissary and her account resembles a narrative of travel "organized by the cumulative, observational enterprise of documenting geography, flora and fauna. The encounter with nature, and its conversion into natural history, forms the narrative scaffolding" (Pratt, *Imperial* 51). Representing the traveler as an explorer meant to reproduce the image of a male hero, and Cochran's narrative replicated this rhetoric in many instances. Thus, becoming an explorer was a male privilege, an image constructed based on gendered principles that reflected patriarchy. Nevertheless, her travel account also displayed a similar instability and heterogeneity that Mills identified in her analysis of the nineteenth-century British women travelers. Pratt suggests the term "anti-conquest" to refer to the rhetoric employed by male travel writers representing their enterprises as innocent and benign interventions all the while asserting their hegemony and superiority. To Pratt, this kind of narrative is inseparable from the "seeing man ... he whose imperial eyes look out and possess" (*Imperial* 7). Cochran subverted this highly masculinized rhetoric to portray a female version of this anti-conquest rhetoric described by Pratt. By relying on male protection, subverting the image of the "seeing man," and feminizing her collecting activities, Cochran's narrative accommodated the uncomfortable presence of a woman impersonating the hero/explorer.

Whether as travelers or scientists, women frequently took advantage of male protection so that they would remain within the limits of their gender constraints. A woman traveling alone was inevitably subjected to questions about her safety and morals and often benefited from the presence of a male travel companion (Harper 18). Likewise, a woman scientist, as history of science has shown, had a much better chance of success through male collaboration, either with a husband, father, or a male mentor. In fact, women who managed to become integrated within the mainstream of the male-dominated world of sciences managed to do so by relying on male protection and mentorship, usually associated with "a progressive male mentor who liberated himself from prevailing gender prejudice and transcended his structural position as a potential oppressor. . . . The effect of such mentor-related integration is that the scientific record of these women will tend to reflect the integrative collaboration rather than the precarious position in science they otherwise would have faced if they had tried to advance without such a protective cover" (Abir-Am and Outram 9–10). Being single and lacking male protection at the Smithsonian, Cochran found the opportunity for collaboration with a male mentor in Brazil.[25] Bertha Lutz and her father, as seen in the letter above, were instrumental in making her voyage possible. Furthermore, Cochran's relationship with them facilitated the prospect of ascertaining both her presence and mobility within the contact zone, both necessary conditions to the establishment of her transatlantic subjectivity.

While in Rio de Janeiro, Cochran was given an apartment to live in the same building where Adolpho Lutz lived with his daughter, making clear that both women were under his protection and mentorship. In fact, during her stay in Brazil, Cochran had access to Lutz's research and infrastructure and was able to work directly with him at the Oswaldo Cruz Institute.[26] Lutz's team assisted Cochran in her field work by planning the excursions and sharing collecting techniques, enabling her mobility across the space. While she stayed in Rio, she would alternate her daily activities with Adolpho Lutz at the Institute with collecting specimens in expeditions around the city. She trusted his judgment and expertise and relied on his guidance to learn how to become a successful field collector. On her first field experience, she commented: "We got a new kind of frog at every stop, and Dr. L. has certainly done some thorough collecting to know where everything is to be found" (24–26). Cochran admitted that Lutz's knowledge was essential to the success of her trip. Moreover, she represented him as a mentor who offered her protection and served her as a bridge to blur the gendered scientific boundaries to which she was subjected. In several entries, she offered many details about their close association and revealed a level of intimacy very close to a familial relationship: "We did not go to the Institute, but Dr. L. dictated some notes on collecting frogs, and then it was lunch time" (24). In fact, while at the Institute, she was always following his directions and her main tasks were to take notes on life histories of frogs from Dr. L.'s dictation, drawing and sketching the tadpoles they collected on a daily basis: "I took my watercolors to the Institute as Dr. L. wants me to sketch the colors of some frogs, still alive, that we got at the Recreio . . . I made two color sketches and part of another, and Dr. L. seems astonished that I can work so quickly, as his own artist, Antonio P., is very slow" (50). While her narrative emphasizes her more feminine abilities, such as watercolor painting, it also evidences her expertise as a scientist capable of drawing living species very accurately and much faster than Lutz's male artist (Mills, *Discourses* 175). Also, she highlighted the fact she was working under Lutz's request and supervision. By depicting a relationship that extrapolated the limits of their professional collaboration, however, she somehow transgressed certain gender hierarchies. For example, after having dinner at his apartment, Lutz invited her to go to the terrace to see the stars on the roof top of the building. She commented: "We made an amusing pair, he in slippers, purple-and-pink pajamas and a felt hat on his scholarly head, me in my black kimono and shuffling green sandals. We sat on the roof for nearly an hour, where it was very pleasant to look down on the brightly lighted Avenida only a block distant, and on the twinkly lights from Niteroi across the bay" (62). In the twentieth century, the image of the scientist that had emerged from the professionalization of science that took place in the previous century was that of a male white man wearing a white robe, whose personality ranged from heroic masculinity to deep eccentricity (Schiebinger, *Has Feminism* 76). It is evident from the passage that their level of intimacy went beyond a mere professional collaboration as they sat in their pajamas on the rooftop of the building for nearly an hour. By depicting Lutz in purple-and-pink pajamas, she dismantled the image of the scientist in the white robe, which is nonetheless subtly recognized when she mentioned his scholarly head. The mocking tone she used cleverly challenged the hierarchies that dictated their mentorship-apprentice relationship and suggested a more equal partnership, subtly reaffirming her presence and capacity to exchange knowledge with him.

After staying two months in Rio exploring the rainforest under Adolpho Lutz's mentorship, on March 8, 1935, Cochran traveled over four hundred miles by train accompanied by Joaquim Venancio, Adolpho Lutz's assistant, and Dr. D., a younger scientist from the Institute, to the state of Minas Gerais.[27] There she explored several locations with the assistance of other scientists from a local branch of the Oswaldo Cruz Institute. The mountains of the central and eastern areas of the state are covered with little vegetation, and its rocky terrain was the perfect site to collect specimens very different from the ones in Rio, many of which had never been described before by scientists at the Smithsonian or elsewhere. As opposed to the familial environment she had experienced in Rio de Janeiro, now she was a woman traveling alone to the countryside with several male companions. Thus, she unintentionally impersonated the role of solitary traveler because a woman traveling unaccompanied by others of her own race would often be perceived as being alone by her audience (Foster and Mills 96). Self-mockery then served as means to guarantee that her wellbeing was not threatened: "We did not need our flashlights to see the road, and Dr. D— began to show the effects by humming Liszt and talking about love. But I felt perfectly safe, for I knew he was thinking of his Nitia, and not about the fat and freckled female striding along by his side" (135). By refusing to present herself in danger, she countered the idea that women traveling alone were seen as sexualized (Foster and Mills 175). As Mills observes in her analysis of Mary Kingsley's travel diary, she often resorted to humor to undermine the conventions of male travel narratives and combined a non-assertive and conforming feminine character with humor (*Discourses* 163).

Pratt suggests that Kingsley is in fact one of the few female travelers who employed a sort of masculine heroic discourse of exploration and discovery: "Through irony and inversion, she builds her own meaning-making apparatus out of the raw materials of the monarchic male discourse of domination and intervention. The result . . . is a monarchic female voice that asserts its own kind of mastery even as it denies domination and parodies power" (*Imperial* 213). Cochran also portrayed panoramic scenes in her narrative and occupied the position of the seeing-man when describing the landscapes: "The moon had just risen behind the rocks over the river bank, and although slightly on the wane, it gave everything a slivery overlay of radiance impossible to describe. The stars gave way before it in the east, but in the west they were bright as ever, especially a deep-blue one that had twinkled at me the whole evening" ("Just a Minute" 135). Once more, Cochran resorted to an aesthetic portrayal of the scene. Her depiction of the sky highlighting the variety of colors, the moon on the center, the stars on the west and east for a moment resemble the rhetoric of the Monarch-of-All-I-Survey described by Pratt, a vivid imperial trope in which "the value of the sight is expressed in terms of esthetic pleasure" (Pratt, *Imperial* 205–6). Nevertheless, the mastery dynamics implied in the relationship between the seer and the sight was disrupted by the presence of a twinkling star, which followed Cochran thorough the evening. Instead of possessing, Cochran was possessed, observed, and protected. She further subverted this imperial aesthetic discourse, using again the same irreverence and irony employed by Kingsley in many instances. As she mocked her own enterprise, she also demystified her predecessors' mastery and fantasy of possession (Pratt, *Imperial* 215). In another instance, she stated:

> We passed a swamp just at dusk, and I saw a heron sitting motionless on a stub, mirrored in the clear, glasslike water which also reflected the perfect range of gray-blue sky shot thru rays of gold from the setting sun. . . . Well, the descent from the sublime to the ridiculous was rather rapid, as such descents most generally are. In ten minutes we had crossed the railroad tracks . . . and were bumping down a narrow grass grown road thru the fields. . . . (68)

Here, the aestheticized representation of the landscape was abruptly demystified and replaced by a mocking tone which went rapidly from contemplating nature to being figuratively almost swallowed by it. In that sense, Cochran's narrative attempted to replicate the "masterful comic irreverence" inaugurated by Kingsley: "Kingsley creates value by . . . rejecting the textual mechanisms values in the discourse of her male predecessors" (Pratt, *Imperial* 214). As Kingsley, Cochran "used a feminine discourse indirectly in ways that challenged many masculine explorer conventions in an effort to create a space for women naturalists in the field" (Harper 211). However, while Kingsley tried to domesticate and normalize the jungle, Cochran emphasized its exoticness as well as her own exoticness, while normalizing her presence there.

Harper points out that Kingsley's narrative presented her travels as an extension of the woman's sphere, the jungle being a non-transgressive, proper place for women (214). Elaborating on Harper's argument, instead of simply domesticating the wildness of the jungle, Cochran presented the possibility of living in two different but parallel worlds which were not necessarily exclusive. To some extent, she assumed the role of social explorer described by Pratt to assert her presence as a woman in the Brazilian society (*Imperial* 157). As she attended dinners and parties, she also performed field work as two separate but co-existing activities. She accomplished that by switching roles throughout the narrative, as she juggled between the tasks of collecting with her male counterparts and having lunch with their wives: "I had been invited to lunch by Mrs. B, and I barely had time to jump into a thin dress before 12:15pm when I was supposed to meet her. I had to hurry back into my collecting clothes right after lunch, for Mrs. D's father had loaned us his car and we were all to go to the Morro Velho gold mine" (82). After a morning of collecting and the afternoon exploring the mine, she had dinner with Dr. M. L.: "The dinner was over at 8pm and then I hurried upstairs and again jumped into my outing clothes, as Dr. M. L. wished to take me out to a good frog-collecting place near the country club. . . . Dr. M. L. and I had great fun dipping for tadpoles. I caught six adult frogs of three species, and a lot of tads and some mollusks and dragonfly larvae" (85). While Kingsley tried to portray the jungle as a safe space for women and played down her unfeminine role as an explorer by keeping her skirt, Cochran cross-dressed to make it clear that she was in fact performing two different roles in two different spheres. In fact, the photograph of herself wearing her collecting outfit depicts a highly masculinized image (figure 4.3). Besides the fact that she was wearing male pants and a very masculine hat, the relaxed position of her body, laying against the wall with her legs crossed, shows that she was confident and comfortable in such a role. Her gaze facing the camera and her subtle smile further emphasized her self-assurance. It is highly doubtful that Cochran would adopt this same position if she were wearing a female dress.

Figure 4.3. Cochran wearing her collecting outfit in Minas Gerais, 1935.
Smithsonian Institution Archives RU 7151 Box 7 Folder 11—1934. Reproduced with permission.

As a matter of fact, proper attire seemed to protect her from being perceived as too exotic within the domestic sphere, which could potentially undermine her femininity. The passage below describes a moment in which, returning from collecting, she was careless when choosing her outfit. Resorting to a self-mocking tone, she remarked:

> I forgot to say that when I changed my wet clothes, I put on my gold blouse, and without thinking I added my silver raincoat and hat, as my other hat was soaked, and with the red color that my face always gets by exercise, I must have looked awfully funny, at least, the children thought so, for they laughed out loud when they saw me, and then . . . had to pinch my coat all over, as if I were a visitor from Mars. . . . Altogether it was quite amusing, and for a while I knew how Barnum and Bailey felt when their circus hit a new town. It's great—for a while—but I prefer mediocrity at that! (112)

This passage describes a particularly meaningful moment of encounter in the contact zone. Her depiction of herself wearing a silver rain coat and hat brings to mind the image of "alien," which seems to be precisely what she was trying to convey. By evoking Barnum and Bailey, an American traveling circus founded in 1871 and famous all over the world, she suggested the extraordinariness of her own image. As Linda Simon observes, historically and across experiences and cultures, the circus has been perceived as "dazzling and fantastic, a living cabinet of wonders, a theatre of the improbable and even the impossible . . ." (41). Acrobats, tiny and gigantic men and women, from the bizarre to the extraordinary, the circus seemed like a free arena to display anything out of the ordinary. Her choice to depict herself as an "alien" associated with the cultural myth of the circus through the eyes of the other presented another possibility to represent herself, one that could potentially invert certain expected cultural roles. Traveling both as a woman and as a scientist, Cochran had to negotiate boundaries to insert herself in two traditions that were perceived as exclusively male. This example shows that she was aware that presenting herself as too exotic, even if she had enjoyed it for a moment, could undermine her authority as a scientist, and she was not willing to risk that. In other words, the passage confirms that cross-dressing between her activities in spaces perceived as male and female was an essential part of her strategy to assert her authority in the narrative. As a matter of fact, the strategy of protecting her femininity while performing field work proved to be effective and provided her opportunities to positively interact with male peers and female friends and build a strong network of collaborators. She used her role as a scientist as an asset when relating to other women: ". . . the registry clerk told me that an English lady who lives at the hotel wanted to meet me . . . Mrs. B—, . . . She is going to be very helpful with suggestions, and she in turn seemed to get a good deal of amusement out of my naturalist tendencies" (78–79). By identifying herself as a "lady with naturalist tendencies" she reaffirmed both her feminine and her scientific personas as possible co-existing roles, although performed differently across the spaces she inhabited. Besides preserving her image as a woman, she also found a more feminized form of practicing her collections, destigmatizing the belief that women could not perform such activities.

Cochran and the Botanist: Collecting Frogs as Women's Business

"Just a Minute, Miss" reveals the details of the relationship between Cochran and Bertha Lutz as both friends and women working as scientists in the field. Cochran referred to Lutz from the very beginning of her narrative and granted her a central role. However, in the diary Bertha Lutz was not the well-known feminist activist who was fighting for the rights of women in Brazil. Rather, she was the Botanist. In fact, the diary does not make any references to her political activities or her position at the National Museum of Rio de Janeiro. This might imply that Cochran did not want to be associated with the feminist movement nor did she want to associate her trip or her collecting activities with the feminist agenda. Also, she avoided any indirect endorsement to Lutz's feminist activities, only emphasizing her scientific skills and interests. Besides, and more importantly, the choice of the word "botanist" suggests that Cochran might have preferred to refer to her by her authority in her own field. The botanist was portrayed as an experienced collector alongside with Joaquim, their black male companion and friend: "These frogs are very agile, and it is much harder to get them than to catch United States frogs. We got two big *Thorofa miliaris*, and the male pricked at my hand with his thumb-spurs in a quite peevish manner. Not many of the frogs we saw got away, thanks to the Botanist" (31–32). Besides, she deliberately added another expert to her expedition, forging a more professional status to their enterprise. Then, beyond their intimate association, the two of them formed a team of specialists united by their professional endeavors. Thus, besides portraying their very close personal relationship, the narrative also focuses on their activities as professional female scientists performing field work while attending to their demands as social explorers in the Brazilian society. Their main goal was to collect frogs, and their collecting incursions served to confer both Cochran and Lutz a strong scientific authority in the narrative.

Collecting new specimens had a central role for the naturalist: "The aesthetic power of specimens and the adventure to collect them in the field were motivations as basic to most naturalists as their desire to discover the order behind nature's wonderful complexity" (Larsen 376). By the same token, field notes were an important part of the task of collecting specimens since they provided details about its specific location and living conditions. Particularly, describing new species entailed meticulous details about where and how they were collected (Larsen 362). Regardless of its apparent innocence, the naturalist mission was a hegemonic project seeking to classify the world within a Eurocentric perspective and it was a highly masculinized activity. Cochran and Lutz, then, subverted this masculinized space of field collection, and instead of going to remote places or to the jungle alone, their collecting activities many times took place at private properties on the surroundings of Rio de Janeiro.[28] Instead of adventuring to the unknown, new specimens could be secured by exploring known and familiar places: "The limitation of women's mobility, in terms both of identity and space, has been in some cultural contexts a crucial means of subordination. Moreover, the two things—the limitation on mobility in space, the attempted consignment/confinement to particular places on the one hand, and the limitation on identity on the other—have been crucially related" (Massey 179). Cochran's and Lutz's ability to perform field work despite their relative limited mobility possibilities posed by their gender empowered their scientific practice and created a space that paradoxically offered them more freedom.

Even if they were performing their collection activities in the backyard of mansions or on rural properties, Cochran refused to portray their collection space as an extension of the domestic sphere, preferring to emphasize the need to switch roles when performing field work, reinforcing the idea that she was performing two complementary roles:

> Supper was a most sumptuous candle-lit affair with an attentive butler. About 9:30pm the Botanist decided to go collecting in the swamp. Although it was still raining heavily, so we put on our riding clothes and boots, and with our lanterns and headlamps left the house. . . . It was wonderful walking through the night, with the sound of the sea breaking just a little way off, and our lights flashing here and there over the shinning rocks on which armies of Bromeliads clung, and all tall trees spreading ghostly parasite-lined branches against the sky in the glare of our lamps. (44)

Her need to wear the right outfit and carry the right equipment reinforced the idea of mobility between two different spaces. Once outside, the space was greatly amplified, as they walked through the night. In a blink of an eye, she transported herself and her reader from a sumptuous dinner to the most exotic jungle. As the exploration progressed, the enduring and dangerous nature of a male scientific exploration emerged in the narrative:

> We turned away from the sea . . . to the edge of the swamp where we heard a fine chorus of frogs. Joaquim strode in wielding his machete, and the Botanist and I followed him, testing our way at every step, for the Lord only knows how deep the water might have been in some places. . . . Huge ferns ten feet tall towered above us, great snaggy vines with terrible thorns an inch long always had to be watched for and avoided, some of the tree trunks also bristled with thorns so that you couldn't put your hand down, while others had nice, smooth, lichen-covered bark that could be picked off to show whole regiments of ants, and sometimes a few daddy-long-legs and spiders as well. . . . The swamp was very beautiful, but the mosquitos were quite troublesome and at midnight the Botanist said she was getting chilled, so we came back to the house and let ourselves in by the back gate. (45)

No passage could offer a better example of the kind of rhetoric Cochran was using and what she was trying to accomplish. She made it sound like the scene was taking place at some unexplored swamp in a remote site somewhere at the farthest reaches of the globe; the image of the machete striking the heavy vegetation, the danger of the swamp, the thorns, the chorus of the frogs, all resemble the expeditions of the male explorers to the unknown. Similar to the example analyzed in the previous section, possessing was portrayed as a mere fantasy in which the image of the explorer/adventurer was deconstructed right away, by the mere presence of the mosquitoes, which abruptly interrupted her fantasy of possession and domination. As much as it may sound ironic and almost pathetic, the collecting activities performed by Cochran and Lutz in private gardens were in fact as productive as the collecting expeditions to the countryside with her male companions. On the evening mentioned above, the group was able to catch at least twelve new species of frogs, including the *Hyla Faber*, the species Lutz dedicated her life to study. In that sense, performing field work in private properties was more than simply a narrative subversion and demystification of the space of scientific explorations: it also produced pragmatic benefits. Thus, Cochran asserted her strong narrative presence by subverting her apparent limited mobility and performing field work across the spaces to which she had access, leveraging these opportunities to generate new knowledge.

Although Cochran preserved the adventurous nature of field work, sometimes she employed a more infantile tone to emphasize their femininity and the possibility of having fun while performing their collecting activities: "The Botanist was feeling in good spirit, so after dinner we ran down to the beach and picked up a lot of sponges, algae and shells thrown up by the recent storm, and I caught a nice, lively, nippy crab . . ." (47). This more feminized way to portray their relationship while practicing such a masculinized activity provided a space for Cochran and Lutz to perform their work in a very particular, yet assertive way. As opposed to her male counterparts, both women felt a certain sentimental attachment to the subject of their research. In her narrative, for example, Cochran often showed compassion toward the landscape and specimens she collected, suggesting a highly feminized scientific practice. For example, when collecting the *Hylas* with Lutz, a culminating moment of scientific discovery in the narrative as they had just uncovered a completely new species, she commented: ". . . on the last nest we saw a female frog sitting, clutching the brim with her long disked toes and fingers, and googling at the light. Such maternal solicitude should be rewarded by continued freedom, so we did not collect her" ("Brazil Bound").[29] This powerful representation of the courageous and defiant behavior of the female frog, who refused to leave her eggs even at the imminent risk of being caught, inspired Cochran and Lutz to empathize with her and feel compelled to reward her attitude. This highly feminized approach is evident not only in Cochran's diary but also in other popular scientific articles she wrote. For example, in 1932 she published an editorial at the *National Geographic Magazine* in which she anticipated this feminized approach to herpetology even before she had performed field collections. The purpose of the article titled "Our friend, the frog" was to explain the intricacies of the animal to the general public. She invited her reader to come to the ravine to contemplate the beauty of the frogs in their natural habitat, describing their colors, the texture of their skins, and the unique features of their bodies. Interestingly, she gave further attention to the agency and non-passive attitude of the female frogs, undermining the gendered conceptions of her non-professional readership. The female frogs, although not singing along with the males, "do not occupy themselves continuously in listening to the chorus in which they cannot participate" (Cochran, "Our Friend" 630). Instead, they leaped and ate insects very skillfully. Similar to the characteristics often attributed to dogs, she represented the frogs in very humanized terms, and described them with adjectives such as intelligent, enthusiastic, and strong willed. Not surprisingly, Cochran also suggested that they could be great pets and explained how they would survive in captivity and make great companions: "Frogs in captivity frequently delight and surprise their owners by their vocalist prowess. They appreciate the radio program, and there is something in the sound of the xylophone which invariable sets the little cricket-frogs to piping. A political speech likewise elicits considerable comment, no matter what the platform may be!" (Cochran, "Our Friend" 649). She made it sound like the frogs could be as good pets as dogs, responding to the environment in very particular and entertaining ways. Furthermore, her article reveals that, despite her feminized way to approach herpetology, she possessed a vast knowledge of the subject, from anatomical to behavioral. In fact, in many other articles and in the personal correspondence she exchanged with Lutz, it is evident that they indeed kept the animals as pets. Their love for them transcended their scientific interest, further emphasizing this very feminized attachment toward them. On a letter to Lutz, she wrote: "I must say goodnight. The frogs in the pool have sung loudly all day. Perhaps they were sending their love to you" (Letter to Lutz, 1942). As scientists, this unusual compassion toward the animals certainly sets them apart from more masculinized forms of scientific practices. That is not to say that men would not feel compassion or keep their own object of study as pets. They certainly could feel similar attachment. But it is very unlikely that they would make such feelings evident in their writings or scientific practices at the risk of undermining their credibility. For Cochran, on the other hand, the feminization of herpetology was a less threatening and competitive way to approach the subject. Additionally, it provided a unique discursive framework within which Cochran would disseminate her knowledge on herpetology to the general public. As a matter of fact, when she returned to the United States from her travels to Brazil in 1935 she was definitely not the same woman who had departed from her country just a few months earlier. The incredible notoriety she achieved in the public opinion upon her return was evident in the press, and she was invited to give several interviews exhibiting the materials she collected as trophies. Her remarks on these interviews relied on the newly acquired authority she obtained on her trip, considering the adventurous nature of her enterprise. In that sense, her travel narrative also comprised this transformation of herself into the "Frog Lady."[30]

ALTERNATE VISIBILITY: THE FROG LADY IN COCHRAN'S TRAVEL NARRATIVE AND IN THE PRESS

"Just a Minute, Miss" portrayed the experience of traveling and performing field work as a rite of passage for Cochran, revealing the process she went through until she became the "Frog Lady" who was acclaimed upon her return to the United States. As she asserted her narrative presence, the meaning of her movements, and the increased potential these movements acquired, the representation of herself within the narrative also changed. Referring back to the aforementioned letter Cochran wrote to Lutz in 1934, she anticipated that collecting specimens in Brazil would be a hazardous and difficult undertaking, and she worried about her lack of skills to carry out the work.

This concern highlighted her complete ignorance regarding field exploration and about South America beyond what she had learned from the books she read. As Cochran explored Brazil, her travel account stressed the empirical knowledge she acquired in her explorations. By moving from one collecting site to another, she attained more experience, becoming more comfortable to perform field work. She also became gradually more confident to make decisions, plan itineraries, and suggest collecting techniques as the narrative progressed. Her transformation was closely related with the establishment of her narrative presence and the consequent authority she acquired as a travel writer and as a scientist.

When she had just arrived in Brazil, her narrative underlined the fact that her knowledge, at that point, was mainly restricted to books and the constraints of the walls of the museum: ". . . for most of the fifteen years during which I had been on the staff of the United States National Museum, I had been studying the fauna of the West Indies, which the zoology books tell us has a great deal in common with that of tropical South America" (Intro). She added that, given this situation, she anticipated that the opportunity to travel to Brazil would be an invaluable experience for her. On her very first few weeks in Rio de Janeiro, as clarified above, she came under the protection and mentorship of Adolpho Lutz, accompanying him to the Institute Oswaldo Cruz Institute and making short excursions, which served as her preparation to become more independent in the following months. These field work expeditions were always planned by Lutz and Cochran never went alone to collect specimens, as she was always escorted by somebody from his team. When undertaking her first excursion with Adolpho Lutz, she wrote: "Dr. L. concluded to go collecting on Tijuca after lunch, and although I had brought no outfit from my apartment, I prepared a few glass vials and three collecting bags, seized my raincoat and sneakers and was ready to go. The trip was marvelous in spite of the rain, for it was my first real experience with a tropical jungle" (25).

Her travel away from Rio de Janeiro to Minas Gerais represented a clear expansion of her collecting space, as she moved from the relatively safer and familial protection of Lutz, to a more independent position. Geographically, Minas Gerais also represented an opportunity of new scientific findings for her. There she proved to be substantially more comfortable in the field and described her collecting activities with more authority and confidence: "I worked as quickly as I could . . . before we quit I was getting one in about twenty-five [frogs]" (81). Barely resembling who she had been when she arrived in Rio just a few weeks earlier, there she impersonated the explorer undertaking a real adventure: "I lay on the pit of my stomach on the slanting sharp edge of a rock, alternatively holding the light for Joaquim and jabbing with the forceps at the beetles myself. It was a great sport, kicking one's legs into the darkness to maintain the proper balance, and imagining a new species (or genus!) at every new find" (90). Besides portraying her incredible physical disposition and emotional excitement to collect and find new specimens, she worked alongside Joaquim, employing unconventional techniques to secure these new specimens. In fact, her relationship with "the champion frog catcher," her traveler companion, was instrumental as he mentored her as these transformations took place. Joaquim, a black man, did not have formal education, but he was considered an expert on herpetology by both Bertha and Adolpho Lutz, and later by Cochran in her diary and many of her later scientific publications. He was also praised by many other scientists of the Oswaldo Cruz Institute for his intelligence, expertise, and ability to find and catch any kind of animal in the field.

Throughout the narrative, her relationship with him becomes an account of the exchange of knowledge in the contact zone. Joaquim was neither white nor a scientist, and his marginalized condition placed him in more equality with Cochran. While Adolpho Lutz represented a male mentor, Joaquim was a peer with whom she could truly exchange knowledge and experience: "I have taught Joaquim a few good things about collecting, but I am sure he has taught me a great many more . . ." (89). By acknowledging Joaquim's expertise, even though he was not a professional scientist, Cochran, once again, challenged the image of the male scientist in a white robe. His techniques, many times improvised, proved to be effective in the field: "Joaquim cut me a stick and showed me how to poke the yellow leaves in search of *Dendrophryniscus* (small frogs)" (156). The symbiotic relationship between him and the animals made it impossible for her to think about Brazilian frogs without associating them with Joaquim and her experiences with him. He taught Cochran how to observe, connect, and see the frogs in a very different manner. When trying to collect some *Elosia*, a small and agile species of frog, she commented:

> They were much too agile to catch—for me, at any rate— but I sat on the edge of the tank and watched them come up to breathe, and then climb straight up the concrete walls for several inches above the water and cling there, and even lunge at a fly or two that happened to wander their way. Joaquim got some later with a hollow bamboo tube he succeeded in getting over them after they dived, as they were much less wary under water. (159)

After the passage above she commented that only by patiently observing the behavior of the frog for several minutes, they were able to see a pattern which led Joaquim to develop a novel technique to catch the animal. Joaquim's non-technical and empirical knowledge was essential in the field, and Cochran learned from the relationship with him a new way to practice science. Joaquim's expertise and singular way to approach science resonated on many of her later writings, in which she mentioned several of his most unconventional techniques allied with his incredibly successful capture rates.

Repeatedly throughout the diary, Cochran evoked the knowledge she had acquired from the books, by comparing and contrasting what she had read to what she was seeing and experiencing. With Joaquim, she concluded, she learned things that could not be learned from any book:

> Joaquim doesn't hesitate a minute in imitating the call, describing the color and telling whether or not the eggs have been found. He made use of glass vials to whistle into, in making some of the most sibilant or metallic calls, and for others he scrapped a piece of wood over an iron pipe for the harsh calls. After lunch we kept on, and it is surprising how much good information I gathered from listening to him jabber in Portuguese. He has taught me more of the language than anybody else in here in Brazil . . . (169)

Joaquim's remarkable empirical knowledge was represented here almost as an extension of his body, as if he were the book from which Cochran was learning. His knowledge was so precise that he could imitate the calls of the frogs, information only available to those who went to the field to hear and record it. By admitting that despite his lack of education, Joaquim was able to teach her more Portuguese than anybody else in Brazil, Cochran acknowledged not only his ability and potential to teach her his empirical knowledge, but also his capacity to teach her more formal subjects as well, even if he used more informal means. He inspired Cochran to impersonate a similar authority, which allowed her to popularize her knowledge on herpetology. Despite the fact that Joaquin's willingness to help and share all his knowledge with her reinforced her superiority and his condition as a colonized subject, by admitting his expertise, she was somehow disrupting his inherent inferiority and granting value to the information he provided.

Increasingly more comfortable in the field, she slowly started to transcend the immobility of her knowledge and the space constraints of her laboratory. Even the gardening tools she used at home served a new purpose in the context of her field explorations: "My forceps and my digging tool, last used to weed my tulips in North America are now very useful for collecting under debris where biting ants or scorpions may be hiding out" (88). In other words, the objects that had a particular application according to her previous experiences now gained a broader meaning, which she had never imagined before. These new experiences demanded a reevaluation of her own beliefs because the knowledge she acquired from the books proved to be insufficient. Thus, her experience as traveler affected her own body and beliefs and provided an

172   *Chapter Four*

opportunity to expand her knowledge so profoundly that she would never be the same again. The more she learned, the closer she was to become the "Frog Lady." The last remark of her travel account confirms that her transformation was concluded. Back in her laboratory, she wrote:

> The expedition is over, and the frogs and fishes and other trophies are safely stowed away in museum jars, and the excitement of the adventure and the sheer beauty of Brazil are already only memories. But sometimes, while I am in the midst of the dry technical writings which are the aftermath of all scientific collecting, the laboratory walls for a moment fade away, and I see again the flash of a humming-bird's wing, the purple beauty of an orchid lighting the dark gloom of the ancient trees, and the fallen fuchsia flowers lying like spilled heart's blood on green Brazilian mosses. (191)

The narrative persona who was now writing this last paragraph of her travel narrative was definitely not the same who traveled to Brazil. The walls of Cochran's laboratory could no longer imprison her, since her imagination, and by extension, the empirical knowledge she acquired, could now provide her with a new perspective, as the dryness of the scientific writing did not bear the same weight for her anymore. Her imagination, which was now able to make the walls of her laboratory fade away, was a manifestation of the new identity she acquired, one that extrapolated the limits of her gendered condition and allowed her to impersonate the "Frog Lady." As a result of this transformation, Cochran took advantage of her alternate visibility to present herself to the media as a female authority in frogs, an image that relied firmly on her travel experience while still preserving her femininity, challenging the pre-conceptions of the society of her time in relation to women and science. Working within the limitations imposed on her by her gender instead of openly defying them, this alternate visibility ultimately allowed Cochran to advance in her career.[31]

Similar to the other women analyzed in this book then, the American scientist took advantage of her unusual alternate visibility in the public sphere, mainly derived from her travel experience. As mentioned, the sudden prestige Cochran acquired after her return from Brazil was evident in the press at the time. Her travel experience validated her position as a transatlantic subject and conferred her an extraordinary authority to speak about herpetology. But instead of using this newly acquired authority to solely write papers that would circulate among the scientific community, she chose to embrace the popularity her travel experience granted to her in the press. She appeared in several newspaper articles exhibiting her collections and sharing her experiences with the general public. Figure 4.4 shows a picture of Cochran when she had just arrived from Brazil in 1935; this remarkable picture evidences the unique image she presented to the press. Displaying a very bright smile on her face and wearing a nice dress, she held her monkey skin as a trophy. Instead of simply demystifying the image of the scientist in the white robe, she presented a female version of this highly masculinized image. The newspaper clippings she collected, which are now in Cochran's personal archives

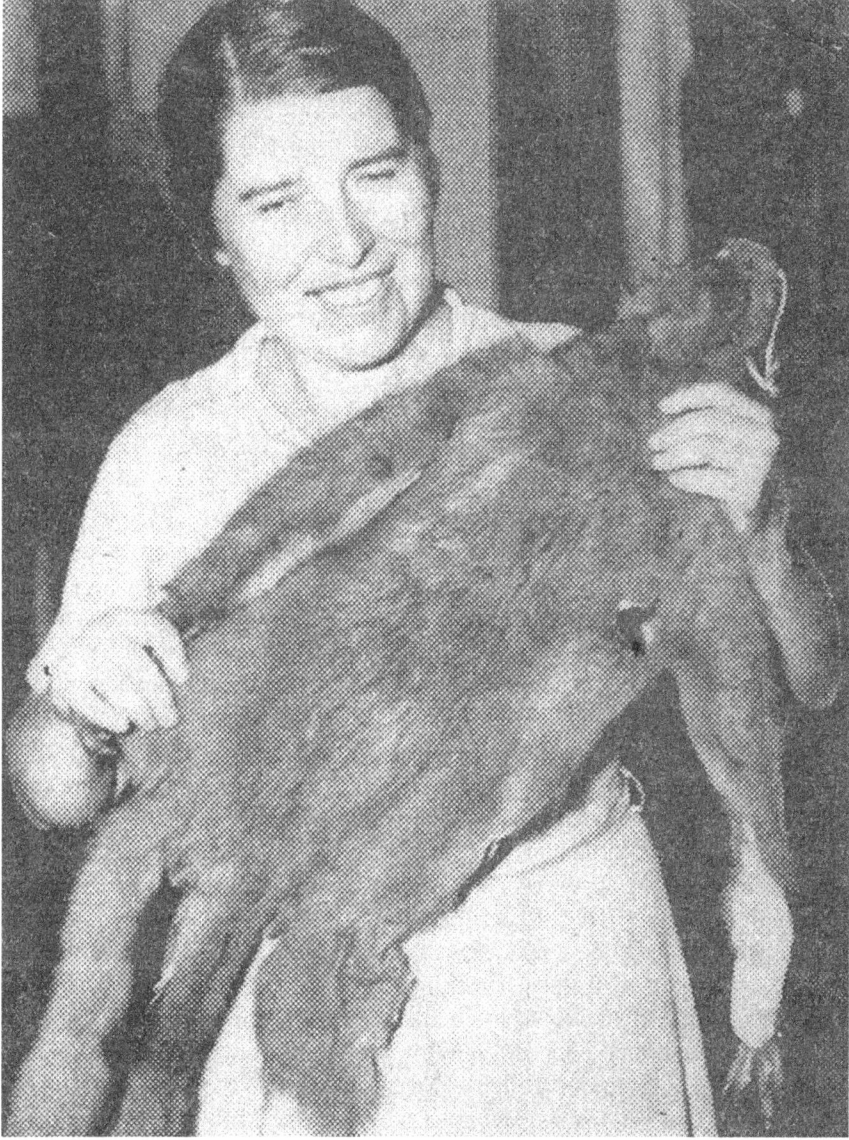

Figure 4.4. Cochran in 1935 exhibiting the skin of a monkey she brought from Brazil.
Smithsonian Institution Archives RU 7151 Box 7 Folder 11—1935. Reproduced with permission.

at the Smithsonian, demonstrate that this prestigious image lasted her entire life and reveal that she made sure to preserve her femininity throughout her career. Her insistence on presenting herself as a woman reinforces the argument that, instead of simply feminizing her scientific activities, she defended that scientific work and women were not opposites and that being a scientist did not mean not to be a woman. She often presented herself as somebody who liked to cook, work on her garden, and take care of her pets. Besides having several cats, she also liked to keep her frogs as pets. Also, she enjoyed emphasizing the fact that her job was fun and did not consume all of her time (Child, A-16). While cultivating in the press an image which combined her field expertise with her femininity, by taking advantage of the experience she acquired from her travels, she popularized science and created a unique space to disseminate her knowledge. Thus, if she could not become a prominent scientist in the Smithsonian Institution, she became the "Frog Lady," an image that blurred gender boundaries and created an alternative way for Cochran to share her knowledge with the public. This image extrapolated the boundaries of her gender, challenging the masculinized image of the scientist, and serving as means to popularize her scientific activities.

Cochran's Last Letter to Lutz: Farewell

Although Cochran was a renowned scientist at the Smithsonian, she still suffered the double standards and under-recognition faced by women scientists of her time. Her travel to Brazil offered her an opportunity to overcome her gender constraints and ascertain her transatlantic subjectivity which would allow her to achieve a remarkable authority as a herpetologist. Her narrative displayed her mobility as well as the many strategies she employed to instate her narrative presence, by engaging with more masculine tropes of travel writing while preserving her femininity. Instead of defying and threatening her male counterparts, she used this authority to gain prominence in the media as the "Frog Lady." With this newly acquired identity, she popularized science and attempted to demonstrate that scientific work could also be performed by women, even if apparently less professionally than men. Nevertheless, although traveling might have assisted Cochran in the task of contributing to the construction of knowledge and participating in science, she was not able to fully overcome her gender constraints in her professional career. She still needed the support of her male counterparts to be promoted and have her work recognized. Upon her return to the Smithsonian, she was overwhelmed with several minor tasks that delayed for fifteen years the publication of her book on the Brazilian frogs. Her promotions at the Smithsonian were given at a considerably slower pace than those of her male counterparts, and she was not promoted to full curator until 1955.[32] Despite the pitfalls of her career at the museum, she felt accomplished and never complained, suggesting her awareness of the limitations she had to face as a woman trying to thrive in the scientific world. In October of 1951 she wrote to Lutz: "I am busy as ever here at the museum, cheerfully doing the work of five people and liking it. I often think of the beautiful places you showed me in 1935 when I was in Brazil" (Letter to Lutz, 1951). The trip to Brazil, mentioned in several letters between Lutz and Cochran, certainly greatly impacted her life. Perhaps, most importantly, this trip provided the opportunity for Cochran to seal her friendship and collaboration with Lutz, a strong tie that lasted her entire life.

In fact, Lutz and Cochran remained active collaborators for more than forty years and exchanged hundreds of letters during their lives. These letters, as I have mentioned, show in detail how they developed a strong friendship. They also disclose an effective channel of exchange of knowledge, support, and experience. The last letter Cochran wrote to Lutz dates from April of 1968, a month before her decease in May of the same year, and it confirms this claim to a great extent. Cochran informed Lutz she had liver cancer and that her prognostic was not very hopeful. She seemed resigned and made a balance of her life:

> I am sorry I have to tell you this, because neither you nor I have many close friends, and you are the oldest and dearest of mine, since we have been in such close association since 1926 and since we used to have such good time together with your father and Joaquim when we went collecting. But I never really wanted to live to a very advanced age—there are problems, you know, when one does not have young relatives to take over, and sometimes, even if one has relatives, they don't always consider your wishes. So I am quite resigned.
>
> Cole Goin and I have got our big manuscript on Colombia frogs in press. . . . I also finished a semi-popular field guide by Putnam on the reptiles and amphibians of the 50 United States . . . I am regretful that I did not get further with my frogs of south and east of Brazil, but Cole Goin may take it over. . . . I had a good many descriptions and measurements made as well as lots of photographs including those of the same type, so perhaps it can help out . . .
>
> Now, Bertha dear, please do not feel sad for me. I've had a very good life and I have done lots of things I liked doing. Although I leave some things undone, perhaps it does not matter. (Letter to Lutz, 1968)[33]

The letter confirms that Cochran never forgot her remarkable collecting trip to Brazil, her close association and friendship with Lutz, and her traveler companion Joaquim. As she recollected her life, she listed her accomplishments and regrets, her major publications, and the work she could not finish despite her best efforts. Furthermore, her desire that her legacy would be continued implied her hope that she would not be forgotten. Her farewell letter

176 *Chapter Four*

leaves us with some unanswered questions though. Would have it mattered if she had finished the "undone"? Would that have changed her legacy? Perhaps it would not matter after all.

NOTES

1. See note 2 in the introduction.
2. Leonhard Hess Stejneger (1851–1943) was a Norwegian-born American herpetologist and zoologist who specialized in vertebrate natural history studies. He gained his greatest reputation with reptiles and amphibians. He was Cochran's mentor and supervisor at the Smithsonian until his death in 1943. For more, see Alexander Wetmore, *Leonhard Hess Stejneger (1851–1943)*. *Nat. Acad. Sci.* 24, (1945). This biography does not make any mention of Cochran's role in his life.
3. For more see Historical Note, Smithsonian Institution Archives, https://siarchives.si.edu/collections/siris_arc_217308.
4. There were only two female scientists employed by the Smithsonian Institution between 1921 and 1938 according to the American Men of Science (Rossetier 224). This number gradually increased over the next few decades, but only in some specific fields. At the Smithsonian, Cochran advanced through the Division of Reptiles and Amphibians, becoming assistant curator in 1927, and associate curator in 1942. The documentation available at the Smithsonian reveal that she was performing the work of full curator since 1950, but the administration only promoted her to that level in 1955 (Smithsonian Archives, RU7231, Box 9). Her promotion requests always mentioned her scientific travel to Brazil (she collected more than 2,000 frogs there), which strongly suggests that the advancement on her career was a result of the success of her trip.
5. Archives of the National Museum of Rio de Janeiro SEMEAR—Seção de Memória e Arquivo—Museu Nacional—UFRJ, Brazil.
6. For a historical account about Cochran's travel to Brazil, see Mariana Sombrio Moraes de Oliveira, "Em Busca pelo campo: *Ciências, coleções, gênero* e *outras histórias* sobre *mulheres viajantes* no *Brasil* em meados do *século XX*,' Dissertation. Campinas: Unicamp, 2014.
7. For Maria Margaret Lopes, Lutz's scientific career cannot be considered apart from her feminist activities because it allowed her to occupy spaces and form networks of scientific sociability beyond the intellectual environment of Rio de Janeiro (Lopes, "Prominence"). In Bertha Lutz's case, simply practicing science and feminism was already a transgression, since she challenged the under-representation of women in the sciences and politics, refused marriage and motherhood, and coupled feminist ideals to a neutral, rational, and objective conception of science in a context in which science was not questioned. For Lopes, as opposed to other women scientists, who had to downplay their gender in order to succeed on the field, Lutz took advantage of her condition as a woman to create an anomalous image of herself that would allow her scientific and feminist activities. She concludes that Lutz created an

image of herself as a strange woman who, without being admitted to the new social space she sought to occupy, was neither a man nor a woman in cultural terms. In other words, she was atypical, not ordinary, and strange. However, Lopes considered that her prominence in the media automatically granted her reputation as a scientist, as she claims that Lutz's feminism fostered her scientific career and granted her visibility as a scientist (2008). Although it is true that her involvement with feminism granted her great visibility in the media, this image was not always favorable and would not be enough to establish her scientific reputation. In fact, this reputation was not automatic and required years of work and negotiation. This argument becomes even more problematic when we consider that her scientific authority was a product of a negotiation that took several years, and even so, she is hardly remembered for her scientific achievements until today. As a matter of fact, as Lopes also admits, to date, Lutz's scientific activities have not been examined by either feminists, historians, or historians of science and there is a lack of recognition of her scientific contributions and many of her works remain unpublished to date.

8. In fact, only three women were invited to join the academy in the first half of the twentieth century: Marie Curie, the famous Polish scientist, the German zoologist Emília Snethlage, who was the director of the Museum Paraense Emílio Goeldi, and the Brazilian-American paleontologist Carlota Joaquina de Paiva Maury.

9. With the help of the archivist Jorge Dias da Silva Junior from the archives of the National Museum of Rio de Janeiro, recently, I uncovered a collection of around 150 letters between Cochran and Lutz from 1926 and 1968 which were never analyzed before. These letters reveal many details about their relationship and the nature of their collaborations (SEMEAR—Seção de Memória e Arquivo—Museu Nacional—UFRJ).

10. An authorization form requesting the purchase of laboratory solutions and scientific publications with the name of Cochran on the back, dated from 1919, is at the Brazilian National Archives (SEMEAR—Seção de Memória e Arquivo—Museu Nacional—UFRJ).

11. Maynard Mayo Metcalf (1868–1940) was a professor of zoology at Johns Hopkins University and a research collaborator in marine invertebrates at the Smithsonian Institution and Waldo LaSalle Schmitt (1887–1977) was the Curator of the Division of Marine Invertebrates and was promoted to Head Curator of the Department of Biology in 1943.

12. Charles William Beebe (1877–1962) was an American naturalist famous for the numerous expeditions and his prolific extensive writing for academic and popular audiences. *Jungle Peace* (1918) was praised both by the scientific and public opinion, especially due the support he received from Theodore Roosevelt.

13. A. Remington Kellogg (1892–1969) was an Assistant Curator of Mammals of the Smithsonian Institution and became Curator in 1941. In 1948, Kellogg was named Director of the United States National Museum and held that post until his retirement in 1962.

14. For a detailed analysis of the content of Lutz's report, see "Honrosas Comissões e o papel educativo do museu moderno: divulgação científica, proteção à natureza e a luta pelo progresso feminino na atuação de Bertha Lutz (décadas de 1920 e 1930)," *Revista Feminismos* 1.2 (2014).

15. In "Just a Minute, Miss," 1935, Cochran makes a reference of a visit of Adolpho Lutz to the Smithsonian in 1925, but it is not clear if Bertha Lutz was with him, although it is very likely because she also went to Baltimore on this same occasion.

16. Alexander Wetmore (1886–1978) was an ornithologist and paleontologist. He was the sixth Secretary of the Smithsonian Institution, from 1945 to 1952. Thomas Barbour (1884–1946) was a herpetologist who as the director of the Harvard Museum of Comparative Zoology from 1927 to 1946.

17. Helen Thompson Gaige (1890–1976), herpetologist at the University of Michigan and longtime editor-in-chief of *Copeia*. Her research concerned the geographical distribution, habitats, and life histories of amphibians. She also assisted in organizing the American Society of Ichthyologists and Herpetologists of which she was named honorary president in 1946. She was married to the entomologist Frederick McMahin Gaige.

18. I was not able to locate Lutz's response to this letter, but it would be interesting to see how she responded to her friend's expectations about her trip to Brazil.

19. "Just a Minute, Miss" was never published in spite of the several submissions to at least five editors between 1935 and 1940. Nevertheless, Cochran did publish a shorter version of the diary called "Brazil Bound: With a Collector's Kit in South America" in *Nature Magazine*, Volume 33, 1940. I have chosen to analyze the unpublished diary here as it offers more details about the trip.

20. As noted in the introduction, although Cochran's travel was not across the Atlantic, the position of the United States in relation to Latin America replicated to a great extent the European imperialist model. For consistency, I will refer to her travels as transatlantic in this chapter.

21. Cochran's diary, in terms of format, is very similar to the travel accounts produced in the nineteenth century. It has an introduction, eighteen chapters, and an appendix. Preceding the introduction is a preface written by Alexander Wetmore, the Assistant Secretary of the United States Museum at the time. The diary has dated entries starting from her departure from New York on January 5, 1935, until her departure from Rio de Janeiro in May of the same year. The first chapter, "On shipboard," describes the days she spent on the boat, her flying fish counting, resembling Graham's journal to a great extent.

22. For more details, see William Ragan Stanton, *The Great United States Exploring Expedition of 1838–1842* (Los Angeles: University of California Press 1975).

23. It is interesting to note Cochran's comment considering that she does not make political observations. Brazilian national identity was constructed based on the mythical miscegenation between indigenous people and European.

24. "Farinha" is a famous Brazilian dish made with tapioca flour, which is served with black beans and rice.

25. It was very difficult for a married woman to carry out original research because the work was systematic, and it involved finding new species (*Uneasy Careers, Intimate Lives* 84).

26. The Oswaldo Cruz Institute was founded in 1908 with the mission of conducting research in parasitology, microbiology, and immunization.

27. Dr. Emmanuel Dias (1908–1962) was a Brazilian scientist specialized in protozoology who investigated the Chagas disease.

28. Visiting and collecting at private gardens would likely not have been possible, however, without Lutz's strong influence as a politician, which granted them access to the most prominent properties in the area. In that sense, Cochran's collection activities were similar to the ones performed by Maria Graham almost a hundred years earlier.

29. I found at least three different versions of Cochran's diary at the Smithsonian archives. The version called "Brazil Bound: With a Collector's Kit in South America" is the source of this citation. This version of her diary is fairly shorter than "Just a Minute, Miss" and was published in *Nature Magazine* in 1940. In fact, in "Just a Minute, Miss" this passage was modified to omit the fact they decided not to capture the female. Instead, it reads: ". . . so it is true that a parent really does guard the egg masses" (36).

30. Several newspaper clippings evidencing Cochran's presence in the press through her life can be found at the Smithsonian Institution Archives, RU 7151, Box 7, Folder 1.

31. This approach was well aligned with the realist approach suggested elsewhere by Rossiter.

32. See M.-B. Leslie, "Women in Science, Historical Edition: Doris Cochran's struggle for promotion at the Smithsonian," *The Clutter Museum*. There are some controversies around Cochran's promotion and the exact dates. The extensive documentation I found in the Smithsonian indicates that she was promoted to full curator in 1955 (see note 4 above).

33. Coleman Jett Goin (1911–1986) was a herpetologist of the Smithsonian Institution who collaborated with Cochran in the last years of her life.

Conclusion

Gender, Science and Authority in Women's Travel Writing: Literary Perspectives on the Discourse of Natural History has sought to analyze specific textual strategies employed by women travelers from the nineteenth and early twentieth centuries who managed to construct a unique authority for themselves in their narratives, overcoming the distinctive gender constraints they had to face to participate in the construction of knowledge. My aim has been to offer new insights to the analysis of women's travel writing to counter and undermine previously held gendered stereotypes that have so often influenced readings of women's contribution to knowledge. Thompson's recent collection of essays *Journeys to Authority: Reassessing Women's Early Travel Writing, 1763–1862* proposes "to convey the public influence and agency that women might garner from travel writing, and the genre's importance as a stepping stone to wider recognition as intellectuals, 'women of letters' and cultural commentators. In this way, women's travel and its subsequent textual representation could become . . . a journey to authority" (133). Building upon Thompson's premise that travel writing was a genre that enabled women to establish their intellectual authorities, this book aimed to study women travelers whose scientific endeavors and contributions have either been overlooked or studied mainly from an exclusively literary perspective without taking into consideration the role they have played in the history of science. Within the specific context of Latin American studies, this book has aimed to elucidate not only the journey to authority undertaken by women travelers but also how such a journey fits within the larger context of the production of knowledge by women in general. This approach takes a step toward bringing a more interdisciplinary perspective to the field of Latin American studies.

Since the seventeenth century, travel and science have been interconnected as both men and women traveling throughout the world wrote their travel accounts, collected materials, and established "scientific" dialogues. Due to politically and socially constructed forces, which defined what was considered scientific, these dialogues required specific political and rhetorical maneuvers (Fulford, Lee, and Kitson 2). Women's engagement with both travel writing and science has always been problematic because their ability to establish such dialogues was mediated by their gender constraints. Lately, many feminist studies on women's travel writing from the nineteenth century have recognized their remarkable presence in and contributions to the genre. These studies have challenged earlier assumptions, which granted to women's travel accounts a lower status in relation to those written by men (Thompson, *Journeys* 132). However, with the shift toward the professionalization of science in the end of the nineteenth century, women and minorities became less involved with science and their contributions to the field were less evident. Although women expressed scholarly and social interest in scientific pursuits at the turn of the century, viable career options, as Harper notes, "were not available, as there was strong social pressure for women to be trained in homemaking" (Harper 222). Therefore, the institutionalization of science that took place throughout the nineteenth century further restricted women's opportunities to participate in the construction of knowledge. In the beginning of the twentieth century, even if they started to have more openings to engage in science and were slowly incorporated into the scientific world, they were nevertheless discriminated against. Their male counterparts continued to resist accepting and acknowledging their contributions to science and they still had to use strategies to negotiate gender constraints and establish their scientific authority. Thus, although the "doors of science" might have been open for women in the early twentieth century, they still had to overcome many of the same barriers faced by their counterparts in the previous centuries to have their work respected and published (Rossiter 128). The similarities among the strategies the women analyzed in this book employed to attain authority indicate that, even if travel narratives had lost some of the prestige they garnered in the nineteenth century, they continued to be an important vehicle to disseminate information and grant authority to the traveler in the first decades of the twentieth century, and women continued to benefit from them (Thompson, *Routledge* 198).

Women interested in making scientific contributions and participating in intellectual debates found in traveling a solution to escape their physical and intellectual confinement and engage in the exchange of knowledge. This was only possible, however, if they were able to establish their transatlantic subjectivity and consequent authority as travelers within their travel narratives.

Mobility alone was not enough for them to obtain and maintain their authority as travel writers. All four women analyzed in this book benefited from the social leverage offered by the transatlantic world between Europe, Latin America, and the United States, and presented their own unique literary, oftentimes feminized, perspective of the natural history discourse to participate in the intellectual debates of their time. Given the constraints to which they were subjected, women travelers needed to constantly negotiate their gendered condition within their narratives to establish their presence and authority as narrators regardless of their nationalities. In that sense, transatlantic subjectivity was not universally accessible. This unique status could only be achieved if a woman traveler, leveraging her gender conditions, was able to carve her narrative authority by strongly establishing her presence as well as her mobility as a narrator, therefore attaching a shifting meaning to her account while evidencing its intellectual potential. By analyzing the work of these four women together, I show a unique perspective of the female transatlantic subject. In that sense, this book has also tried to articulate the idea that women's participation in science needs to be reevaluated to encompass their apparently less professional contributions as they were a consequence of the limited opportunities they had to perform scientific work. The women analyzed here leveraged the prominence they achieved as writers and used a newly acquired alternate visibility to share their own perspectives on science. As Rossiter claims, rather than fighting their discriminatory condition, women had to find less competitive fields in which male presence was not too overwhelming (138). This alternate visibility allowed them to express their ideas employing literary genres considered more appropriate and less threatening to their male counterparts, such as letters, diaries, biographies, and periodical publications, as was the case for all the women analyzed here. Thus, as transatlantic writing subjects, these women became influential and achieved the authority to challenge and reshape recognized scientific ideas and viewpoints. By doing so, they managed to establish, with different levels of recognition, a name for themselves in predominantly male fields of study.

Travel writing as a genre has evolved over time and across cultures. In that sense, analyzing travelogues produced by subjects originated from places outside of Europe and North America is an important tool to augment critical models that tend to focus on the genre solely as a vehicle of empire and colonization (Thompson, *Routledge* xviii). This book sought to unveil the intellectual value of the work of American and European women travel writers and the broader implications of their contributions to the formation of nineteenth- and twentieth-century transatlantic intellectual currents. By analyzing women travelers from both sides of the Atlantic, it is possible to construct a more comprehensive critical model that better explains the fundamental strategies employed by them in their attempts to participate in intellectual discussions. Within this framework, narrative devices such as the alignment with imperial tropes become mere specific instantiations of rhetorical tools meant to establish a transatlantic subjectivity. As I have stated in the introduction of this book, rather than an attempt to homogenize these women, bringing them together was an effort to evaluate to what extent certain textual mechanisms enabled these travelers to overcome the cross-cultural immobility that limited their opportunities to engage in the intellectual debates of their time, despite their race or place of origin. That is not to say that their race or class were not relevant nor that they did not engage in the imperial rhetoric of travel writing. Quite the opposite, they all engaged with the discourses surrounding them while negotiating their own authority as writers. I proposed here that for European and American women travelers, the imperial superiority implicated in the hegemonic rhetoric of travel writing could also represent a possibility to establish themselves in terms of their own difference, negotiating their intrinsic gendered inferiority. Latin American women equally managed to establish their difference and superiority within their travel narratives, also negotiating their own gender constrains. Regardless of their origin, Latin American women were still able to set themselves apart, constructing an identity as "outsiders," which is a strong indicator that their European and American women counterparts, for the most part, engaged in this rhetoric of imperial superiority for a similar reason. By carefully articulating a network of influential local contacts who perceived their otherness as a characteristic that granted them a broader and hence valuable perspective, they secured a social status not previously available to them. Then, even if these women travelers employed hegemonic tropes in their writings, their goal was not exclusively to reaffirm notions of empire and colonization. Instead, they challenged and reassessed these imperial perspectives and used them to construct their own authority as writers of travel narratives. Then, analyzing women's approach to travel writing is also an opportunity to propose new theoretical frameworks departing from the analytical models that have permeated travel writing studies over the last two decades.

Finally, examining the connections among these travelers is an attempt to include gender as a category of significance in the understanding of the social production of scientific knowledge (Bleier 5). If we accept that science is a social and historical product constructed predominantly by men, analyzing the way different social groups approached it allows an alternative perspective of the subject: ". . . by splitting women by categories, there is no she, no singularity, but a sea of differences" (Haraway 106). Although gender, class, race, and nationality are all unavoidable conditions of observation, they are in fact "forced on us by the terrible historical experience of the contradictory social realities of patriarchy, colonialism, and capitalism" (Haraway 14). As Donna Haraway suggests, women's studies must explore the possible affinities and connections that might actually impact history locally and globally: "The politics of difference that feminists need to articulate must be rooted in a politics of experience that searches for specificity, heterogeneity, and connection through struggle.... Feminism is collective; and difference is political, that is, about power, accountability, and hope. Experience, like difference, is about contradictory and necessary connection" (109). In other words, the similar strategies the women travelers analyzed in this book employed in their travel accounts underscore the connections among them, not their differences. Focusing on these connections might offer a more productive tool to understand the role of women in the history of sciences. Thus, this book has attempted to propose a theoretical approach to analyze the travel writing of women which, while acknowledging their differences, prioritized the connections between their strategies, goals, and achievements.

The under-representation of women in the history of sciences and in the construction of knowledge is a universal problem. In order to further uncover and better understand their role, a more comprehensive dialogue between the sciences and the humanities is needed. It is clear that women travelers and scientists had to overcome many barriers to have their work respected and published well into the twentieth century. This realization is important not only because it raises awareness about the situation of these women but also because it evidences the need of bringing to light the silenced voices lost to history. This book is an attempt to reclaim women's participation, and to study more thoroughly their scientific contributions because this is the only viable way to accomplish what Joan W. Scott suggested many years ago when she called on historians and others to "make women visible as active participants, and create analytic distance between the seemingly fixed language of the past and our own terminology" (50). My comprehensive analysis shows how transatlantic travels continued to make it possible for women to overcome certain social limitations and achieve substantial recognition abroad both in the nineteenth and the twentieth centuries. We cannot, however, limit ourselves to the recovery of women of science who were forgotten, or to keeping track of their contributions over time: "If we view the scientific enterprise as a cultural and social activity, then we can recognize that our present practice is not the only way science could have evolved. Therefore, we can envision the possibility of a different practice being carried out by a specific cultural group, and also conceptualize the possibility of future change" (Hudson 269).

As Haraway explains, feminists have to reappropriate science in order to define what is "natural" for themselves (23). She adds that natural sciences are a political practice—"a weaving of multi layered meanings in the social working out of what may count as explanation" (82). Some critics have suggested that historically feminist scholars have paid less attention to the sciences than to other disciplines perhaps due to a lack familiarity with the topic (Maynard 2). Now, science is finally becoming an area of concern for feminism and women studies. There is now widespread interest in understanding why women often do not pursue careers in the fields of Science, Technology Engineering, and Mathematics (STEM). In order to understand where we are, we must first understand how we got here. This is the only way we will be able to propose new paradigms and transform obsolete models, thereby creating more opportunities for women in scientific fields and in society at large. This book is one of the first steps in that direction.

Credits

COVER ART

Painting of Costa Rican Frogs by Doris Cochran. Reproduced with permission from the Smithsonian Institution Archives (SIA2014-00026a).

CHAPTER 1

Parts of the article "Crossing Boundaries into a World of Scientific Discoveries: Maria Graham in Nineteenth-Century Brazil" (2012) are reproduced with permission from Taylor and Francis Ltd. (http://www.informaworld.com).

Figure 1.1—Dragon tree by Maria Graham and by Humboldt. *Journal of a Voyage to Brazil and Residence there, During Part of the Years 1821, 1822, 1823, 135. Atlas pittoresque du voyage: vues des Cordillières.* Amsterdam: Theatrum Orbis Terrarum, 1910, plate 69.

Figure 1.2— Graham's *Scripture Herbal* front page and her illustration of the Bramble. *Scripture Herbal*, London, 1842, 44.

Figure 1.3—*Escallonia Callcottiae* and *Wahlenbergia Grahamae* © The Board of Trustees of the Royal Botanic Gardens, Kew. Reproduced with the consent of the Royal Botanic Gardens, Kew.

CHAPTER 2

Figure 2.1—Portrait of Gómez de Avellaneda by Fernando de la Costa (1859–1864). Reproduced with permission from the Archives of the Museo Nacional del Romanticismo, Spain.

Figure 2.2—Retama Plains. *A voyage in the Sunbeam: Our home on the ocean for eleven months.* Annie Allnutt Brassey, 1878, p. 24.

CHAPTER 3

Figure 3.1—Watercolor of Nísia Floresta. Reproduced with the consent of Gabriela Motta.

Figure 3.2—Courses offered at the Collège de France in 1849–1850. Reproduced with permission from the Archives of the Collège de France.

CHAPTER 4

Quotes from Doris Cochran's unpublished diary "Just a Minute, Miss" are reproduced with permission from the Smithsonian Institution Archives (RU 7151—Series 1, Box 2, Folder 5).

Quotes from the correspondence between Bertha Lutz and Doris Cochran are reproduced with permission from the Museu Nacional (Brasil). Seção de Memória e Arquivo. Fundo Bertha Lutz, 1927–1968.

Figure 4.1—Doris Cochran at her desk at the Smithsonian, 1934. Reproduced with permission from the Smithsonian Institution Archives (96–955).

Figure 4.2—Bertha Lutz and Adolpho Lutz during field work in Rio de Janeiro, 1935. Reproduced with permission from the Museu Nacional (Brasil). Seção de Memória e Arquivo. Fundo Bertha Lutz, 1927–1968.

Figure 4.3—Cochran wearing her collecting outfit in Minas Gerais, 1935. Reproduced with permission from the Smithsonian Institution Archives (SIA2019-000772).

Works Cited

Abir-Am, Pnina G. and Dorinda Outram. "Introduction." *Uneasy Careers and Intimate Lives: Women in Science, 1789–1979.* New Brunswick: Rutgers University Press, 1987.

Acker, Joan. "Hierarchies, Jobs, Bodies: A Theory of Gendered Organizations." *The Gendered Society Reader.* Ed. Michael S. Kimmel. Oxford: Oxford University Press, 2000.

Akel, Regina. *Maria Graham: A Literary Biography.* New York: Cambria Press, 2009.

Albin, María C. *Género, poesía y esfera pública: Gertrudis Gómez de Avellaneda y la tradición romántica.* Madrid: Trotta, 2002.

Appelbaum, Nancy, Anne Macpherson, and Karin Rosemblatt. *Race and Nation in Modern Latin America.* Chapel Hill: University of North Carolina Press, 2003.

Anderson, Monica. *Women and the Politics of Travel, 1870–1914.* Cranbury: Fairleigh Dickinson University Press, 2006.

Barman, Roderick J. *Brazil: The Forging of a Nation, 1798–1852.* Stanford: Stanford University Press, 1988.

———. "Brazilians in France, 1822–1872: Doubly Outsiders." *Strange Pilgrimages: Exile, Travel, and National Identity in Latin America, 1800–1990s.* Eds. Ingrid E. Fey and Karen Racine. Wilmington: Scholarly Resources Inc., 2000.

Beer, Gillian. "Travelling the Other Way." *Cultures of Natural History.* Ed. N. Jardine, J. A. Secord, and E. C. Spary. Cambridge: Cambridge University Press, 1997.

Benjamin, Marina. "Elbow Room: Women Writers on Science, 1790–1840." *Science and Sensibility: Gender and Scientific Enquiry, 1780–1945.* Oxford and Cambridge: Basil Blackwell, 1991.

Bennett, Jennifer. *Lilies of the Hearth: The Historical Relationship between Women & Plants.* Ontario: Camden House, 1991.

Bertucci, Paola. "The In/visible Woman: Mariangela Ardinghelli (1730–1824) and the circulation of natural knowledge between Paris and Naples." *Isis* 104 (2013): 226–49.

Bird, Dúnlaith. "Travel Writing and Gender." *The Routledge Companion to Travel Writing*. Ed. Carl Thompson. London: Routledge, 2016.

Birke, Lynda. "Life as We Have Known It: Feminism and the Biology of Gender." *Science and Sensibility: Gender and Scientific Enquiry, 1780–1945.* Oxford and Cambridge: Basil Blackwell, 1991.

Birkett, Dea. *Off the Beaten Track: Three Centuries of Women Travellers.* London: National Portrait Gallery Publications, 2004.

Bleichmar, Daniela. "A Visible and Useful Empire: Visual Culture and Colonial Natural History in the Eighteenth-Century Spanish World." *Science in the Spanish and Portuguese Empires: 1500–1800.* Ed. Daniela Bleichmar, Paula De Vos, Kristin Ruffine, and Kevin Sheehan. Stanford: Stanford University Press, 2009.

Bleier, Ruth. *Feminist Approaches to Science.* New York: Pergamon Press, 1986.

Brassey, Annie Allnutt. "A Voyage in the Sunbeam: Our Home on the Ocean for Eleven Months." London: Longman, Green, and Co., 1878.

Bravo, Michael T. "Ethnological Encounters." *Cultures of Natural History*. Eds. N. Jardine, J. A. Secord, and E. C. Spary. Cambridge: Cambridge University Press, 1997.

Buzard, James. *The Beaten Track: European Tourism, Literature, and the Ways to "Culture," 1800–1918.* Oxford: Oxford University Press, 1993.

———. *Disorienting Fiction: The Autoethnographic Work of Nineteenth-Century British Novels.* Princeton: Princeton University Press, 2005.

Caballero, Soledad M. "For the Honour of Our Country: Maria Dundas Graham and the Romance of Benign Domination." *Studies in Travel Writing* 9.2 (2005): 111–31.

Caesar, Terry. "South of the Border: American Travel Writing in Latin America." *The Cambridge Companion to American Travel Writing.* Ed. Alfred Bendixen and Judith Hamera. Cambridge: Cambridge University Press, 2009.

Cantor, Geoffrey and Sally Shuttleworth. *Science Serialized: Representations of the Sciences in Nineteenth-Century Periodicals.* Cambridge: MIT Press, 2004.

Cañizares-Esguerra, Jorge. *Nature, Empire, and Nation: Explorations of the History of Science in the Iberian World.* Stanford: Stanford University Press, 2006.

Chard, Chloe. *Pleasure and Guilt On the Grand Tour: Travel Writing and Imaginative Geography, 1600–1830.* Manchester: Manchester University Press, 1999.

Clark, Steven. *Travel Writing and Empire: Postcolonial Theory in Transit.* London: Zed Books, 1999.

Cochran, Doris. "Our Friend the Frog." *National Geographic Magazine*, 1932.

Cologero, Steve. "Why Positivism Failed in Latin America." *Latin American Positivism.* Ed. Gregory D. Gilson and Irving W. Levinson. New York: Lexington Books, 2013.

Comte, Auguste. *Sept lettres inédites d'Auguste Comte a Nisia Brasileira.* Rio de Janaeiro: Siège central de l'Apostolat positiviste du Brésil, 1988.

Corson, Hiram. *An Introduction to the Study of Robert Browning's Poetry.* Boston: D.C. Heath and Co. Publishers, 1889.

Cresswell, Tim and Tanu Priya Uteng. "Gendered Mobilites: Towards an Holistic Understanding." *Gendered Mobilities.* Ed. Tim Cresswell and Tanu Priya Uteng. Aldershot: Ashgate, 2008.

Dettelbach, Michael. "Humboldtian Science." *Cultures of Natural History*. Ed. N. Jardine, J. A. Secord, and E. C. Spary. Cambridge: Cambridge University Press, 1997.

Denegri, Francesca. "Desde la Ventana: Women 'Pilgrims' in Nineteenth-Century Latin-American Travel Literature." *The Modern Language Review* 92.2 (1997): 348–62.

Dias, Gonçalves. "I-Juca Pirama." *Poemas de Gonçalves Dias*. Ed. Péricles Eugênio da Silva Ramos. São Paulo: Cultrix, 1980.

"Duvernoy, Georges Louis." *A Dictionary of Biography, Past and Present. Containing the chief events in the lives of eminent persons of all ages and nations*. Ed. Benjamin Vincent. London: Ward, 1877.

Ezama Gil, Ángeles. "Los relatos de viaje de Gertrudis Gómez de Avellaneda." *Anales de Literatura Española* 23 (2011): 323–35.

Farley, David. "Modernist Travel Writing." *The Routledge Companion to Travel Writing*. Ed. Carl Thompson. London: Routledge, 2016.

Felski, Rita. *The Gender of Modernity*. Cambridge: Harvard University Press, 1995.

Ferrús Antón, Beatriz. *Mujer y literatura de viajes en el siglo XIX: Entre España y las Américas*. Valencia: Universitat de València P., 2011.

Figarola-Caneda, Domingo and Emilia Boxhorn. *Gertrudis Gomez de Avellaneda: biografía, bibliografía e iconografía, incluyendo muchas cartas, inéditas o publicadas, escritas por la gran poetisa o dirigidas a ella, y sus memorias*. Madrid: Sociedad general española, 1929.

Floresta Brasileira Augusta, Nísia. *Opúsculo humanitário*. Ed. Peggy Sharpe. São Paulo: Cortez Editora, 1989.

———. *Cartas*. Ed. Constância Lima Duarte. Florianópolis: Editora Mulheres, 2002.

———. *Itinerário de uma viagem à Alemanha*. Florianópolis: Editora Mulheres, 1998.

———. *Três anos na Itália seguidos de uma viagem a Grécia*. Natal: Edu-RN, 1998.

———. *Trois ans en Italie suivis d'un voyage en Grèce: par une brésilienne*. Paris: E. Dentu, 1864.

———. *Inéditos e dispersos de Nísia Floresta*. Ed. Constância Lima Duarte. Natal: EDUFRN, 2009.

———. *Le Brésil: par Mme. Brasileira Augusta*. Paris: Librairie André Signier, 1871.

Floresta Brasileira Augusta, Nísia and Mary Wollstonescraft. *Direitos das mulheres e injustica dos homens*. Ed. Constância Lima Duarte. São Paulo: Cortez, 1989.

Forsdick, Charles. "Travel and the Body: Corporeality, Speed and Technology." *The Routledge Companion to Travel Writing*. Ed. Carl Thompson. London: Routledge, 2016.

Foster, Shirley and Sara Mills. *An Anthology of Women's Travel Writing*. Manchester: Manchester University Press, 2002.

Foucault, Michel. *The Archaeology of Knowledge*. London: Tavistock, 1974.

———. *The Order of Things: An Archaeology of the Human Sciences*. New York: Vintage Books, 1994.

Fraser, Nancy. "Rethinking the Public Sphere: A Contribution to the Critique of Actually Existing Democracy." *Social Text* 25 (1990): 56–80.

Fulford, Tim, Debbie Lee, and Peter J. Kitson. *Literature, Science and Exploration in the Romantic Era: Bodies of Knowledge*. Cambridge: Cambridge University Press, 2004.

Garcia, Rodolfo. "Introduction." *Correspondência entre Maria Graham e a Imperatriz Dona Leopoldina e Cartas Anexas by Maria Graham.* Rio de Janeiro: Biblioteca Nacional, 1940.
Gerassi-Navarro, Nina. *Women, Travel, and Science in Nineteenth-Century Americas: The Politics of Observation.* New York: Palgrave, 2017.
Gilbert, Sandra M. and Susan Gubar. *The Madwoman in the Attic: The Woman Writer and the Nineteenth-Century Literary Imagination.* New Haven: Yale University Press, 1979.
Gilson, Gregory, D. "Latin America and Logical Positivism." *Latin American Positivism.* Ed. Gregory D. Gilson and Irving W. Levinson, New York: Lexington Books, 2013.
Gómez de Avellaneda, Gertrudis. *Autobiografía y cartas.* Ed. Lorenzo Cruz de Fuentes. Madrid: Diputación Provincial de Huelva, 1996.
———. *Memorias Inéditas de La Avellaneda.* Ed. Domingo Figarola-Caneda. La Habana: Biblioteca Nacional, 1914.
———. *Diario íntimo.* Buenos Aires: Ediciones Universal, 1945.
———. "Mi última excursión por los Pirineos." *Obras: Tomo VI (Miscelánea).* La Habana: Aurelio Miranda, 1914.
———. *Cartas inéditas y documentos relativos a su vida en Cuba de 1859 a 1864.* Ed. José Augusto Escoto. Matanzas, 1911.
———. *Carta de Dª Gertrudis Gómez de Avellaneda dirigida a S. M. la Reina, acusando a Rivera de haber herido de muerte a su esposo, Diputado de la Nación, 1858.*
———. "Álbum cubano de lo bueno y lo belo." Habana: Imp. del Gobierno y Capitania General, 1860.
Gotch, Rosamund Brunel. *Maria, Lady Callcott: The Creator of "Little Arthur."* London: John Murray, 1937.
Graham, Maria. *Journal of a Voyage to Brazil, and Residence there, During Part of the Years 1821, 1822, 1823.* London: Longman, 1824.
———. *Journal of a Residence in Chile During the Year 1822, and a Voyage to Brazil in 1823.* Ed. Jennifer Hayward. Charlottesville: University of Virginia Press, 2003.
———. *Scripture Herbal.* London: Longman, 1842.
———. *Correspondência entre Maria Graham e a Imperatriz Leopoldina e Cartas Anexas.* Trans. Américo Jacobina Lacombe. Belo Horizonte: Itatiaia, 1997.
———. "Letter to the President and Members of the Geological Society in Answer to Certain Observations Contained in Mr. Greenough's Anniversary Address of 1834." London: T. Brettel, 1834.
———. "An Account of Some Effects of the Late Earthquakes in Chili." *Transactions of the Geological Society.* 2nd ser. 1.2 (1824): 413–15.
Hagglund, Betty. *Tourists and Travellers: Women's Non-Fictional Writing about Scotland, 1770–1830.* Bristol: Channel View Publications, 2010.
———. "The Botanical Writings of Maria Graham." *Journal of Literature and Science* 4.1 (2011): 44–58.
Hammond Matthews, Charlotte. *Gender, Race and Patriotism in the Works of Nísia Floresta.* Woodbridge: Tamesis, 2012.

Haraway, Donna Jeanne. *Simians, Cyborgs, and Women: The Reinvention of Nature.* New York: Routledge, 1991.

Harper, Lila Marz Harper. *Solitary Travelers: Nineteenth-Century Women's Travel Narratives and the Scientific Vocation.* Madison: Rosemont Publishing, 2001.

Harter, Hugh A. *Gertrudis Gómez de Avellaneda.* Boston: Twayne, 1981.

Haulman, Kate. *The Politics of Fashion in Eighteenth-Century America.* Charlotte: University of North Carolina Press, 2011.

Hayward, Jennifer. "No Unity of Design: Competing Discourses in Graham's Journal of a Residence in Chile." *Journal of a Residence in Chile During the Year 1822, and a Voyage to Brazil in 1823.* Ed. Maria Graham. Charlottesville: University of Virginia Press, 2003.

———. "Latin America." *The Routledge Companion to Travel Writing.* Ed. Carl Thompson. London: Routledge, 2016.

Hooker, William Jackson. *Botanical Miscellany: Containing Figures and Descriptions of Such Plants as Recommend Themselves by Their Novelty, Rarity, or History, or by the Uses to Which They Are Applied in the Arts, in Medicine, and in Domestic Economy; Together with Occasional Botanical Notices and Information.* London: John Murray, 1830.

Horta Duarte, Regina. "Olhares estrangeiros: viajantes no Vale do Rio Mucurí." *Revista Brasileira de História* 22 (2002): 267–88.

Hudson, Gill. "Unfathering the Thinkable: Gender, Science and Pacifism in the 1930s." *Science and Sensibility: Gender and Scientific Enquiry, 1780–1945.* Oxford and Cambridge: Basil Blackwell, 1991.

Humboldt, Alexander von. *Researches Concerning the Institutions & Monuments of the Ancient Inhabitants of America: With Descriptions and Views of Some of the Most Striking Scenes in the Cordilleras.* Trans. Helen Maria Williams. London: Longman, Hurst, Rees, Orme & Brown, J. Murray & H. Colburn, 1814.

———. *Views of the Cordilleras and Monuments of the Indigenous Peoples of the Americas.* Ed. Vera M. Kutzinski and Ottmar Ette. Chicago: University of Chicago Press, 2012.

Humboldt, Alexander von and Aimé Bonpland. *Personal Narrative of Travels to the Equinoctial Regions of America, During the Years 1799–1804.* Trans. Thomasina Ross. London: H.G. Bohn, 1852.

———. *Aspects of Nature, in Different Lands and Different Climates with Scientific Elucidations.* London: J. Murray, 1850.

———. *Atlas pittoresque du voyage: vues des Cordillières.* Amsterdam: Theatrum Orbis Terrarum, 1910.

Hulme, Peter and Tim Youngs. *Introduction to The Cambridge Companion to Travel Writing.* Ed. Peter Hulme and Tim Youngs. Cambridge: Cambridge, 2001.

Hunter, Melanie. "British Travel Writing and Imperial Authority." *Issues in Travel Writing: Empire, Spectacle, and Displacement.* Ed. Kristi Siegel. New York: Peter Lang, 2002.

Ianes, Raúl. "La esfericidad de papel: Gertrudis Gómez de Avellaneda, la condesa de Merlín, y la literatura de viajes." *Revista Iberoamericana* 63 (1997): 209–18.

Jacinto, Lizete and Eugenia Scarzanella. "Introducción: curar y enseñar." *Género y ciencia en América Latina: mujeres en la academia y en la clínica (siglos XIX–XXI)*. Frankfurt: Iberoamericana, 2011.

Jardine, Nicholas and Emma Spary. "The Natures of Natural History." *Cultures of Natural History*. Ed. N. Jardine, J. A. Secord, and E. C. Spary. Cambridge and New York: Cambridge University Press, 1997.

Kirkpatrick, Susan. *Las románticas: Women Writers and Subjectivity in Spain, 1835–1850*. Berkeley: University of California Press, 1989.

Kölbl-Ebert, Martina. "Observing Orogeny–Maria Graham's Account of the Earthquake in Chile in 1822." *Episodes* 22.1 (1999): 36–40.

Korte, Barbara. "Western Travel Writing, 1750–1950." *The Routledge Companion to Travel Writing*. Ed. Carl Thompson. London: Routledge, 2016.

Lammers, Thomas G. "Phylogeny, Biogeography, and Systematics of the Wahlenbergia fernandeziana Complex." *Systematic Botany* 21 (1996): 397–415.

Larsen, Anne. "Equipment for the field." *Cultures of Natural History*. Ed. N. Jardine, J. A. Secord, and E. C. Spary. Cambridge: Cambridge University Press, 1997.

Leiss, William. *The Domination of Nature*. Montreal: McGill-Queen's University Press, 1994.

Leopoldina. Maria. *Cartas de uma Imperatriz*. Ed. Bettina Kann and Patrícia Souza Lima. São Paulo: Editora Estação Liberdade, 2006.

Lightman, Bernard. *Victorian Popularizers of Science: Designing Nature for New Audiences*. Chicago: University of Chicago Press, 2010.

Lindsay, Claire. *Contemporary Travel Writing of Latin America*. New York: Routledge, 2010.

Lima Duarte, Constância. *Nísia Floresta: vida e obra*. Natal: Editora Universitária, 1995.

———. *Nísia Floresta: uma mulher à frente do seu tempo*. São Paulo: Mercado Cultural, 2006.

———. *Nísia Floresta: A primeira feminista do Brasil*. Florianópolis: Ed. Mulheres, 2005.

Lins, Ivan. *História do Positivismo no Brasil*. São Paulo: Editora Nacional, 1967.

Lopes, Maria Margaret. *O Brasil descobre a pesquisa científica: Os museus e as ciências naturais no século XIX*. São Paulo: Hucitec, 1997.

Lopes, Maria Margaret, and Irina Podgorny. "The Shaping of Latin American Museums of Natural History, 1850–1990." *Osiris* 15 (2000): 108–18.

Luna, Claudia. "Nísia Floresta: Una viajera brasileña en el viejo mundo." *Viajeras entre dos mundos*. Ed. Sara Beatriz Guardia. Dourados: UFGD, 2012.

Luna Peixoto, Ariane and Tarciso de Souza Filgueiras. "Maria Graham: anotações sobre a flora do Brasil." *Acta Botânica Brasilica* 22.4 (2008): 992–98.

Lutz, Bertha. *Função educativa dos museus*. Ed. Guilherme Miranda, Maria José Santos, Silvia Estevão, and Vitor da Fonseca. Rio de Janeiro: Museu Nacional, 2008.

Lyell, Charles. *Principles of Geology: Being an Enquiry How Far the Former Changes of the Earth Surface Are Referable to Causes Now in Operation*. London: John Murray, 1835.

Martínez Pinzón, Felipe. *Una cultura de invernadero : trópico y civilización en Colombia (1808–1928)*. Frankfurt: Iberoamericana, 2016.
Martins Castro, Luciana. "A contribuição de Nísia Floresta para a educação feminina: pioneirismo no Rio de Janeiro oitocentista." *Outros Tempos: Dossiê História e Educação* 7.10 (2010): 237–56.
Massey, Doreen. *Space, Place, and Gender*. Minneapolis: University of Minnesota Press, 1994.
Maynard, Mary. *Science and the Construction of Women*. Ed. Mary Maynard. New York: Routledge, 2003.
Meliá, Juan Tous. *La Medida de Teide: Historia, descripciones, erupciones y cartografía*. San Cristóbal de la Laguna, 2015.
Méndez Rodenas, Adriana. *Transatlantic Travels in Nineteenth-Century Latin America: European Women Pilgrims*, Lewisburg: Bucknell University Press, 2014.
Mills, Sara. *Discourses of Difference: An Analysis of Women's Travel Writing and Colonialism*. London: Routledge, 1991.
———. "Knowledge, Gender, and Empire." *Writing Women and Space: Colonial and Postcolonial Geographies*. Ed. Alison Blunt and Gillian Rose. New York: Guilford, 1994.
Míseres, Vanesa. *Mujeres en tránsito: Viaje, identidad y escritura en Sudamérica (1830–1910)*. Chappel Hill: University of North Carolina Press, 2018.
Nachtomy, Ohad. "Leibniz and Kant on Possibility and Existence." *British Journal for the History of Philosophy*. 20.5 (2012): 953–72.
Nenzi, Laura. "Pilgrims." *The Routledge Companion to Travel Writing*. Ed. Carl Thompson. London: Routledge, 2016.
Nugent, Thomas. *The Grand Tour: Containing an Exact Description of Most of the Cities, Towns, and Remarkable Places of Europe*. London: 1749.
Nunes, Cassiano. "Gonçalves Dias e a estética do indianismo." *Luso-Brazilian Review* 4.1 (1967): 35–48.
Olin Ireland, Norma. *Index to Women of the World from Ancient to Modern Times: Biographies and Portraits*. Westwood: Faxon Co., 1970.
Orr, Mary. "Pursuing Proper Protocol: Sarah Bowdich's Purview of the Sciences of Exploration." *Victorian Studies* 49.2 (2007): 277–85.
Pérez-Mejía, Ángela. *A Geography of Hard Times: Narratives about Travel to South America, 1780–1849*. Trans. Dick Cluster. New York: University of New York Press, 2002.
Picon Garfield, Evelyn. *Poder y sexualidad: El discurso de Gertrudis Gómez de Avellaneda*. Atlanta: Rodopi, 1993.
Poole, Deborah. *Vision, Race, and Modernity: A Visual Economy of the Andean Image World*. Princeton: Princeton University Press, 1997.
Pratt, Mary L. *Imperial Eyes: Travel Writing and Transculturation*. London: Routledge, 1992.
———. "Las mujeres y el imaginario nacional en el siglo XIX." *Revista de Crítica Literaria Latinoamericana* 19:38 (1993).
Raj, Kapil. "Introduction." *The Brokered World: Go-Betweens and Global Intelligence, 1770–1820*. Sagamore Beach, MA: Science History Publications, 2009.

Ramacciotti, Karina Inés and Adriana María Valobra. "Modernas esculapios: acción política e inserción profesional, 1900–1950." *Género y ciencia en América Latina: mujeres en la academia y en la clínica (siglos XIX–XXI)*. Ed. Lizette Jacinto and Eugenia Scarzanella. Frankfurt: Iberoamericana, 2011.

Rhodes Gollo, Rodney. "The Birth of a New Political Philosophy: Religion and Positivism in Nineteenth-Century Brazil." *Latin American Positivism*. Ed. Gregory D. Gilson and Irving W. Levinson. New York: Lexington Books, 2013.

Rose, R. S. "Brazil's Military Positivists: Another Myth in Need of Explosion?" *Latin American Positivism*. Ed. Gregory D. Gilson and Irving W. Levinson. New York: Lexington Books, 2013.

Rossiter, Margaret. *Women Scientists in America: Struggles and Strategies to 1940*. Baltimore: Johns Hopkins University Press, 1984.

Said, Edward. *Orientalism*. New York: Pantheon Books, 1978.

Sanchez Llama, Iñigo. *Galería de escritoras isabelinas: La prensa periódica entre 1833 y 1895*. Madrid: Cátedra, 2000.

Sapriza, Graciela. "Ciencia, política y reforma social: esperanzas y conflictos de la primera médica del Uruguay, Paulina Luisi (1875–1950)." *Género y ciencia en América Latina: mujeres en la academia y en la clínica (siglos XIX–XXI)*. Ed. Lizette Jacinto and Eugenia Scarzanella. Frankfurt: Iberoamericana, 2011.

Sawicki, Jana. "Identity Politics and Sexual Freedom: Foucault and Feminism." *Feminism and Foucault: Reflections on Resistance*. Boston: Northeastern University Press, 1988.

Scanlon, Geraldine. *Polémica feminista en la España contemporánea (1686–1974)*. Madrid: Akal, 1986.

Scatena Franco, Stela Maris. *Peregrinas de outrora: viajantes Latino-americanas no século XIX*. Florianópolis: Ed. Mulheres, 2008.

Schiebinger, Londa. *Plants and Empire: Colonial Bioprospecting in the Atlantic World*. Cambridge: Harvard University Press, 2004.

———. "Creating Sustainable Science." *The Gender and Science Reader*. Ed. Muriel Lederman and Ingrid Bartsch. New York: Routledge, 2000.

———. "Gender and Natural History." *Cultures of Natural History*. Ed. N. Jardine, J. A. Secord, and E. C. Spary. Cambridge and New York: Cambridge University Press, 1997.

———. *Has Feminism Changed Science?* Cambridge: Harvard University Press, 1999.

———. *The Mind Has No Sex? Women in the Origins of Modern Science*. Cambridge: Harvard University Press, 1989.

———. *Nature's Body: Gender in the Making of Modern Science*. Boston: Beacon Press, 1993.

Schriber, Mary Suzanne. *Writing Home: American Women Abroad, 1830–1920*. University of Virginia Press, 1997.

Scott, Joan Wallach. *Gender and the Politics of History*. New York: Columbia University Press, 1988.

Secord, James A. "Knowledge in Transit." *Isis* 95.4 (2004): 654–72.

Sharpe-Valadares, Peggy. "Introdução." *Opúsculo humanitário.* Ed. Peggy Sharpe-Valadares. São Paulo: Cortez Editora, 1989.
Shteir, Ann B. *Cultivating Women, Cultivating Science: Flora's Daughters and Botany in England, 1760 to 1860.* Baltimore: Johns Hopkins University Press, 1996.
———. "Botany in the Breakfast Room: Women and Early Nineteenth-Century British Plant Study." *Uneasy Careers and Intimate Lives: Women in Science, 1789–1979.* Ed. Pnina G. Abir-Am and Dorinda Outram. New Brunswick: Rutgers University Press, 1987.
Siegel, Kristi. "Introduction." *Issues in Travel Writing: Empire, Spectacle, and Displacement.* Ed. Kristi Siegel. New York: Peter Lang, 2002.
Simon, Linda. *The Greatest Shows on Earth: A History of the Circus.* London: Reaktion Books, 2014.
Smith, Sidonie. *Moving Lives: 20th-Century Women's Travel Writing.* Minneapolis: University of Minessota Press, 2001.
Smethurst, Paul. "Discoverers and Explorers." *The Routledge Companion to Travel Writing.* Ed. Carl Thompson. London: Routledge, 2016.
Sombrio, Mariana Moraes de Oliveira. "Em Busca pelo campo: Ciências, coleções, gênero e outras histórias sobre mulheres viajantes no Brasil em meados do século XX." Dissertation. Campinas: Unicamp, 2014.
Sommer, Doris. *Foundational Fictions: The National Romances of Latin America.* Berkeley: University of California Press, 1991.
Souza Maia, Ludmila de. "Viajantes de saias: gênero, literatura e viagem em Adèle Toussaint-Samson e Nísia Floresta (Europa e Brasil, século XIX)." Dissertation. Campinas: Unicamp, 2016.
Stepan, Nancy Leys. *Picturing Tropical Nature.* Ithaca: Cornell University Press, 2001.
Thompson, Carl, Betty Hagglund, and Esme Coulbert. *Maria Graham Project.* Nothingan University. 2007. Web. 5 May 2014.
Thompson, Carl. "Introduction." *The Routledge Companion to Travel Writing.* Ed. Carl Thompson. London: Routledge, 2016.
———. "'Journeys to Authority.' Reassessing Women's Early Travel Writing, 1763–1862." *Women's Writing* 24:2 (2017): 131–50.
———. "Earthquakes and Petticoats: Maria Graham, Geology, and Early Nineteenth-Century 'Polite' Science." *Journal of Victorian Culture,* 17:3 (2012): 329–56.
Torres, Claudia and Mónica Szurmuk. "New Genres, New Explorations of Womanhood: Travel Writers, Journalists, and Working Women." The Cambridge History of Latin American Women's Literature. Eds. Ileana Rodríguez and Mónica Szurmuk. Cambridge: Cambridge University Press, 2015.
Torquato Lima, Stélio. "O indianismo e o problema da identidade nacional em 'A Lágrima de um Caeté,' de Nísia Floresta." Dissertation. U Federal da Paraíba, 2008.
Turnbull, David. "Boundary-Crossings, Cultural Encounters and Knowledge Spaces in Early Australia." *The Brokered World: Go-Betweens and Global Intelligence, 1770–1820.* Ed. Simon Schaffer, Lissa Roberts, Kapil Raj, and James Delbourgo. Sagamore Beach: Science History Publications, 2009.

Valente, Waldemar. *Antecipação de Pernambuco no Movimento da Independência*. Recife: MEC, 1974.
Van Den Abbeele, Georges. *Travel as Metaphor: From Montaigne to Rosseau*. Oxford: University of Minnesota Press, 1992.
Varejão, Marcela. "Nísia Floresta e a emancipação mental brasileira." *Género y ciencia en América Latina: mujeres en la academia y en la clínica (siglos XIX–XXI)*. Ed. Lizette Jacinto and Eugenia Scarzanella. Frankfurt: Iberoamericana, 2011.
Watts, Ruth. *Women in Science: A Social and Cultural History*. London: Routledge, 2007.
Youngs, Tim. "Introduction." *Travel Writing in the Nineteenth Century: Filling the Blank Spaces*. Ed. Tim Youngs. London: Anthem Press, 2006.

ARCHIVAL MATERIALS

Child, Margaret. "Capital Careers." *The Evening Star*, September 7, 1948. Smithsonian Institution Archives, Washington, D.C. RU 7151, Box 7, Folder 9.
Cochran, Doris. "Just a Minute, Miss," 1935. Smithsonian Institution Archives, Washington, D.C. RU 7151, Box 2, Folder 5.
———. "Brazil Bound: With a Collector's Kit in South America." *Nature Magazine*, v. 33, 1940. Smithsonian Institution Archives, Washington, D.C. RU 7151, Box 7, Folder 9.
———. Letter to Adolpho Lutz. February 11, 1928, *Adolpho Lutz's Papers and Correspondence*. Archives of the National Museum of Rio de Janeiro (SEMEAR – Seção de Memória e Arquivo, UFRJ).
———. Letter to Bertha Lutz. December 15, 1933, *Bertha Lutz's Papers and Correspondence*. Archives of the National Museum of Rio de Janeiro (SEMEAR – Seção de Memória e Arquivo, UFRJ).
———. Letter to Bertha Lutz. January 23, 1930, *Bertha Lutz's Papers and Correspondence*. Archives of the National Museum of Rio de Janeiro (SEMEAR – Seção de Memória e Arquivo, UFRJ).
———. Letter to Bertha Lutz. June 3, 1934, *Bertha Lutz's Papers and Correspondence*. Archives of the National Museum of Rio de Janeiro (SEMEAR – Seção de Memória e Arquivo, UFRJ).
———. Letter to Bertha Lutz. June 13, 1942, *Bertha Lutz's Papers and Correspondence*. Archives of the National Museum of Rio de Janeiro (SEMEAR – Seção de Memória e Arquivo, UFRJ).
———. Letter to Bertha Lutz. October 23, 1951, *Bertha Lutz's Papers and Correspondence*. Archives of the National Museum of Rio de Janeiro (SEMEAR – Seção de Memória e Arquivo, UFRJ).
———. Letter to Bertha Lutz. April 13, 1968, *Bertha Lutz's Papers and Correspondence*. Archives of the National Museum of Rio de Janeiro (SEMEAR – Seção de Memória e Arquivo, UFRJ).

Floresta, Nísia. Letter to George-Louis Duvernoy. August 13, 1852, *George-Louis Duvernoy Papers*. Central Library–National Museum of Natural History, Paris (Bibliothèque centrale du Muséum national d'histoire naturelle), Ms 2743/116-117.

———. Letter to George-Louis Duvernoy. March 24, 1855, *George-Louis Duvernoy Papers*. Central Library–National Museum of Natural History, Paris (Bibliothèque centrale du Muséum national d'histoire naturelle), Ms 2743/116-117.

———. "Frog Collecting in Brazil." Smithsonian Institution Archives, Washington, D.C. RU 7151, Box 2, Folder 1.

"Frog Lady." *The American Magazine*, August 1956. RU 7151, Box 7, Folders 14-15. Smithsonian Institution Archives, Washington, D.C. RU 7151, Box 7, Folder 9.

Graham, Maria. *Life of D. Pedro*. 1835. Manuscript. National Library of Rio de Janeiro.

"Lady Expert Has Kind Word, Useful Hints for the Frogs." *Unidentified Source*, August 28, 1956. Smithsonian Institution Archives, Washington, D.C. RU 7151, Box 7, Folder 9.

———. "Letter to Sir William Hooker." Archives of the Kew Gardens Library, April 11, 1824, *Directors' Correspondence XLIII,* 1824.

Lutz, Adolpho. Letter to Doris Cochran. January 4, 1938. Smithsonian Institution Archives, Washington, D.C. RU 7151, Box 7, Folder 10.

Lutz, Bertha. Letter to Doris Cochran. October 22, 1940. Smithsonian Institution Archives, Washington, D.C. RU 7151, Box 7, Folder 11.

Shelton, Elizabeth, "Dr. Cochran: Curator of Curious Pets." *The Washington Post* August 25, 1956. Smithsonian Institution Archives, Washington, D.C. RU 7151, Box 7, Folder 9.

Smith, Waldo. Letter to Doris Cochran. November 28, 1939. Smithsonian Institution Archives, Washington, D.C. RU 7151, Box 7, Folder 12.

"Snakes Alive! Here's a Woman Who Prefers Them that Way." *Minneapolis Morning Tribune*, November 2, 1953. Smithsonian Institution Archives, Washington, D.C. RU 7151, Box 7, Folder 9.

"Women Scientist Back with Ton of Specimens." *Washington Post*, August 15, 1935. Smithsonian Institution Archives, Washington, D.C. RU 7151, Box 7, Folder 14.

Index

Académies des Sciences, Curie membership denial from, 5
"An Account of some Effects of the Late Earthquakes in Chili [sic]" (Graham, M.), 40
adventure hero, Mills and Foster on, 30
Agassiz, Elizabeth Cary, 10
Agassiz, Louis, 3, 116, 129
Akel, Regina, 19n4, 38
Albin, Maria C., 60
Album Cubano de lo Bueno y de lo Bello magazine (Album), of Gómez de Avellaneda, 16, 69–70, 79, 82–84, 87n37; "La Cueva de las Brujas" in, 72–75; sections of, 71; writers for, 91n76
de Alencar, José Martiniano, 97, 98, 130nn6–7
"Al Partir" (Gómez de Avellaneda), 53
alternate visibility, of women authors: Ardinghelli on, 15; of Cochran, 168–74; of Floresta, 107–12, 127–29; Rossiter on, 183
America: Humboldt on nature of, 4, 21, 61, 117; Humboldt voyage to, 3, 34, 60
Anderson, Monica, 149–50
anti-conquest rhetoric, Pratt on, 158
Ardinghelli, Mariangela, 15

d'Arouet, François-Marie, 132n20
de Artega y Loinaz, Heloysa, 57, 59
Auber de Noya, Virginia Felicia, 72–75, 88n49, 89n65
Aublet, Jean Baptiste, 35
Augustin Serres, Etienne Reynard, 132n20
authority, 181; of Cochran, 150, 152, 163–64; in contact zone, 10; of Floresta, 107–12; Gilbert and Gubar on women literary, 63; of Gómez de Avellaneda, 16, 69, 82–84; Graham, M., negotiation of, 15, 21, 29–34, 40, 45–46; of Humboldt, 34; Hunter on imperial, 61; imperialist identity and, 10; Mills on, 8–9

barbarism vs. white civilization discourse, 4, 117–18; on Latin America, 58
Barbour, Thomas, 147, 178n16
Barman, Roderick J.: on D. Pedro II, 97; on France and Brazil connections, 101
bearleaders, on Grand Tour, 122–23
Beebe, Charles William, 144, 177n12
Beethoven, Ludwig von, 129
Bell, Charles N., 3, 116
Benjamin, Marina, 54

Bertucci, Paola, 15
biographical information: on Cochran, 140–41; on Floresta, N., 94–96; on Graham, M., 22–23; on Gómez de Avellaneda, G., 54–55; on Hooker, 50n18; on Lutz, B., 142
biographies, Graham, M., use of, 16
Bird, Isabella, 108–9
Birke, Lynda, 104
Birkett, Dea, 41
Bleichmar, Daniela, 65
Bonaventure Orfila, Mathieu Joseph, 132n20
Bonifácio de Andrada, José, 26, 97
Book of Botanical Illustrations (Graham, M.), 46
Botanical Gardens in Latin America, 3, 33, 48n1, 50n19
Botanical Miscellany (Hooker), 46
botanist, Graham, M., as, 18, 42
botany: feminization of, 7, 42–43; Graham, M., observations in, 29, 31–33, 38, 41, 46; Shteir on, 45
Bowdich, Sarah, 39–40
Bramble: Graham, M., on, 43, *44*; Hasselquist on, 43
Bravo, Michael T., 51n27
Brazil: Barman on France connection with, 101; birthplace of Floresta, 94; Cochran and monkey skin from, *173*, 173–74; Floresta educational reform goal in, 106; Graham, M., travel in, 22–23; history of, 97; racial miscegenation in, 98, 154; Rio Seco family in, 25–26, 49n11; scientific travels and explorations of Cochran in, 146, 149–56, 178n19; travel narratives of Graham, M., in, 15–16; women secondary role in, 98
Brazil Bound: With a Collector's Kit in South America (Cochran), 178n19
Brazilian Academy of Sciences, 144
Brazilian Federation for Feminine Progress, of Lutz, B., 143
Brazilian Species of Hyla (Lutz, B.), 144

Bremer, Fredrika, 9
Le Brésil (Floresta), 128
Breton, Adela, 9
Bridgewater Treatises (1833–1840), 79–80
Browning, Robert, 154, 155
Buzard, James, 64

Caesar, Terry, 148
Calderón de la Barca, Frances, 10
Callcott (Lady). *See* Graham, Maria
Callcott, Augustus Wall, 23
"Canção do Exílio" (Gonçalves Dias), 97–98, 120
Cañizares-Esguerra, Jorge, 3
Carnegie Corporation, 146
Castel Sant'Elmo, Floresta description of, 126
Catt, Carrie Chapman, 146
cemeteries, Gómez de Avellaneda visiting of, 62, 85n22
Cepeda, Ignacio de, 54–55
Chamberlain, Henry, 49n11
Chard, Chloe, 122
Chateaubriand, François-René de, 98, 119, 130n9
Chile earthquake, Graham, M., on, 40–41, 51n26
civilizing mission, Pratt on, 58
Cochran, Doris Mable, 8, 14, 18, 19n3, 139; alternate visibility of, 168–74; authority of, 150, 152, 163–64; biographical information about, 140–41; Brazil monkey skin and, *173*, 173–74; Brazil scientific travels and explorations, 146, 149–56, 178n19; in collecting outfit, 161–63, *162*; diaries of, 149, 157, 164, 167, 178n21, 179n29; as "Frog Lady," 157, 168–74; gender limits, 157–64; hegemonic superiority of, 153–56; on herpetology, 1, 17, 141, 146, 167–68; as illustrator, 140–41; imperialist identity alignment by, 152; last letter to Lutz, B., 174–76;

Lutz, A., supervision of, 158–59, 169–70; Lutz, B., mutual interest with, 144–49; Lutz, B., relationship with, 140–49, 170; as Smithsonian Institute herpetologist, 17, 141, 146, 176n4; at Smithsonian Museum of Natural History, 141, *142*; as transatlantic eye-witness, 154; transatlantic subjectivity of, 140; U.S. Ex., alignment by, 152–53
Colégio Augusto school, of Floresta, 96, 99–100
Collège de France, Floresta attendance at, 101, 102
Comte, Augusto, 81, 101, 137n64; Floresta relationship with, 128–29; positivist ideas of, 128–29, 131n17
Conselhos à minha filha (Floresta), 99–100, 104
Consigli a mia figlia (Floresta), 96
Constant, Benjamin, 131n17
contact zone: authority in, 10; defined, 9; Graham, M., freedom in, 31; Graham, M., social networks in, 23–29, 47; Mills on, 9, 61; mobility with movement within, 12; Pratt on, 9, 23
Contemporary Travel Writing of Latin America (Lindsay), 10
Correspondência entre Maria Graham e a Imperatriz Dona Leopoldina e Cartas Anexas.(Graham, M.), 23, 49n4
counterpublic spaces, Fraser on, 87n39
Cousin, Victor, 79
Creole, in Latin America: elites, on barbarism vs. white civilization discourse, 4, 117–18; Pratt on scientific travels and national identities of, 3
Cresswell, Tim, 13, 19n7
"La Cueva de las Brujas" (Auber), 72–75
Curie, Marie, 177n8; Académies des Sciences membership denial to, 5
Cuvier, Georges, 101, 105, 131n16

Darwin, Charles, 81, 88n52
Denegri, Francesca, 113
The Descent of Man, and Selection in Relation to Sex (Darwin), 81
diaries: of Cochran, 149, 157, 164, 167, 178n21, 179n29; of Floresta, 93, 109, 110, 115–16; of Graham, M., 22–23, 35; Hagglund on, 51n31
Diario de la Marina Cuban newspaper, 64, 68, 86n24
Dias, Antônio Gonçalves. *See* Gonçalves Dias, Antônio
Direitos das mulheres e injustiça dos homens (Floresta), 96, 98, 99, 103, 104
discourse: barbarism vs. white civilization, 4, 58, 117–18; Foucault on, 4; natural history, 4; religious, 42, 80
discrimination, against women scientists, 182
D. Pedro I (emperor), 26, 97, 131n17; Graham, M., as tutor to daughter of, 23, 50n14
D. Pedro II (emperor), 131n17; Barman on, 97; financial support from, 98, 130n10
dragon tree, Graham, M., and Humboldt on, 35–37, *36*
Duarte, Constância Lima, 19n4, 129n3, 130n13, 134n25
Dumas, Alexandre, 137n64
Dundas, David, 22
Dundas, George, 22
Dundas, Maria. *See* Graham, Maria
Duvernoy, George-Louis, 124, 131n16; Floresta friendship with, 101, 103, 105, 112; Floresta pilgrimage to tomb of, 113–15

education: Floresta as educator, 18, 94–96; Grand Tour nature and, 123; lack of, for Latin American women, 7, 105; Michelet on women, 127;

model for girls, of Floresta, 17, 97–100
Endowment for International Peace, 146
Enlightenment period, 3; Latin America nature and, 117; Voltaire and, 132n20; women scientific work during, 23
Escallonia Callcottiae, Graham, M., plant of, 46, *47*
Espina, Concha, 10
Europe: Floresta life in, 96; Floresta on landscape of, 111–12, 118; Gómez de Avellaneda arrival in, 57–58; Schiebinger on, 59–60; women status in, 24
European travelers: Floresta as, 100–107; Mills on, 2
evolutionary narratives, Felski on, 126
exotic nature, of Latin America, 116–17

de Faria Rocha, Manuel Augusto, 95
Felski, Rita, 126
feminist movement, 6, 7, 139–40; Lutz, B., involvement with, 142–43, 176n7
feminists: on gendered inequalities, 34; Haraway on, 186
feminization: of botany, 7, 42–43; of natural history, 14
Ferrús Antón, Beatriz, 9, 19n4
Field Museum of Natural History, 46
financial support, from D. Pedro II, 98, 130n10
Flora Brasiliensis, Martius collection of, 47, 51n30
Floresta, Nísia, 8, 14, 16, 93, 95, 129, 130n6; alternate visibility of, 107–12, 127–29; authority of, 107–12; Brazil birthplace of, 94; Brazil educational reform goal of, 106; Castel Sant'Elmo description by, 126; Colégio Augusto school of, 96, 99–100; Collège de France attendance by, 101, *102*; Comte relationship with, 128–29; death of, 96; diaries and letters of, 109, 110, 115–16; Duvernoy friendship with, 101, 103, 105, 112; as educator, 18, 94–96; on European landscape, 111–12, 118; Europe life of, 96; Europe travel by, 100–107; grandiose expressions of, 118–19; Grand Tour and, 17, 121–27; Humboldt mentorship of, 124; *Itinéraire* of, 96, 112–15, 135n37; on lack of education and women inferiority, 105; Monarch-of-All-I-Survey rhetoric of, 111, 112, 120; on narrative for education model for girls, 17, 97–100; Paris residence of, 100–101; pseudonyms of, 94, 108, 128; on sublime, 121; as transatlantic eye-witness, 116; transatlantic subjectivity of, 107–12; *Trois ans en Italie* by, 96, 115–21; Vesuvius Volcano and, 119, 124–25; watercolor portrait of, *95*; on women equal rights, 99
Forsdick, Charles, 12
Foster, Shirley, 19n5, 110, 155; on adventure hero, 30
Foucault, Michel, 4
Fowler, Amy, 142
"Fra Lippo Lippi" (Browning), 154, 155
France: Barman on Brazil connection with, 101; Gómez de Avellaneda in, 60–61
Franchi (Marquis), 35
Fraser, Nancy, 87n39
French Pyrenees, Gómez de Avellaneda on, 64–65, 67, 87n35, 119
"Frog Lady," Cochran as, 157, 168–74
Fulford, Tim, 8, 40, 51n20

Gaige, Helen Thompson, 178n17
Garfield, Picon, 79, 90n68, 90n71
gender constraints, 183; male protection and women, 158–59
gendered characteristic, of space, 13
gendered condition negotiation, 13–14, 183

gendered inequalities, feminists on, 34
Gendered Mobilities (Uteng and Cresswell), 19n7
gendered scientific discourse, Schiebinger on, 5, 34, 105
gender limits: Cochran on, 157–64; in Spain, 63
gender roles negotiation, for mobility, 12
A General View of Positivism (Comte), 131n17
A Geography of Hard Times (Pérez-Mejía), 3, 116–17
Gerassi-Navarro, Nina, 10
Gertrudis Gómez de Avellaneda (Harter), 84n5
Gilbert, Sandra M., 39, 59; on patriarchal literary standards, 71; on women literary authority, 63
Goin, Coleman Jett, 175, 179n33
Gómez de Avellaneda, Gertrudis, 8, 9, 14; Album magazine of, 16, 69–74, 79, 82–84, 87n37, 91n76; cemeteries visited by, 62, 85n22; Cepeda relationship with, 54–55; de la Costa portrait of, *55*, 84n6; *Diario de la Marina* articles of, 64, 68; on Europe arrival, 57–58; in France, 60–61; on French Pyrenees, 64–65, 67, 87n35, 119; Heredia as tutor to, 54; Humboldt and Heredia dialogues with, 54; hurricane during voyage of, 53; literary authority of, 69, 83; *Memorias* of, 16, 53, 57–63, 67, 68; "Mi última" of, 16, 56, 64–69; move to Madrid, 55; networks and authority of, 16, 82–84; periodical writings of, 69–82; religious discourse and, 80; on Retama Plains volcano, 73, 73–74; Sabater marriage to, 55; scientific knowledge and, 69–70; Sommer on, 67–68; on sublime, 66; tourist representation by, 64–65; transatlantic subjectivity of, 16, 56, 61, 68, 83; transatlantic travels of, 57–63; travel narratives of, 56; Verdugo marriage to, 55; women's inferiority opposition by, 81; writer path of, 18, 54–56

Gonçalves Dias, Antônio, 97, 120, 130nn6–7; D. Pedro II financial support to, 98

Gonçalves Pinto Lisboa, Dionísia. *See* Floresta, Nísia

Gonçalves Pinto Lisboa, Dionísio: assassination of, 95; as Floresta's father, 94

Graham, Maria, 8, 9, 14, 51n21; authority negotiation and, 15, 21, 29–34, 40, 45–46; biographical information on, 22–23; biographies and religious books used by, 16; botanical observations of, 29, 31–33, 38, 41, 46; as botanist, 18, 42; on Bramble, 43, *44*; Brazil travel by, 22–23; Brazil travel narratives of, 15–16; on Chile earthquake, 40–41, 51n26; contact zone freedom, 31; contact zone social networks, 23–29, 47; diaries of, 22–23, 35; as D. Pedro I daughter's tutor, 23, 50n14; on dragon tree, 35–37, *36*; Hayward journal publication of, 49nn4–5; Hayward on male criticism, 39, 49n8; Hooker collaboration with, 45–46; on Humboldt dragon tree, 35–37, *36*; on Humboldt sepulchers of Guanches, 37–38; imperialist identity of, 15, 22, 24, 47–48; Lammers on, 46; on landscape, 119; male force alignment by, 24; male protection lack for, 40; Maria Leopoldina friendship with, 25–28, 49n11, 50nn12–13; masculine sciences world and, 21–22, 34–39; plant specimens discovery by, 23, 45–46, 47, *47*; Pratt on explanatory language of, 36–37; racial statements of, 24–25; religious discourse use by, 42; Rio de Janeiro social networks in, 25–26, 49n11; as social

explorer, 16, 28–34, 48, 50n15;
Soledad Caballero on, 49nn4–5, 60;
sugar cane plantation visit by, 29,
41, 50n17; superiority position of,
25–27; transatlantic subjectivity and,
29–34, 41, 43, 48; work of, 39–48
Graham, Thomas, 22
Grand Tour: bearleaders on, 122–23;
Chard on, 122; educational nature of,
123; Floresta and, 17, 121–27
The Grand Tour (Nugent), 122
Greenough, George, 41
Gubar, Susan, 39, 59; on patriarchal
literary standards, 71; on women
literary authority, 63

Hagglund, Betty, 51n31
Hammond Matthews, Charlotte, 19n4,
130n10, 131n18; on Floresta, 94
Haraway, Donna Jeanne, 185; on
feminists, 186
Harper, Lila Marz, 182; on Kingsley,
161; on travel narratives for women
scientific discoveries, 5
Hasselquist, Fredric, 43–44
Hayward, Jennifer, 19n4; Graham, M.,
journal publication by, 49nn4–5;
on Graham, M., male criticism, 39,
49n8; on industrialization, 152
hegemonic superiority, 184; of Cochran,
153–56
Helvétius, Claude Adrien, 132n20
Heredia, José Maria, 53, 84n2; as
Gómez de Avellaneda tutor, 54
herpetology: Cochran on, 1, 17, 141,
146, 167–68; Joaquim as expert in,
170–71
history, of Brazil, 97
Hobbes, Thomas, 123
Hoffman, Ella, 9
Hooker, William, 29, 45–46, 50n13,
51n21; biographical information on,
50n18
Hugo, Victor, 129, 137n64
Hulme, Peter, 34

Humanitarian Opuscule (Floresta), 103
von Humboldt, Alexander, 49n6, 54, 72,
75–76, 88n52, 110, 116; on America
nature, 4, 21, 61, 117; America
voyage of, 3, 34, 60; authority of, 34;
barbarism vs. white civilization and,
4, 117–18; on dragon tree, 35–37,
36; Floresta reference to, 124; Hulme
and Youngs on, 34; Pratt on, 34; on
sepulchers of Guanches, 37–38; on
sublime, 66, 93, 111
Hunter, Melanie, 61
hurricane, during Gómez de Avellaneda
voyage, 53
Hyla Faber frog, Lutz, B., study of,
144, 166

idealist strategies, for women scientists
inclusion, 6
illustrator, Cochran as, 140–41
imperial authority, Hunter on, 61
imperialist expansion, natural history
for, 2–3
imperialist identity: alignment with,
152, 184; authority and, 10; Cochran
alignment with, 152; of Graham, M.,
15, 22, 24, 47–48; Pérez-Mejía on
women, 24; of Tristán, 24
Imperial Museum, 50n12
industrialization, Hayward on, 152
Inglis, Frances Erskine, 9
institutionalization, of science, 7
Instituto Oswaldo Cruz, 158, 169–70,
179n26
International Women's Suffrage
Alliance, 143
Iracema (de Alencar), 98
Isabel de Borbón (queen), 88n43
Itinéraire d'un voyage en Allemagne
(*Itinéraire*) (Floresta), 96, 112,
135n37; on Duvernoy tomb
pilgrimage, 113–15

Jacobina, Américo, 49n4
Jardine, Nicholas, 2

Joaquim, as herpetology expert, 170–71
Journal of a Residence in Chile during the Year 1822, and a Voyage from Chile to Brazil in 1823 (Graham, M.), 40
Journal of a Voyage to Brazil and Residence there, During Part of the Years 1821, 1822, 1823 (Graham, M.), 23
Journeys to Authority: Reassessing Women's Early Travel Writing, 1763-1862 (Thompson), 181
Jungle Peace (Beebe), 144, 177n12
"Just a Minute, Miss" (Cochran), 140, 149, 164, 168, 178n19; reason for name of, 151–52

Kant, Immanuel, 112–13
Kellogg, A. Remington, 145, 178n13
Kingsley, Mary, 21, 159–60, 161
Kirkpatrick, Susan, 71
Kitson, Peter J., 8, 40, 51n20
knowledge: Gómez de Avellaneda and scientific, 69–70; production of, natural history discourse and, 4; restrictive, 6
Kölbl-Ebert, Martina, 41

de la Costa, Fernando, 55, 84n6
"Lágrima de um Caeté" (Floresta), 130n6, 130n12
Lammers, Thomas G., 51n29; on Graham, M., 46
Langford, John, 49n1
Latin America, 2; barbarism of, 58; Botanical Gardens in, 3, 33, 48n1, 50n19; Caesar on perception of, 148; Enlightenment period and, 117; exotic nature of, 116–17; nature control and, 3; patriarchal system in, 7; women lack of education in, 7, 105
League for the Intellectual Emancipation of Women, 142
lectotype, 47, 51n29

Lee, Debbie, 9, 40, 51n20
de León, Fray Luis, 79, 90n68
"Life of D. Pedro" (Graham, M.), 23, 49nn4–5; on botanical observations, 29, 38, 41
Lightman, Bernard, 70, 77–78, 87n41
Lindsay, Claire, 10
Linnaeus, 43, 165
literary authority: Gilbert and Gubar on, 63; of Gómez de Avellaneda, 69, 83
Living Amphibians of the World (Cochran), 141
Locke, John, 123
London Geological Society, 40
Lopes, Maria Margaret, 176n7
Luna, Cláudia, 94
Lutz, Adolpho, 142, *143*, 178n15; Cochran under supervision of, 158–59, 169–70
Lutz, Bertha Maria Júlia, 17, 139, *143*; biographical information on, 142; Brazilian Federation for Feminine Progress formed by, 143; Cochran last letter to, 174–76; Cochran mutual interests with, 144–49; Cochran relationship with, 140–49, 170; feminist movement involvement by, 142–43, 176n7; *Hyla Faber* frog study by, 144, 166; Lopes on, 176n7; as suffrage movement leader, 142–43
Lyell, Charles, 41

male protection: Graham, M., lack of, 40; women gender constraints and, 157–59
male racial superiority, 14; Graham, M., alignment with force of, 24; women alignment with, 24
males, women scientists compliance with, 147
Mansilla, Eduarda, 10
"Mapping the Unknown: European Women Travelers in Humboldt's New World" (Méndez Rodenas), 50n16

Maria da Gloria (princess), 23, 50nn12–13
Maria Leopoldina (empress), Graham, M., friendship with, 25–28, 49n4, 49n11, 50nn12–13
masculine sciences world, Graham, M., and, 21–22, 34–39
Massey, Doris: on gendered characteristic of space, 13; on mobility constraints, 12
Matto de Turner, Clorinda, 9–10, 110
Mélanges de botanique et de voyage (Petit-Thouars), 38–39
Memorias inéditas de La Avellaneda (*Memorias*) (Gómez de Avellaneda), 16, 53, 57–63, 67, 68
Méndez Rodenas, Adriana, 9, 19n4, 50n16; on Graham, M., dragon tree account, 36–37; on Latin American women travelers, 108; on pilgrimage narratives, 133n23, 134n32; on transatlantic perspective, 11, 13
Metcalf, Maynard Mayo, 144, 177n11
Michelet, Jules, 127
Mills, Sara, 2, 13–14, 19n5, 49n7, 129, 155; on adventure hero, 30; on authority, 8–9; on contact zone, 9, 61; on male force alignments, 24; on women discursive constraints, 39; on women travel writer scientific posture, 110
Míseres, Vanesa, 11, 13, 19n4; on transnational imaginary, 11
"Misterios del aire" (The Mysteries of the Air) (Zenea), 76–77
"Mi última excursión a los Pirineos" (Mi última) (Gómez de Avellaneda), 16, 56, 64–69
mobility, in travel narratives, 183; Cresswell and Uteng on, 13; Forsdick on, 12; gender roles negotiation for, 12; Massey on constraints in, 12; by movement within contact zones, 12; space definition and regulation, 12

Molina, Silvia, 10
Monarch-of-All-I-Survey rhetoric, of Floresta, 111, 112, 120, 160
de Montoya, Laura, 9
Moritz Rugendas, Johann, 128
"La mujer" (Gómez de Avellaneda), 80
Mujeres en tránsito: Viaje, identidad y escritura en Sudamérica (Míseres), 11
"Las mujeres y el imaginario nacional en el siglo XIX" (Pratt), 84n4
Mujer y literatura de viajes en el siglo XIX: entre España y las Américas (Antón), 9
Murphy, Patricia, 81

National Geographic Magazine, 167
National Library of Madrid, 82
National Library of Rio de Janeiro, Graham, M., manuscript in, 23, 49n4
National Museum of Rio de Janeiro, 146, 177n9
native, Latin American: lack of civilization presentation of, 4, 117–18; Pérez-Mejía on, 4, 117
natural history, 1; Bleichmar on, 65; discourse, production of knowledge in, 4; feminization of, 14; for imperialist expansion, 2–3; post-structuralist feminist approach to, 8; reality in, 2
naturalist missions, Pratt on, 165
negotiation: gendered condition, 13–14, 183; of gender roles, for mobility, 12; Graham, M., authority, 15, 21, 29–34, 40, 45–46
Nugent, Thomas, 122

"Oda al Niagara" (Heredia), 53, 84n2
Opúsculo Humanitário (Floresta), 102–3, 104, 106; travel narratives in, 107
Orr, Mary, 39–40

de Paiva Maury, Carlota Joaquina, 177n8

Palhares-Burke, Maria Lúcia Garcia, 130n13
Pan American Conference, Lutz, B., at, 143
passion for the tropics, Stepan on, 2
patriarchal literary standards, Gilbert and Gubar on, 71
patriarchal society, scientific discourse agenda of, 5
patriarchal system, in Latin America, 7
Peregrinas de outrora: viajantes latino-americanas no século XIX (Scatena Franco), 9
Pérez-Mejía, Angela, 3, 4, 19n4, 116–17; on women imperialist identity, 24
Personal Narrative of Travels to the Equinoctial Regions of America (Humboldt), 34, 38, 72, 75–76, 88n52
Petit-Thouars, Aubert du, 35, 38–39, 51n22
pilgrimage narratives, 113; Méndez Rodenas on, 133n23, 134n32
Piñeyro, Enrique, 71
plant specimens discovery, by Graham, M., 23, 45–46, 47, *47*
Poole, Deborah, 110–11
Porter, Denis, 133n23
positivist ideas: of Comte, 128–29, 131n17; of Floresta, 137n64; of Varejão, 129
post-structuralist feminist approach to, 8
Pratt, Mary Louise, 38, 84n4, 125; anti-conquest rhetoric and, 158; on civilizing mission, 58; contact zone and, 9, 23; on Creole elite and scientific travels, 3; explanatory language, of Graham, M., and, 36–37; on Graham, M., as social explorer, 50n15; on Humboldt, 34; on Kingsley, 160; Monarch-of-All-I-Survey of, 160; naturalist missions and, 165; social explorer and, 28, 50n15; on travelers, 2, 111; travel narratives heterogeneity of, 6
presence, in travel narratives, 12; on both sides of Atlantic, 13; gendered condition negotiation in, 13–14; Said on, 13
Principles of Geology, Graham, M., report in, 41
pseudonyms, of Floresta, 94, 108, 128
Puga, Maria Luisa, 10
Pyramus de Candolle, Augustin, 51n28

racial miscegenation: in Brazil, 154; Sommer on Brazil, 98
Racine, Jean-Baptiste, 132n20
Raj, Kapil, 82–83
Real Academia Española, Gómez de Avellaneda as member of, 56, 84n7
realistic strategies, for women scientists inclusion, 6–7
religious books, Graham, M., use of, 16
religious discourse: Gómez de Avellaneda and, 80; Graham, M., use of, 42
research, Rossiter on women scientists, 6, 18n2, 139, 141
restrictive knowledge, 6
Retama Plains volcano, *73*, 73–74
rhetorical and political construct, in scientific discourse, 182
Rio de Janeiro: Floresta Colégio Augusto school in, 96, 99–100; Graham, M., social networks in, 25, 49n11
Rio Seco family, Graham, M., social networks with, 25–26, 49n11
Rivera, Antonio, 82
Rossiter, Margaret: on alternate visibility, 183; American women scientists research by, 6, 18n2, 139, 141; male compliance with women scientists, 147

Sab (Gómez de Avellaneda), 55, 67–68
Sabater, Pedro, 55
Said, Edward, 13, 129
de Saint-Hilaire, Auguste, 128

Sanborn, Helen, 9
Sánchez Llama, Iñigo, 70–71, 88n45, 88nn42–43
Scanlon, Geraldine, 80
Scatena Franco, Stela Maris, 9, 19n4, 67, 84n9, 86n33, 110
Schiebinger, Londa, 59–60; on gendered scientific discourse, 5, 34, 105; on post-structuralist feminist approach to, 8; on women scientists, 150
Schmitt, Waldo, 144
Schönlein, Johann Lukas, 132n20
science: Benjamin on women writers on, 54; Birke on gender and, 104; botany, 7, 29, 31–33, 38, 41, 42–43, 45, 46; herpetology, 1, 17, 141, 146, 167–68, 170–71; institutionalization of, 7; professionalization of, 182. *See also* women scientists
Science, Engineering, and Mathematics (STEM) fields, 186
scientific careers, 6
scientific discourse: patriarchal society agenda, 5; rhetorical and political construct in, 182; Schiebinger on gendered, 5, 34, 105; women inferiority perception in, 5
scientific knowledge, Gómez de Avellaneda and, 69–70
scientific theories, on women incapable of academic tasks, 5
Scintille d'un'anima brasiliana (Floresta), 96
Scott, Joan W., 185
Scripture Herbal (Graham, M.), 42, 44
sepulchers of Guanches, 37–38
Shteir, Ann B., 23; on botany, 45
Simon, Linda, 163
Smith, Adam, 123
Smithsonian Institute, Cochrane as herpetologist of, 17, 141, 146, 176n4
Smithsonian Museum of Natural History, Cochran at, 141, *142*

Snethlage, Emilia, 177n8
social explorer, Graham, M., as, 16, 28–34, 48, 50n15
social networks, 184; in contact zone, of Graham, M., 23–29, 47; of Graham, M., with Rio Seco family, 25–26, 49n11
Soledad Caballero, Maria, 19n4; on Graham, M., 49nn4–5, 60
Sommer, Doris, 67–68; on Brazil racial miscegenation, 98
Souza Maia, Ludmila, 132nn18–19
space: defined and regulated, for women, 12; Foster and Mills on, 19n4; Fraser on counterpublic, 87n39; Massey on gendered characteristic of, 13
Spain, gender limits in, 63
Spanish Romanticism, 55
Spary, Emma, 2
Stejneger, Leonhard, 141, 145, 146–47, 176n2
STEM. *See* Science, Engineering, and Mathematics
Stepan, Nancy Leys, 2
sublime: Floresta on, 121; Gómez de Avellaneda on, 66; Humboldt on, 66, 93, 111
suffragist movement, 6, 7, 139–40; Lutz, B., as leader of, 142–43
sugar cane plantation visit, by Graham, M., 29, 41, 50n17
superiority: Graham, M., position of, 25–27; hegemonic, 153–56, 184; male racial, 14, 24
Szurmuk, Monica, 19n4, 108, 110

Terra, Gabriel, 7
Thompson, Carl, 41, 108, 181; on travel narratives, 150
Torre, Claudia, 108
tourist: Buzard on experience of, 64; Gómez de Avellaneda representation as, 64–65

Transactions of the Geological Society, Graham, M., report in, 40–41
transatlantic eye-witness: Cochran as, 154; Floresta as, 116
transatlantic perspective, Méndez Rodenas on, 11, 13
transatlantic subjectivity, 11–12, 184; of Cochran, 140; of Floresta, 107–12; of Gómez de Avellaneda, 16, 56, 61, 68, 83; Graham, M., and, 29–34, 41, 43, 48
Transatlantic Travels in Nineteenth-Century Latin America: European Women Pilgrims (Méndez Rodenas), 9
transnational imaginary, Miseres and, 11, 13
travel narratives: Anderson on, 149–50; Denegri on, 113; of Gómez de Avellaneda, 56; Graham, M., Brazil, 15–16; mobility in, 12–13, 183; in *Opúsculo Humanitário*, 107; pilgrimage, 113, 133n23, 134n32; Pratt on heterogeneity of, 6; presence in, 12–14; Thompson on, 150; for women scientific discoveries, 5
Travels in West Africa (Kingsley), 159–60
Tristán, Flora, 9, 49n9, 125; imperialist identity of, 24
Trois ans en Italie, suivis d'un voyage en Grèce (Floresta), 96, 115–21
Turnbull, David, 83

United States Exploring Expedition (U.S. Ex.), Cochran alignment with, 152–53
Uteng, Tanu Priya, 13, 19n7

Valentine, Waldemar, 49n11
Varejão, Marcela, 129
Venancio, Joaquim, 159
Verdugo, Domingo, 55, 82
Vesuvius Volcano, 119, 124–25

Viaje de Recreo (Matto de Turner), 110
"El viajero americano" (Gómez de Avellaneda), 54, 84n1
Views of Nature (Humboldt), 66
"A Vindication of the Rights of Women" (Wollstonecraft), 99
Voltaire. *See* d'Arouet, François-Marie
von Martius, Karl Friedrich Philipp, 50n12
von Spix, Johann Baptist, 50n12
Voyage Pittor-esque dans le Brésil (Moritz Rugendas), 128

Warburton, Henry, 40
Warren, John Esaias, 3, 116
Weld, Charles Richard, 87n35
Wetmore, Alexander, 146, 147, 178n16, 178n21
W.grahamiae Hemsl, Graham, M., plant of, 47, *47*
Wollstonecraft, Mary, 99, 130n13
women: Brazil secondary role of, 98; European status of, 24; Floresta on equal rights of, 99; gender constraints and male protection of, 158–59; Gilbert and Gubar on literary authority of, 63; Gómez de Avellaneda opposition to inferiority of, 81; inferiority perception, scientific discourse and, 5; male racial superiority alignment by, 24; Michelet on education of, 127; Mills on discursive constraints of, 39; Pérez-Mejía on imperialist identity of, 24; in STEM fields, 186; strategic networks for expertise, 14; Youngs on travels of, 47–48. *See also* gender
Women, Travel, and Science in Nineteenth Century Americas: The Politics of Observation (Gerassi-Navarro), 10
women scientists: discrimination against, 182; during Enlightenment,

23; inclusion strategies for, 6–7; male compliance with, 147; Rossiter research on, 6, 18n2, 139, 141; Schiebinger on, 150; travel narratives for discoveries of, 5

Youngs, Tim: on Humboldt travels, 34; on women travels, 47–48

Zambrana Valdés, Ramon, 77
Zenea, Juan Clemente, 76–77

About the Author

Michelle Medeiros is an assistant professor of Spanish at Marquette University. Her research interests include women's travel writing in the nineteenth and twentieth centuries, Latin American and Hispanic literatures, gender and women studies, and history of science. She is particularly interested in unveiling women's participation in the construction of knowledge.

www.ingramcontent.com/pod-product-compliance
Lightning Source LLC
Chambersburg PA
CBHW070830300426
44111CB00014B/2503